TIME
TO GO
HOME

TIME TO GO HOME

Rabbi Meir Kahane

Nash Publishing
Los Angeles

Library of Congress Catalog Card Number: 72-90884
Standard Book Number: 8402-1306-9

Published simultaneously in the United States and Canada
by Nash Publishing Corporation, 9255 Sunset Boulevard,
Los Angeles, California 90069.

Printed in the United States of America.

First Printing.

*This is, perhaps, the most important book
I shall ever write,
for it may save many lives.
It is, surely, the saddest
—for it may not.*

*It is dedicated with loyalty
to the America that gave so many millions
freedom, democracy, and a new life;
with deepest respect and love for what it has been,
and with a somber sense of loss and tragedy
for what it has become
in the hands of fools and knaves.*

CONTENTS

TIME TO GO HOME

What a pity,
that that which is lost
cannot be found again.
—Talmud

PART I
THE
REALITY OF
JEW-HATRED

CHAPTER 1: CLOUDS ON THE HORIZON

Once upon a time, the rabbis of the Talmud gathered together, as they were wont to do, and in the midst of their discussion the question was thrown out:

"Would it not have been better for man never to have been created?"

And, the Talmud tells us, the House of Hillel and Shammai, both filled with men of intellect, depth, and wisdom, discussed and debated the question at great length. Was the puny life of man—so filled with trouble and weariness, with the pursuit of his daily bread at the cost of the sweat of his brow, with the vicious cycle of laboring-so-that-he-might-eat-so-that-he-might-have-the-strength-to-labor-again-the-following-day, with the aberrations of rage, frustration, and hate—really worth the gift of life? A gift of life to

3

which he clings with an instinct that enables him to prefer the deepest agony rather than extinguish the
light of survival? On and on the discussion ranged and
finally—in weary resignation—the rabbis of Israel
agreed:

It would have been better, surely, for man had he
never been created, but, since it was ordained that he
should come into the world, let him constantly search
his deeds.

The life into which Divine Providence has thrust man is,
indeed, a subject that too often poses the inscrutable question:
Why? And the lack of meaning that so often surrounds ordinary
life is multiplied a thousandfold in the face of the waves of
wars, horrors, fratricide, upsurgings of primeval brutality and
cruelty that from time to time—and with growing frequency—
intrude upon the lives of men. We are, indeed, men whose lives
are insecure, who come from dust and thereto return and who,
in the words of the High Holy Day prayer book are "like the
potsherd that breaks, the grass that withers, the shadow that
passes, the cloud that vanishes, the breeze that blows, the dust
that floats, the dream that flies away."

Knowing the brief duration of the candle of life and the pains
and trials that accompany us on our too-short journey, we cling
to the joys and happiness that pass our way along the road and
seek to make them a permanent part of our stay on earth. We
flee from pain, and cleave to whatever pleasures we can find.

We also run from reality and cling to illusion.

We see that which we want to see; we shut our eyes to that
which will upset our dreams. We refuse to speak the unspeakable and think the unthinkable and prefer to walk forward with
blind determination while rationalizing to ourselves that all is
good and will never change. We strike out against those who
shake our castles in the sky and rail against those who prick our
illusions. A Jeremiah is never welcome and a Cassandra is
shouted down lest their message penetrate our minds and chill

our hearts. We prefer the bearers of good tidings and do not question too deeply their veracity. We applaud those who tell us that the unthinkable is precisely that and that the prophet of doom is, in reality, a victim of paranoia and a gloomy misreading of events. Grant us the warming fires of hope, we cry, so that we may be protected from chill reality. Let us see lambs where lions prowl lest we be eaten, and let us see light where blackness reigns lest we stumble.

And so we refuse to see that which we will not see, since that which is too terrible to contemplate is easily overlooked and thus not brought to mind, while that which, happily, is not allowed to come to consciousness will, hopefully, cease to exist. It is a situation that partakes of the very nature of the human beast and one that, if endemic to all humans is, a hundred and thousand times more, a part of the nature of the Jew.

Buffeted by every storm and indeed, every whim and fancy of the world into which he was thrust so reluctantly; the ultimate victim of every madness and inhuman permutation; the logical sacrificial lamb for every sin and abomination on this earth; bearing upon his body and psyche the scars of history and the slings of outrageous misfortune—the Jew sees in every harbor an end to terror and in every kind word a harbinger of the Messiah's arrival. History is no longer a guide to what may be and a compass for proper direction. It becomes, instead, an opponent not to be studied but to wrestle with, so that we might point out in what ways its lessons are not applicable in the present instance. With great sophistry, and in the best pilpulistic tradition, every new event is distinguished from all others that were ever part of the Jewish experience, and the past becomes irrelevant rather than becoming a prologue to it—a key to understanding the present. Every point of difference is exaggerated, and each glaring similarity is ignored or laboriously explained away. Hope springs eternal in the Jewish breast, so beaten and bruised in the past that it yearns for a final solution of tranquility lest it come face to face with yet another final solution born in the mind of yet another tyrant.

What has happened is that our past enemies have succeeded, not only in destroying large numbers of us, from time to time, but also in assuring the success of future enemies and our own continued destruction as we, in response to past horrors, refuse to recognize the possibility of future horrors and fail to take appropriate measures to deal with them.

Instead of turning to the reality of danger the Jew turns upon those who warn him of that danger. The enemy is not the one who will destroy us, but the one who terrifies us so by his alarming warnings that we still exist in a society where people are capable of intending that destruction. We grow livid with rage as we hear the prophets of doom; we tend, continually, to throw our Jeremiahs into the pit. But the angrier we grow and the more fiercely we rail and the more violent we become at the audacity of prophets of doom—the clearer are the indications that in the bottom of our hearts—in that secret hideaway where man closets up his hidden of hiddens, in the place where man buries the essence of things that are too painful to be seen by the outside world, in the subterranean recess of our consciousness where Truth, bitter and brutal, resides—we know. We know before the clairvoyant speaks; we know despite our efforts to shut him—and our true selves—down. We know the reality of the world against the Jew and the inevitable outcome of that struggle in every harbor that once seemed so safe. And because we know it we cannot allow ourselves to hear that to which we dare not listen.

But we must. There is an obligation upon one who has evidence to testify, and there is an even deeper imperative commanding the intended victim to hear those words, no matter how unpleasant or painful they may be. The plain, brutal, and tragic fact is that the potential for a wave of total Jew-hatred sweeping the United States exists today, and a second Holocaust, rivaling that of Europe, is an emphatic possibility whose roots are already deeply imbedded in the political, social, economic, and psychological realities of America today. In short, not only can it happen in the United States, it has already begun to move along that road. "Who is wise?" the rabbis ask. "He who foresees that which will be." It is time for the Jew to become wise and to see that which is written in the book of American Jewish destiny. The hand writes on the wall and only the foolish and fearful will not desire to read its message: Jew, it is time to go home.

There are those who, reading these words, will conclude that I am a partner to those whose lives center daily on vilifying, condemning, and plotting the destruction of the United States. Nothing could be further from the truth. I possess a deep love for the country of my birth, an immense respect for its human and social accomplishments unequaled by any other power, and a true appreciation of what she has given me and all her individual citizens. No other nation possessing its immense power would have refrained from using that power for tyrannical, world domination. No other government has tried so sincerely, if naively, to set its own house in order through reform and changes. I do not see America as the land of fascism incarnate, peopled by individuals and rulers who cunningly plot against victims both within and without its borders. I love the land of my birth and thank it for all that until now it has given me, my people, and all those who have so benefited from its freedom and sense of fair play.

There are indeed those who see the United States as a bête noire, the evil colossus, and the thrust behind all that is wrong on this earth. In a world that houses the abominations of Moscow and Peking and abides the oppression of freedom in Asia, Africa, and in much of Europe, such people are either incredibly ignorant or inexcusable knaves. To say that there is nothing imperfect in this society, and that the American republic has never sinned, would be to be guilty of the same kind of stupidity. But if one believes that in this world there has ever been, or that there exists today or ever will, a society free of poverty, hatred, bigotry, and selfishness, he has wandered into some other world. "For the inclination of man's heart tends toward wickedness from his youth"; these words of the Bible find confirmation in the eternal corruption, selfishness, hatred, and inequities of every society, no matter how different its ideological base or how pretentious its claims to perfection.

So the American society has within it deep imperfections—but no more than others and, mostly, a great deal less. The individual freedom it granted its citizens was, for years, the envy of all, and the great dream of those who dwelt in the political and economic prisons of almost every nation in the world was to find the means to emigrate to the New World. In this land men could voice their opinions and gather together to translate those views into active reality. In this land paupers knew that hard work and determination blended with intelligence and skill could lift them from depths to untold heights. The barriers of birth and privilege that existed here were far lower than in any other place on this earth; the weaknesses and evils that were found here were amenable to change and reform by determined men no longer faced with a secret police and a law that served tyrants.

Few understood this better than the Jew who fled from an Old World of legal disability and semilegal pogroms, from grinding poverty and religious hatred, from hoplessness to hope, from terror and insecurity to confidence and opportunity. He may have come to the slums of New York's lower East Side, but he knew that a higher level of living was attainable if he but willed it and worked toward it. He knew that the antipathy and hostility to him that often barred his way existed, but he also knew that this was a society which permitted him to speak out and protest and change that which he considered evil. America was a Golden Land for the Jew; here his talents were developed in an atmosphere of freedom and competition, and here he prospered in all that he turned to. "And the Children of Israel were fruitful and multiplied and increased and became exceedingly mighty and the land was filled with them." America! The Children had found another harbor; Israel had found yet another messianic era.

This is no longer true. The Golden Land is no longer golden

for the Jew today as it was yesterday, and tomorrow it will be worse.

One need not deny the truth of the American dream as it was and, as in great measure, it still is, to understand, at the same time, what the future holds. One need not disparage the past to realize the difference in what the future will be. America's greatness during its first 200 years is there for history to record in eternal splendor, and no one can erase it. Alas, that which was is not necessarily that which shall be, and a glorious past is no longer a guarantee of an honorable end. I wish to Heaven that it were not so. How much one would give for it not to be so! But there is a terrible vision that haunts me and gives me no rest. Having spoken the historical truth about American liberty and freedom, one cannot escape the sight of a terrible specter of changing times and values, of bitterness and fear, of frustration and anger, of economic, social, and political upheaval. The ghost of the American Christmas future chills the beholder as he sees within it the destruction of all the republican stability and the unraveling of the social democratic framework of American life. There is an evil mood roaming the streets and psyche of America today. It is a mood that I do not envision as being modified or overcome. It appears that it will only grow worse and that the days of democracy and the American dream are numbered. The dream is turning into a nightmare, and the sheltering harbor's placid waters are turning dark, sullen, and stormy. The final chapter, I fear, is being written to the idyll of the Jew in America, for when democracy and freedom go under it is the Jew who is the first to suffer. He is the goat for Azazel; he is the sacrificial lamb; he is the one, always, who is crucified for the sins of others.

Time moves swiftly in our era, more swiftly than ever before; events occur with breathtaking speed leaving in their wake dazed and uncomprehending victims. That time is moving today; it is running out. The Jew must begin to make plans, for a fire is beginning to rage and he will be consumed by it. The time to be wise is when the danger is not yet apparent to all;

9

afterwards, it is too late. The time to react and to save oneself is when the sun is still shining and the dark cloud on the horizon is still so insignificant and distant that it appears to have little relevance to one's own sunny afternoon. That is the time to recognize the approach of the storm and to escape its inevitably relentless anger. Above our heads, today, the dark clouds are gathering, and only the wilfully blind will refuse to recognize the storm that they portend. The thunder in the background that grows louder and the far-off flashes of deadly lightning speak to us in unmistakable language: Jew, it is time to go home. It is time to return to Israel.

The pity is that we are not prepared to hear or to agree. The fleshpots of the New World draw us to them today quite as irresistibly as their Egyptian counterparts held our forefathers thirty-five centuries ago. The good life is such a deadly opponent of good sense, that reason and logic become prey to the material cravings of our bodies, and we allow ourselves to be convinced that it cannot happen here. Because of this the Jew will instinctively react to warnings of danger with anger and fear, the anger and fear of men who are terrified by the thought that their entire lives might be uprooted and undergo total change. The warning will be ignored and universally condemned, and those whose voices will be heard the loudest in that condemnation will be the leaders of the Jewish community ranging over an entire spectrum of violent reaction. Mockery, personal attacks, anger, defamation, learned sermons and lectures will be aimed at the alarmists, clearly disproving their "irresponsible and paranoid" fears, followed by excommunication from every official and responsible institution of Jewish respectability of those who "only encourage anti-Semitism."

This predictable outcry of condemnation on the part of official leadership poses the most dangerous threat of all. For they are the ones who can influence the American Jew and ease his fears; they can anesthetize his insecurities and sooth his worried brow.

And they will. They will tell him that such talk is panicky madness and assure him that all is well. They will tell him that

10

non-Jews now like him despite their knowledge that this is stupid nonsense. They will convince him that America is not Germany and that the magic amulet of constitutional guarantees will ward off all evil. They have it in their power to convince the American Jew not to fear, not to make plans to leave, not to save himself. And they will.

Thirty-five years ago we suffered through a similar paralysis of will and it took six million lives. It was the decade of the 1930s and a giant of our times paced the cities and towns of Europe. Anguished and distraught he was driven by demons and wracked by the agony of his own vision of the apocalypse. Zev Jabotinsky—the founder of the Jewish Legion of World War I, the first Jewish fighting unit since the days of Bar Kochba; the maximalist Zionist par excellence, who cried out for a sovereign Jewish state with a Jewish majority in the land of Israel at a time when such a thing was unfashionably dangerous; instiller of Jewish pride and strength into the hearts of his Betar youth movement and the Zionist Revisionist organization he founded; spiritual father of the fighting Jewish underground, the Jewish national liberation movement; the idol of millions of poor and forlorn Jews in Eastern Europe—Jabotinsky raced through the *shtetlech* and cities of a continent that would soon sink into a night of horrors such as had never before gripped this unhappy planet, and cried out to his beloved and foolish Jews:

> Get yourselves moving, Jews, get moving. There is no time. A fire is burning, get out. Liquidate the exile before the exile liquidates you.

Jabotinsky saw what others could not or would not. His opponents used to taunt him with the charge that "when the whole world looks at the clock and sees '6:00' Jabotinsky sees '12:00.'" It was true. While others saw nothing strange, Jabotinsky saw the terror, the hatred, the death, the extermination. But he was a tragic figure, a strange specter who walked about seeing and hearing what remained invisible to others. He was, perhaps, foredoomed to fail.

Many years earlier, a younger Jabotinsky had listened as an elderly, weary, and wiser Max Nordau told him:

> You do not understand the Jew. A non-Jew will go into the street, look up at the sky and see an ominous cloud. He will immediately run into his house and get an umbrella.
> Not so the Jew. He must first catch pneumonia. . . .

The wrath of Jewish leadership throughout the world was poured upon Jabotinsky's head. "Irresponsible" was the least of the epithets aimed at him; the famous Yiddish writer Sholom Asch rose in all his righteous indignation to declare: "Woe unto a nation that has leaders such as these!" How irrelevant to the slaughtered that Asch, sixteen years and six million Jews later in May 1952, told a Jerusalem newspaper conference: "I am deeply sorry that I fought the evacuation plan of Jabotinsky." His sorrow, and that of all the other Jewish leaders who survived the Holocaust of which Jabotinsky had warned them and for which he was pilloried, did little to revive those who had died of Jewish pneumonia.

Let us not repeat the horrible mistake of yesteryear; there are involved yet another six million. Instead, let us listen to the argument for the evacuation of American Jewry, and weigh the reasons. Let logic and good sense outweigh emotion and self-interest. Let us understand that the non-Jew dislikes the Jew, a dislike that under proper conditions explodes into hatred. Let us at least be willing to listen rather than stop our ears so that they cannot become vehicles for our discomfort. If not for ourselves then at least for our children and theirs, let us reason together.

Again, I say: There is a dark cloud on the horizon of the American Jewish future. It signals a storm such as we have never yet seen. It warns of the beginning of the end for the American Jewish community. The time to leave is now, while there is yet time. Now is the time to go home, to return to the land of Israel.

CHAPTER 2: JEWISH ATTITUDES TO JEW-HATRED

A tale is told of a rabbi who was visited by a poverty-stricken Jew. It was in the midst of the frigid Russian winter and the pauper had no money for firewood to warm himself and the shivering bodies of his wife and children. The one man who could donate the necessary sum of money immediately was a wealthy miser from whom squeezing money was as difficult as the proverbial splitting of the Red Sea.

The rabbi went out into the bitter cold, his body lashed by the howling gale that swept out of the Siberian east. The snow came down in a thick sheet of whiteness that shut the world from view. Stumbling toward the house of the miser the rabbi pounded on the door. The wealthy man was astounded to find the rabbi at his door and exclaimed:

"Come in, rabbi, come in, it is freezing."

> But the rabbi remained where he was and as the bitter cold seized both the miser and his guest in its icy grip and while the chilling winds cut like a knife into both their bodies, he began to describe in great detail the terrible need for firewood to warm the pauper's home.
>
> "Yes, yes, I understand," cried the miser through chattering teeth and shivering body, "but surely we can talk about this inside where it is warmer."
>
> "No," said the rabbi. "Once we get into the warmth my description of the bitter plight of that Jew will become unreal and meaningless. Only standing here, where you yourself shiver from the cold, can you understand the plight of your fellow Jew...."

Only those who have themselves undergone the experience of suffering and deprivation can understand its full and awful impact. Only the Jew can appreciate the exquisite historical horror of what it has meant to be a Jew and to suffer under the tyranny of government and the animalism of the mob. Only he can appreciate what it meant—as a Jew—to flee the agony of the Old World and find new hope and opportunity in the New. The czar took his child from him at the age of eight to serve in the army for twenty-five years; the bitter winter sapped his energy while bitterer poverty clutched at his existence; the Russian pogromist sought his body and the Russian church his soul; he was cramped into a Pale of Settlement that did not allow him to live in the cities, to send his sons to universities, or to acquire land or meaningful wealth; blood libels and massacres appeared from time to time to take his life and property.

And so, when America beckoned, as did that incredible statue in New York harbor that symbolized the one opportunity in this life to escape from the misery, despair, and hatred that was his daily lot, the European Jew seized the chance and ran toward his garden of Eden to eat of the tree of opportunity. He was not the first of his people to have come to North America. Preceding him by 200 years were the Jewish refugees of that era, the Sephardim of Brazil, descendants of those people who fled the Inquisition, that intolerant manifestation of man's inability to allow those whose beliefs differ from his own to live with him in brotherhood.

No one today, not even the grandchildren and great-grandchildren of those who set foot on Ellis Island and who, figuratively, kissed the soil of a New Land of Freedom, can begin to appreciate what America meant to the Jews who escaped from the Old World. Given an atmosphere of freedom to develop their talents, an opportunity to engage their minds and industry, the latitude to create, invent, and expand their abilities, the Jews climbed swiftly up the ladder of economic, political, and social progress. Every legal disability was removed from his path to enable him to enjoy the fruits of complete equality; in time, it appeared to him that all de facto barriers also fell. The Jew was to be found in every major political party and held high offices under both. His children entered all schools. They filled the institutions of higher learning and the professions, the sciences, and the arts. His wife, liberated from her kitchen, pranced about in mink and played Mah-Jongg. His home was moved from the crowded city to the expansive and expensive suburbs, and freedom and equality were, daily, translated into every meaningful facet of his life.

Little wonder that he came to believe with a full and complete faith in the principles that created this paradise. He believed totally in the efficacy of democracy, in the magical powers of liberalism, in the ultimate victory of full equality for all, in the success of secularism that negated religion as a meaningful standard by which to judge human beings. He was fully convinced that here existed a melting pot which stirred all American citizens together and broke down barriers, misunderstandings and hatreds. He believed in all these things and worked for their enshrinement in the American Parthenon; and every day that passed was further evidence to him that anti-Semitism, if not totally eradicated, was a weak and meaningless thing, on its way to extinction in the New Eden.

The American Jew is convinced that Jew-hatred is a dying

phenomenon in America, that it cannot happen here. His conviction is bolstered by an impressive and undeniable quarter of a century of absence of any meaningful Jew-hating organization, of astounding progress for Jews in every walk of life, of the disappearance of all legal and almost all social barriers to Jewish enjoyment of total equality, of opportunity in almost every conceivable aspect of employment, housing, and political advance. This progress, proof of which is at our fingertips in the reams and reams of Jewish organizational statistics and in the everyday eyes of the beholder, is proof positive to most American Jews and every one of their established organizations that the American principles of democracy, equality, and liberalism embodied in constitutional guarantees as interpreted by the Supreme Court have transformed the United States into a permanent bulwark against significant Jew-hatred and an eternal haven for the Jew.

It is, of course, a dangerous error. There has been no basic change in the dislike that vast numbers of people feel for the Jew, and the virus of Jew-hatred continues to infect millions of Americans despite the fact that it has lain dormant and passive for so long. There is a reason for the ostensible demise of anti-Semitism during this era. Indeed, there are two basic reasons for the apparent death of Jew-hatred. They are both most temporary phenomena and their passing is only now beginning to be seen and felt.

Twenty-five years ago the world opened the doors of the extermination camps and was shaken to its very foundation. Even a universe such as our own, which has passed through so many abominations in its existence that it has long since grown callous to almost every horror, was ashen-faced when it beheld what modern man had done to the Jew. The cold and carefully planned destruction of an entire people, the horror of the gas chambers and the crematories, the sickening emaciated bodies, created a revulsion on the part of the world against those who were responsible for such a thing. The terrible Holocaust and its accompanying horrors created a temporary embargo on Jew-hatred in America; it was simply unthinkable that people should publicly mouth or advocate hatred against the Jew while the stench of Auschwitz was still in the nostrils of America. And, indeed, the State of Israel came into being on the emotions generated by Auschwitz.

The American Jew benefited from the Holocaust. Progress and equality were given him by a world and a country stricken with guilt at the thought that fellow Christians could have done such a thing. It was, perhaps, to be expected since, after every world disaster, the Jew can look forward to having his wounds licked by world sympathy. Each massacre and every pogrom brings forth shocked pity for the Jew—this is how he has tended to purchase positive world public opinion. Nevertheless, the fact remained that Jew-hatred became, for a time, a temporary parish relegated to the muttering of men who drank too much and the aberrations of a handful of unfeeling fanatics. The rest, shaken by the Horror, felt compelled to repay the debt to the dead by way of their living kinsmen. Jew-hatred suffered a serious reversal; it became unfashionable. But a reversal is not a total defeat, and fashions change. Jew-hatred was relegated to the inner recesses of the mind and covered over, but it was only awaiting the passage of time for man to forget and for his pangs of conscience to give way to moral amnesia.

There was another reason that hatred of the Jew seemed to be a vanishing thing. Twenty-five years ago, the war was followed by an era of prosperity unmatched in the annals of this country or the world. A people that had come out of the depression into a war economy that filled their pockets with dollars, but offered them little to spend it on, now went on an explosive spending spree that saw all the good things of life within the reach and grasp of tens of millions of Americans. At the same time, America emerged from the world conflict relatively unscathed whereas every other major country lay prostrate and bleeding, their economic capacity and industrial potential either in total ruin or desperately in need of rebuilding with huge transfusions of capital.

In this situation of unparalleled lack of competition, America was handed a golden opportunity to monopolize the world's markets that lay open to its products with few to challenge it. American trade boomed and business reaped huge profits. Jobs were plentiful, and nearly every American home wallowed in material goods to exceed their wildest dreams. Americans rode in their own cars and often owned two; they purchased television sets and many owned small boats on which they spent weekends; incredible numbers were able to purchase their own homes, far from the crowded cities; electrical appliances of all kinds made life more beautiful and freed the housewife for leisure and pleasure; vacations became longer and more frequent; entertainment and sports occupied more time than ever before; Americans luxuriated in the good life and everything was beautiful.

When people's bellies are stuffed and their pockets are filled, Jew-hatred is hardly an urgent or pressing thing. It is not that the emotion vanishes; it is rather that it is not uppermost in people's minds. When times are good people dislike Jews quietly; when things are not so good they dislike them loudly; and when things are critical they hate them violently—and act on their hate. The jackals who prey on hate and frustration prosper in times of crisis. But a steak in the broiler and a sleek new car in the garage dilute the appeal of the demagogue. The paradox is that fat pickings come during lean times while good times are lean ones for the haters.

It is not necessarily true that only an economic crisis can bring about a Hitler, but some crisis there must be. If it is not an economic one, then the political, social, or psychological one must be so deep and traumatic as to find the people desperately yearning for an escape to stability and authority. None of this was present to a sufficient degree during the first twenty-five years following the end of the Second World War and, because of this, Jew-hatred floundered on the rock of good times.

The guilt of Auschwitz and the good times of an economic boom—these, and not the efficacy of democracy, liberalism, and education—were responsible for the seeming demise of Jew-hatred in America. These gave the Jew a quarter of a century of unparalleled prosperity, equality, and opportunity. They also fed his self-delusion, and may have contributed to the blindness that could destroy him.

For let us be very clear about what has happened. Times are changing and the two dams that have held back the flood of Jew-hatred are beginning to crumble and vanish into history. There is no longer any feeling of guilt engendered by Auschwitz. Those who are too young to remember the trauma of its discovery are totally untouched by any pangs of conscience. Those who once felt this guilt have been relieved of it by the natural passage of time and by the rise of the State of Israel.

The incredible creation of the Jewish state, with its "new Jew" whose military prowess has become legendary, effectively built up a new image in the mind of the non-Jew. No longer was the Jew weak, a victim of oppression and in need of the sympathy, support, and pity of the world. Now, he was a vigorous fighter and—praise Heaven for having rid us of the need to feel guilty—even an aggressor! With immense eagerness much of the Christian world rushed forward to condemn the Jew as a rapacious seizer of territory, an expeller of refugees, as bellicose, aggressive, and guilty of all the things about which the world had, for so long, felt guilty towards him. There is a *need* today to see the Jew as a victimizer rather than a victim since this relieves the Christian world of the awesome guilt for the Six Million. In brief, the safe and secure days have come to an end when non-Jews trod carefully in the presence of the Jew lest they offend him, when the cry, "anti-Semitism," was enough to send people into a panic and forced doors of equality open to the Jew—not because people were nice or good or just, but because they felt guilty. The Six Day War not only destroyed Arab armies, it also laid to rest Christian guilt.

At the same time, the great economic bubble has burst— irrevocably. America will never see again the awesome prosperity, the bubbling belief in permanent happiness, the ebullient spirits and, above all, a United States as free of competition as before. Business will face grave difficulties in the struggle for world markets in competition with other economic powers, as the European Common Market, West Germany, and Japan; it will face a growing profit squeeze at home as it is caught, on the one hand, between demands for higher wages on the part of workers (who outdraw their Japanese and West German peers awesomely) and, on the other, the need to keep prices from rising lest products be priced out of the market (again, because of the high wages that are paid). Unemployment will go up as business attempts to increase profits by cutting labor costs through layoffs and as the demand for the goods they produce declines. This in turn will cause another wave of slackened demand and the cycle will continue, growing ever more vicious. And as the era of good feeling that was created by the era of good times fades away the arrested cancer of dislike for Jews will fester and grow and turn into hate—fed by all the fear, anger, and frustration that economic insecurity creates; fueled by all the other sudden social, racial, psychological cries and upheavals that have been thrust upon the American of our times.

The dams have burst and though we are not drowning yet—nor, for that matter, have we even become conscious of the fact that our feet are wet—the wheel has already begun to turn. The Jew, upon returning home from burying his dead, eats an egg at the first meal. He does so as an object lesson that life is a wheel that is constantly turning. Today we are on top and life is good; tomorrow the wheel turns and we are on the bottom. For the Jew the wheel of fortune has kept him on top for a quarter of a century. It has now begun to move in the other direction.

Why are we so clever for others and such fools for ourselves? Why do we refuse to acknowledge that, under the best of circumstances, the non-Jew does not like the Jew?

What has happened to the Jew in country after country—the hatred, persecution, pogrom, and extermination that have followed him into every land in which he was quantitatively large or qualitatively influential and highly visible—can occur in America, too. For hatred of and disaster for the Jew depend upon things that are all too universal; the nature of man, historical hostility to the Jew, the explosion of Jew-hatred that waits only to be triggered off by crisis or crises.

Those who say that America is different and that it cannot happen here fly in the face of historical precedent. There is a presumption that disfavors them, that cries out its logical contradiction of their views. It has always happened to Jews in the past, and those who claim that America is different are under a difficult obligation to rebut a presumption of guilt. It is not those who say that it is probable that it *will* happen here who have a burden of proof cast upon them, but those who say it will not.

There were, indeed, those who said—and truly believed—that Weimar Germany was different. After all it was not Czarist Russia! True, it was merely Germany. The natural laws and conditions that drove Germans to do what they did, exist in great measure in America today. The potential for an American disaster and holocaust begin with the very nature of man.

CHAPTER 3: MAN

In the end there remains only individual Man. Whether a society remains committed to the democratic process; whether freedom and liberty are granted; whether justice, fair play, and tolerance are respected; whether tyranny and mob rule are rejected; whether authoritarianism, the police state, the concentration camp and gas chamber are vetoed; whether love overcomes hate; whether uppermost is rationalism or fanaticism, decency or savagery—all depend, in the end, upon the whim and fancy of individual man.

Those who believe that it is the form of government that is the deciding factor, make a great mistake. Those who think that the world can be made better by changing the system will be as disillusioned as were all their predecessors. A world does not become better, more decent or less hate-filled merely by changing from monarchy to republic, from oligarchy to parliament, from mercantilism to laissez-faire, from capitalism to socialism, from gold standard to silver, from New Deal to Fair Deal to New Society, from tariff to free trade, or from any form to any other form. The tragedies of the world do not stem primarily from the evil of the system but from the faults within the character, personality and ethics of the one who runs and supports the system—individual man.

In the end, the problem is not a political, economic, or social, but a moral one. Goodness can only come from one who is good and a system which is run by selfish and cruel people must emerge selfish and cruel; a system by any name given it will smell evil as long as it is run by selfish people. Hatred and pogrom are quite as capable of occurring under a people's government as under a czar, and authority is chosen quite as easily under Weimar as under a kaiser. In the end people will choose a good and just society if they are good and just. If they are not, let us not delude ourselves, they will choose selfishly, on the basis of self-interest and, quite consciously, they will choose the most obscene and cruel regime if they are desperate enough and truly believe that this is their sole path to a better life.

In the end there is only Man. He decides whether a nation will go into the long dark night of tyranny, not the fact that his country has a constitution committed to democracy. He will opt for decency or the gas chamber despite all the "traditions" and precedents of the past. It is not the system that shapes man but man who shapes, rejects, or approves the system. It is not a question of political science but of morality, ethics, and the nature of man.

To the extent that he disciplines himself and learns to sacrifice his base instincts and selfish desires, the state that he chooses and creates will emerge in that image. If he is indeed prepared to sacrifice for the common good, ready to understand the complexity of problems that do not yield easy and instant answers, attuned to the moral and ethical horrors of religious and racial and ethnic bigotry, then the state that he creates will be one thing. If he is unwilling to choose the greater good over the narrow one; if he values his stomach over democracy; if he opts for security at the expense of freedom; if he is prepared to sacrifice his fellow human being to assuage his hunger and material poverty; if he is a slave to his passions, his anger, his frustrations, bitterness, envy, and hatred; if he is too weak or undisciplined to reject the siren call of the demagogue, the traditions and guarantees written into constitutions will not matter, his society and state will plunge into the long, dark, night of tyranny and terror.

Indeed, there is a strong argument for believing that it is precisely a liberal democracy with its power to the people which most inevitably turns on its weak minority; for if the people, with all their passions, weakness, materialism, and narrow and base interests control power, they are less ready to think in greater and more noble terms than some who are inspired by the spirit of noblesse oblige. Mobs that control a country think and feel like mobs. They also act like mobs, and their irrational, selfish, narrow interests move them easily down the lynch-path of searching out and destroying the most convenient scapegoat.

All this is axiomatic for man, wherever he is and whatever his background. It is no different for the individual citizens of the United States. What America will be tomorrow; what path it will choose; whether democracy will grow or collapse before a tide of totalitarianism all depend upon the strength or weakness of the American individual and upon his decision that, in turn, will be the product of a particular sense of ethics, character, and will.

The American is no different from any other human creature, despite his birth in a land with a tradition of democracy. He is a captive of the essence that is man, and his is the nature of men everywhere. He is no better and no worse than the individual in Weimar whom we so foolishly have turned into some abnormal demon armed with immoral horns and tail. It behooves us to remember this, for it is the foundation of foundations of the study of political behavior. It is our compass and sextant.

Democracy and freedom are, indeed, huge and imposing structures, but they rest on a terribly unsure and wavering foundation called man who is a prisoner of his character, ego and will, a captive of his very essence. What is the prognostication for man's reaction in time of crisis? What can we expect from him? What is the political forecast for an American wracked by extensive crisis? Not a very happy one.

One of the great myths that arose in the not-too-distant past was the one that proclaimed the essential *goodness* of man. It was a mystical belief that, somehow, there existed within the soul of man or the masses of men that peculiar ability to divine Truth. It was a creed that gave man a perception and intellectual divining rod that would, that must, invariably reject evil and falsehood and cleave to justice and goodness.

From this essential liberal belief there arose a supernatural belief in the power of the democratic system to sift from within itself all blemishes and aberrations. It saw the vote as a certain way of ultimately casting freedom and justice into the seats of political power. The masses would, in the end, choose that which was correct, and democracy, by its very nature, would regain for man, Paradise lost.

From all this came forth staunch liberal opposition to censorship and suppression of any and all views, no matter how heinous they might be. In the naive bloom of a political spring that heralded the era of bourgeois democracy, self-confidence in the wisdom and sagacity of the people came into being, in the wisdom that would inevitably reject the madness and the siren song of the tyrant. Let the extremist speak, it was urged, let the totalitarian babble. Reason and science were king, and man had within him the ability to perceive the error, stupidity, and menace in the call of the wild. Fascists? Let them propogate. Communists? Allow them their pitiful efforts. The masses will never follow; man's ultimate wisdom must conquer; the people may be trusted to use their sense of reason and good judgment.

And so there arose the confident, arrogant belief in the supremacy of decent, rational, wise man. There grew the assertion that freedom included the right to speak and organize, influence and work to destroy that freedom; that democracy demands the granting of right to the authoritarian to use its very processes and its guarantees to bury it, since there was no possibility that the masses of people would be swayed by him.

Yes, yes, a hundred times yes, shouted the comfortable civil libertarian from the heights of his fog-shrouded intellectual sanctuary. Far from the madding reality, safe from the laboratory of life as it is, the rational, liberal, democrat looked down upon those on the Right and Left, dedicated to the overthrow of freedom; watched them grow stronger and bolder; beheld the obvious truth that, given the opportunity, they would seize power, enslave and exterminate, plunge nations and the world into the darkness of a long night, and that the world might never again see the light of free day. And in the face of all this, he solemnly invoked the right of freedom for those who would destroy it.

This is not an event of antiquity. We behold them today, still, not a whit bothered by their eternal partnership with colossal error, everlastingly dusting themselves off following yet another fall before the reality of life, and preparing to take yet another fling into yet another intellectual hole. We behold them still, today, carrying into battle the battered and tattered flag of yesteryear, with all the ancient and tortured arguments upon it. They are well known. "It is the right of every man, no matter how heinous his view to advocate that belief; by silencing him we do precisely what he would do; true democracy is the insistence that all men be granted freedom without reservation; and above all, the people may be trusted to use their reason and good judgment to reject the tyrant. It cannot happen here."

They are not new arguments. Intellectuals in Germany and Italy argued so as they defended the right of Hitler and Mussolini to destroy political legality. Liberals in Czechoslovakia believed it when they gave the Communists the right to be elected to office. One presumes they all had some misgivings as they were carted off to the concentration camps. One can imagine a pang of sorts as they gave the tyrants rope to hang themselves and with which they themselves were strung up.

They are not new arguments and yet we hear them once again.

One is tempted to weep, because in this is mirrored all the ignorance and futility and immaturity of our times. Here is the lesson that all the blood and misery and tragedy of a war that took thirty million lives has taught us nothing. Those who are so convinced that they are upholding the principles of democracy are merely parroting and regurgitating all that bankrupt intellectuals of our times have hammered into them. Once again it becomes clear that the only permanent lesson of history is that there are no permanent lessons and that man never learns from the past, but rushes to repeat all the mistakes of his ancestors.

History is full of quixotic visionaries, muddled liberals, and foolish children who proclaimed the freedom of men to destroy freedom, and who declared their intention to defend that right to the death. Generally, their wish was fulfilled. The blood of countless innocent victims flows through the sea of history, victims of tyrants and confused democrats who helped those tyrants to power.

The naive belief that somehow the people will always see the truth and, following it, reject the men of evil, has been refuted a hundred, nay, a thousand times—not the least in our days.

Where was the good judgment of the German who voted for Hitler? Where was the good sense of the Italian as he cheered the rape of Ethiopia? Why do one-third of the Italian people vote Communist and the Cuban peasants idolize Castro?

There can never be a guarantee of democracy; there can never be an assurance that people will choose freedom. It is self-interest that guides us, and who is to say where it will lead us in the future? Who can be sure of the temper of the people in time of economic crisis? Who is willing to guarantee naziism's rejection?

The tyrants and racists who succeeded in destroying half of Europe did so through the blindness of those who learned nothing from history. One grows cold seeing that it is happening all over again.

Man is not perforce decent, rational, or wise. He may not be wicked or hopelessly cruel, but surely his first commitment is to

28

himself and, time after time, his instincts are selfish in times of crisis. It takes a strong man to reject a tempting solution to grave and serious problems. It takes a man of immense character and decency to turn down an offer to fill his belly and regain his security and that of his family in return for his neighbor's hide. It takes a man of great moral willpower to reject the hater and the demagogue when his own life is filled with agony, frustration, and desperation and he is offered a way out—the price being merely his fellow citizen's liberties and freedom. It takes more than ordinary people to turn down an offer of the good life with payment taken from someone else. Such men are not found in great abundance. They are the products of training, restraint, discipline, and willpower, and we have never lived in an era when such things have been less abundant or popular.

Ours is an age of weakness, not strength, a time when men are filled with a desire to do their "thing," when to pursue pleasure is the pursuit of the Holy Grail. Such an era is a time of paucity of inner strength and ability to sacrifice. At such a time we willingly sacrifice freedom for security. At such a time, weakness breeds insecurity, insecurity breeds fear, fear breeds desperation, and desperation leads to hate, irrationality, and violence. It is a time when man flees from unstable freedom that casts upon him responsibility and the need to make decisions. It is a time when liberty abdicates in favor of the strong man on the horse. It is a time when man searches for an enemy and a scapegoat. He usually has little trouble in finding one.

It is not evil that drives man to do evil things, but weakness and fear. It is not immorality that moves him to silence and paralyzed impotence when his neighbors are being led away, but fear for himself and the life he has so carefully and laboriously built. But this fear, and the silence it generates, will, in the end, aid and abet in the killing and destruction of innocents. Evil does indeed triumph because of the silence of decent people.

Civilization, all too often, is merely a garment that man learns to wear over his nakedness. In no way does that pseudo-civilization remove the nakedness; in no way does it make any fundamental change in the essence of that nakedness. It merely covers and obscures from view that which remains fundamental and real, and that reality—that nakedness—consists of the basic ego, selfishness, anger, brutality, frustration, envy, and hatred that lies within the breast and mind of the creature—greater than the angels and lower than the beast—called man. Too often, we mistake politeness and savoir faire for genuine goodness. It is a great error.

If it does not cost man much to be good, he will be so. The test of the really decent person is when decency and morality become expensive. Depressingly, we have seen man fail the test of righteousness when the price he has to pay is exorbitant.

What will America do at the moment of truth? The precedent of history is not a happy one and those who claim that America is different must rebut the presumption of man's guilt.

The fate of the American Jew rests not upon constitutional guarantees nor upon a flood of crises that are inundating America and the violent reaction of the average citizen to them. Each one of these crises is staggering but, alone, might very well be withstood. Coming as they do, together, they pose a terrible challenge to the ability and the strength of the American to stand up to them and a threat to the survival of the classic historical scapegoat—the Jew.

America is wracked by racial, political, military, social, psychological, and economic crises. There is grave doubt, that grows more serious with every passing day, that it can solve them. If it cannot, the Jew will not survive in the United States. The probability of a frightened, frustrated, desperate, weary, bitter, and angry American turning into a violent hater who will follow the demagogues and haters, is a real one. If he does, the primary target and the major victim will be the Jewish scapegoat. The fate of the American Jew rests upon his understanding, clearly, the crises in the midst of which he stands, their seriousness, and the probable inability of the American masses to rise above their passions and self-interest. Jew-hatred and a potential Holocaust are the terrible germs that are being nurtured in the culture of weakness and violence of contemporary American crises. It is important that we study and analyze them so that we may coldly and clearly realize why the future for the American Jew is a bleak one, and why it is time to go home.

It is important that we know these crises and understand the violence and the potential for violence that lie in the warp and woof, in the marrow, in the historical past and the all-too-real present of American society. It is this violent reality that can explode—as it is triggered by crisis—into a horror equal to the one we beheld in Europe.

CHAPTER 4: VIOLENCE

Let us not play games. The fact of the matter is that America is a violent country. It is peopled with violent individuals and boasts a violent past and tradition. That violence can be triggered and explode against the Jew under the proper circumstances of crises and at the proper time. America, the violent; how often the Jew overlooks it.

Side by side with the America that the Jew always saw and preferred to emphasize was that other America, the one that he rarely encountered and that he discounted. It was the America of violence, burgeoning dissatisfaction, and upheaval. The Jew, raised in a tradition of peace and shrinking from violence, was separated from the huge masses of the lower socioeconomic non-Jews both geographically and psychologically. He had little realization that violence was an integral part of the society of which he was a part, that violence was perhaps a growing expression of a modern, free, disjointed society, and that it was found, to a far greater extent than he believed, in the psyches and emotions of large numbers of people.

Having climbed from the lower depths of social and economic existence, he could not know or understand that others who were deprived and discriminated against or who were unable to attain economic advantage were discontented, angry, and frustrated, and ready to resort to physical upheaval, revolt, wild lashing out, looting, and revolution. He surely did not believe that any such thing could be tied to Jew-hatred. Instability, revolution, violence in the streets, the upheaval of an ordered society, hatred and calls to action against the Jew— these were endemic to the Old World. America, pragmatic and reformist, democratic and composed of multitudes of different nationalities, was different. Certainly, Jew-hatred, the product of ignorance and religious intolerance, the result of tyranny and misunderstanding, could never be a meaningful thing in a land that was the direct contrast to all these evils. Jew-hatred could not flourish in a soil of democracy, equality, and stability, and these factors were a permanent aspect of the American scene.

In reality, however, violence, threats to the stability of the social and democratic fabric, general racial and religious hatred, and hatred of the Jew, in particular, are deeply rooted into the American scene and the brief history of this country is filled with numerous instances when they have emerged from just beneath the surface to besmirch the American soul. We would do well to remember them and to bear in mind, also, that they loom again at this moment as an emerging and clear and present danger to America and its Jews.

We have already seen the violent reactions in a number of communities, communities that are the avant garde of the coming New Reaction. There have already been attacks upon Blacks attempting to integrate schools, and school buses have been blown up. There have already been riots against Blacks in reaction to attempts to instill quotas for minorities in the construction industry. There have already been rampaging workers who have attacked long-haired students, and other groups that have attacked homosexuals. There have been rampaging mobs using sports victories as excuses for looting and smashing and raping. Black mobs have burned down neighborhoods and white mobs have smashed them in return. Schools have been closed down, time and time again, by racial clashes. A city in the Midwest has been the scene of actual guerrilla warfare between whites and blacks, and the hatred hangs low and ominous for all to see. Homes purchased by Blacks in all-white neighborhoods have been burned down and integration marchers stoned and attacked. Sports events between whites and blacks have already been the scenes of fighting and at least one major scene of beatings and rape. A Cabinet member has been attacked by leftists on campuses. Teachers and students have already been beaten and raped and whites and blacks in schools divide into hostile enemy camps.

And Jew-hatred? Surely, there's no lack of incidents of physical Jew-hatred: an elderly Long Island couple tormented for twelve (!) years with broken windows, paint spraying, and eggs thrown at the house, lights ripped out and anti-Jewish slogans daubed on the fence; over 170 synagogues desecrated in a brief span of a few years; and it is impossible to estimate the number of incidents never reported to the police for fear of "making things worse." Fires and bombings of synagogues in Rochester, New York, Long Island, New York City, Boston, Philadelphia and countless other places; swastikas daubed on Jewish homes and centers; the numberless youngsters beaten up because they are Jewish and insulted because of their background; cemeteries that are vandalized and desecrated; all the incidents we know about and all the hate we know is there.

One of the most significant indicators of the real presence of Jew-hatred may be found in the relatively new spate of radio talk shows involving phone calls to the studio from the audience.

Jews are heremetically sealed from the reality about them. Living in ghettos without walls, for the most part associating almost totally with other Jews or with non-Jews on their best behavior, they have not the slightest idea of the true feelings of the non-Jew about them. It is not they who walk into the neighborhood bar and listen to the rising pitch of voices as the liquor goes in and the truth comes out. They simply do not know what most non-Jews think of them. If they did they would be stunned and frightened. All the envy and resentment that are given life and sustenance by the crises of our time erupt in the sanctuary that is the tavern and in the whiskey and beer culture. The Jew is not present. The Jew does not know nor hear. He is at home in his gilded ghetto and, to him, all is well with the world and its Jews.

But listen to the radio talk shows that have given haters the opportunity to vent their feelings on the air to listening millions and the anonymity to screw up their courage to begin. One listens, and catches for an instant a brief look at the hell that looms ahead, a momentary glance into the ugly, sordid, soul of the hater.

"This is not Germany." Indeed, it is not. It is America. It is a land with a history and tradition of lusty violence, cruelty, and murder. A large proportion of those who long ago arrived here were hardly of the most genteel and sensitive nature. The endless wilderness that stretched before the newcomers, the frontier that beckoned with all its vastness and lack of restraints, gave birth to an unbridled violence where life was cheap and gunning a daily thing. The West, with its shootings, its posses and its easy death, was an integral part of the American scene and its folklore absorbed the violence so casually accepted and eagerly enjoyed. Indeed, its outlaws—cruel, common and vicious—became, and still remain, folk heroes for us. Both sheriff and outlaw symbolize the excitement of violence that is so American. (In countries with a much longer history, the violent heroes of wars and myth were enshrined in a distant past, and exerted a less immediate impact.) The names of the outlaws and their bands are well known: Billy the Kid, the James brothers, the Younger brothers, William Quantrill, and the bloody raids in Kansas; the massacres of Indians and the vigilante lynchings of barely accused and untried persons. All these, in the frontier of America, gave rise to a tradition that accepted shooting and death as everyday events. Violence and its perpetrators were, at least unofficially, folk heroes.

And we forget too quickly the eruption of violence and cruelty in both South and North: not only in the lynching of three terrified foreigners in the tiny town of Dry Diggings, California of 1849, but in the draft riots in New York City during the Civil War that saw mobs swarm through the streets hunting down Negroes (and killing thirty) while burning, looting, and destroying; not only in the lynching of blacks, symbolized by the death of Mack Parker in Mississippi in 1959, but the lynching of Leo Frank in Atlanta, amid horrible outbursts of anti-Semitism; the 1943 race riots against Mexicans in California that saw thousands of people surging through the streets in search of "zoot suiters"; and the World War II race riots against blacks in Detroit. Violence is the way of life for youth gangs that roam the streets fighting, knifing, shooting, and killing out of boredom, racism, and hate. It is expressed in the organized crime that made Chicago and Capone American symbols; in the inexplicable beatings of infants by their own parents, a syndrome that sees thousands of battered children yearly—not all of them surviving—and others left hungry, chained, and neglected. It is revealed in the incredible cruelty and violence on the part of young, terribly young, children, a cruelty that sees not just killing but a sadistic burning of drunks; in the daily television programs and movies we love so much with their violence, murder, and sadistic brutality; in senseless vandalism and beatings of people. It is present in the students flocking to beaches and festivals and exploding into fights and wild, aimless violence; in the toys of death our children play with daily. It is inherent in the alarming number of multiple murders by individuals who go berserk and kill three, four, five, and more, people who invariably show no signs of violence or aggression previous to the murders. It is present in the total collapse of respect for authority, and in the disappearance of fear of defying or attacking authority—in the physical assaults on teachers by students and the murderous attacks upon police. America is a country which was born in the freedom to be violent, and whose wealth and materialist concept of the good life has fed that bent to violence. The American is a violent man, far more so than the German, and his history proves it a thousand times over. The fact that this violence has flared up, despite two oceans that saved this nation from external enemies and despite a long history of peace and security, is not a good omen.

And then there is a special danger in every violent and brutal society—the police officers. The men who have been given the legal right to use guns beat people to enforce their will. Blessed with many decent men, these forces are also cursed with too many others who are dangerous to democracy, who only wait for an opportunity to do violence. Only the totally isolated can contend that there does not exist a mentality in America among so many policemen that can tomorrow transform society into a cruel Gestapo-like atmosphere. Only those who have not seen police charging brutally and violently into a crowd, beating arrested individuals in police cars and station houses, speaking about Blacks and Jews quietly to each other over coffee, joining fringe hate groups as shown by the vast past membership of policemen in the Coughlin movement, and mistreating prisoners in state and federal prisons alike, can deny that little people yearn for the opportunity to lord it over their fellow creatures.

There are none so dangerous as those who come out of the masses with little breeding and intellectual capacity. All their frustrations and hates are vented legally. Here is their opportunity legally to act out their fantasies, to release their explosive hate and bitterness. How many little people—given power—plunge those under them into catastrophe! How much sadism and terror are enclosed within the little minds and hearts of little people! The blue and the gray shirts are too easily exchanged for brown and black. The potentially sadistic and brutal SS men are not unique to Germany. In every country and among every people they can be found among the frustrated and malcontented of the unprivileged masses.

Is not Kent State a sign? Are not the colleges barometers?

Are not all the incidents of unnecessary brutality clear indications? Indeed, they are.

America the violent, the record is there for all to see and, worriedly, to contemplate. And there is also the America that—with all its democratic traditions and constitutional guarantees—already has a solid history of Jew-hatred.

CHAPTER 5: LOOKING BACK

Even at a time when the number of Jews was small, and Jew-hatred in America insignificant, it nevertheless manifested itself early in America. The Know-Nothing movement—the first, great, native-born hate movement—had poor pickings in a country with a vast frontier and opportunities for all. Nevertheless it grew, and vented its spleen, not only upon the newly arriving Catholics, but upon the tiny handful of Jews. Among its leaders whose anti-Jewish feelings were not hidden were men like William G. Brownlow, the abolitionist Thaddeus Stevens, and Henry Wilson, destined to become the vice-president of the United States under Grant.

The Civil War brought forth shocking anti-Jewish statements by three of the Union's top generals—Sherman, Halleck, and Grant—culminating in the latter's infamous General Order 11 of December 17, 1862:

> The Jews as a class violating every regulation of trade established by the Treasury Department and also department orders, are hereby expelled from the department and held in confinement within 24 hours from the receipt of their order.
>
> Post commanders will see that this class of people be furnished passes and required to leave. . . .

At this time, Jews numbered 150,000 of a white population of 27 million—barely more than half of one percent of the total. When the great immigrations from Europe began in the last quarter of the nineteenth century, bringing with them large numbers of East European Jews, the festering, latent resentment and hatred moved into the open.

The era of "genteel," social Jew-hatred is dramatized by the turning away of one of the most prominent American Jews, Joseph Seligman, from the exclusive Grand Union Hotel in the resort town of Saratoga. It was only the beginning. By the 1880s, private schools, camps, hotels, and the Union League Club began to bar Jews. It was a policy that continued and extended into colleges and universities right through the end of World War II where, in the face of Auschwitz and "good times," it receded for a while beneath the surface. It was in this period that the most dangerous native manifestation of potential upheaval, violence, and Jew-hatred came into being. To this day, the vast majority of liberals and radicals look upon it as a good and vital force, and efforts are being made to resurrect it in our times.

The Populist movement of the late nineteenth and early twentieth centuries was, undoubtedly, a people's movement. It was one that cried out for the farmers, the workers, the discontented and the "outs." It has a warm place in the hearts of "progressive" people and is lauded as an example of a "people's movement" endowed with natural qualities of purity, wisdom, honesty and justice. It was also blatantly Jew-hating.

The Populists, who rolled up an impressive if disunified coalition of discontented farmers and workers from the Civil

War till World War I, railed against "monopoly, the gold trust, the aristocratic millionaires who . . . generally purchased their elections in order to protect the great monopolies they represent; the hopelessly and shamelessly corrupt Democratic and Republican Parties; the parasites." Above all, they lashed out at the "conspiracy entered into between the gold gamblers of Europe and America." A picture was built up of the little farmer and worker of America at the mercy of international bankers and monopolists who used gold to oppress, and to retain their privileges. They may have called for a better life for the little people; they may have wished to dismantle the monopolies; they may have advocated socialism and the nationalization of the railways and utilities; they may have called for a graduated income tax; they may have demanded labor's right to organize, but they were also a vehicle for the most violent and vicious Jew-hatred in America to surface until that time.

It was not for nothing that the Associated Press reporter who attended the 1896 Populist Convention in St. Louis noticed, "as one of the striking things," "the extraordinary hatred of the Jewish race. It is not possible to go into any hotel in the city without hearing the most bitter denunciation of the Jews as a class and of the particular Jews who happen to have prospered in the world."

The words and writings of leading Populist figures like Mary Lease, Coin Harvey, and Ignatius Donnelly are filled with representations of Rothschild and Wall Street conspiracies against the people. Populist literature as well as that of the widely read *Police Gazette* and *Puck* again and again depicted the Jew as both rich banker and anarchist. One could find hatred of the Jew arising in the writings of a man like Henry Adams and the leading socialist who wrote: "Our era may be called the Jewish era. . . . 'Jewism' to our mind best expresses that special curse of our times, 'Speculation.' " When Grover Cleveland could be branded by a leading Populist as "the agent of Jewish bankers and British gold," it is not surprising that a Populist like Georgia's Tom Watson could become one of the most notorious of the American Jew-haters as we shall soon see.

What does the lesson of Populism, with its ideology of "the people" and that notion's total irrelevancy to Jew-hatred, hold for our times? Surely, a thing to be carefully considered.

As Jews grew in population and became a more visible force, discrimination against them grew and began to encompass large areas of life. Jews began to encounter restrictive covenants, a refusal by landlords to rent them apartments, and vandalism when they moved into new areas. Large numbers of the best colleges and universities made little effort to hide the fact that they had quotas for admission of Jews, and it was immensely difficult for a Jew to become a doctor or an engineer. Discriminatory employment practices were common, and young Jews looking for jobs as clerks and secretaries were turned down in favor of non-Jews, leading Jacob Schiff to resign from the board of directors of an employment agency which, ironically, barred Jews from jobs. Newspapers openly ran ads that stated "Christians only," and, as the Depression made competition for jobs acute and white-collar jobs were at a premium for Jews, many a Jewish girl wore a cross prominently displayed in order to make her struggle a little easier.

And for just a moment, the veil was lifted to reveal the potential for physical expression of Jew-hatred in the 1913 lynching of Leo M. Frank. Frank, a Jewish resident of Atlanta and president of the local B'nai Brith, was accused of having raped and murdered a young girl who worked in his pencil factory. Limited strictly to the evidence of an illiterate worker who later confessed to the crime himself, the trial was a disgrace and a sham. The crowds that gathered outside yelled "Lynch the Jew" and "Crack that Jew's neck." Frank's lawyers received threats, "If they don't hang that Jew we'll hang you." The jury was threatened with lynching if it did not "hang the damned sheeny."

Eventually, the mob burst into the prison and dragged Frank away to be hanged. It was Tom Watson, the Populist who had polled a million votes as candidate for vice-president of his People's Party, who was largely responsible for the execution. It was Watson who aroused the emotions of the workers with his continuous characterization of the murdered girl as "the little factory girl." In sharp contrast stood the accused:

> Frank belongs to the Jewish aristocracy and it was determined by rich Jews that no aristocrat of their race should die for the death of a working girl.

And after the lynching, Watson again wrote:

> Let Jew libertines take notice! Georgia is not for sale to rich criminals.

And upon the death of Tom Watson in 1922, Eugene Victor Debs, the Socialist who led the struggle for a better life for the masses, wrote his widow:

> He was a great man, a heroic soul who fought the power of evil his whole life long in the interest of the common people and they loved and honored him.

By the end of World War I, America had begun to experience a vast change. Millions of Americans had been overseas, and a great shift from the farm to the city had begun. Traditions were beginning to fall, the frontier was closed as an open place for opportunity and as a safety valve, and economic and social problems began to grow. The Jew was now in America in the millions, and the demand to shut the gates to East European immigration became a roar that was obeyed by Congress. Along with the social and economic discrimination, there arose for the first time a serious movement dedicated to physical Jew-hatred. Spurred on by the tensions of the times, the Ku Klux Klan, despite its lack of sophistication and leadership, despite the inherent drawbacks in its total inability to appeal to both city and farm, North and South, grew to the point where it had millions of members. The Klan was so strong and it reflected such powerful voices in the American community that it split the Democratic Convention of 1924. There, William McAdoo, the strongest candidate for the nomination, pandered to the agrarian and Fundamentalist vote by lashing out at "sinister, unscrupulous, invisible government which has its seat in the citadel of privilege and finance in New York City." A demand by Al Smith that they repudiate the Klan by name was defeated by one vote. It was only the good times of the Coolidge era that put a sudden stop to further Klan growth outside the South.

On May 22, 1920, one of the most famous Americans of his time wrote a front-page editorial in the newspaper that he owned, *The Dearborn Independent.* It was titled: "The International Jews: The World's Problem." The man was Henry Ford and, for ninety-one consecutive issues (until he erred by defaming an individual Jew), the International Jew continued to spew forth its hate. It was Ford who helped to popularize, as never before, the *Protocols of the Learned Elders of Zion,* a crude forgery that purports to outline a Jewish plot to take over the world.

For months and months Ford described Jews as being "lewd and erotic" accusing them of corrupting American gentiles with liquor and jazz, and of being draft-dodgers during World War I. For seven years the attacks continued, lashing out at the "flabby tolerance" of Americans for Jews, praising the Klan for its attacks upon Jews and predicting the "exodus" of Jews from America. Thanks to Ford, anti-Jewish writings and ideas were made available to millions of Americans. The years passed and Jews survived, but the seeds of hate were sown as never before, and the traditional American tolerance had suffered a serious blow. It was incalculably weaker than it had been, and the next decade was to deliver it a shattering blow, averting disaster only by the narrowest of margins.

The Great Depression descended upon America with a suddenness and unexpectedness that was psychologically devastating. Suddenly the good life and the fun times were over with a loud and sickening crash. People's savings and dreams were wiped out. Jobs evaporated into thin air. Farmers were angry, and all were frightened. The system came under attack as never before, and capitalism and the democratic system were no longer things to be accepted without question but rather to be looked at with doubts previously unheard of.

People wondered about revolution in America, and angry voices of extremism rose to become an antidemocratic force more powerful than had ever been possible before in this country. A mixture of populism and fascism began to emerge under the charismatic Huey Long, senator from Louisiana, the Kingfish. It was a bullet in Long's belly that put an end to the man who would have liked to take America down the long road to totalitarianism. In his place, arose another man who could not duplicate Long, but who gave a voice to Jew-hatred, who gathered millions into his Christian Front movement, and who posed a threat to democracy and Jews in this country that was only eliminated by the coming of World War II.

Millions of people listened to Father Charles E. Coughlin's weekly radio program. In it he attacked both greedy capitalism and communism. This was an American kind of fascism that began to be woven, having all the elements of the populism of the prairie, farms, and factories, and in it the Jew was the chief target. Christian Fronters beat up Jews in Brooklyn, and a whole series of vicious Jew-hating groups arose that called for violent fascist revolution and elimination of Jews. These groups were led by men like William Dudley Pelley and his Silver Shirts; Lawrence Dennis, probably the brightest and most intellectual of the haters; James Banahan and his Iron Guard; the Yorkville Nazi Joe McWilliams and his American Destiny Party, which openly terrorized Jews—and, in the midst of all this—there arose a small group of American intellectuals and well-known names who had become disillusioned with democracy and saw in Hitler's naziism and Italy's fascism a "wave of the future." And that was, indeed, the title of the best-seller written by Anne Morrow Lindbergh and a theme that her husband, Charles, advocated over and over again until World War II began.

The war effectively ended all this, as well as the swaggering German-American Bund that openly goose-stepped in New York and in other cities. It was the war that ended the Depression and the desperate search for jobs that were nonexistent, and it was the war against the foreign Nazis and Fascists that put an end to the rapidly growing homemade Nazis and Fascists. It was the war that put a stop to the Jew-hatred that had grown beyond belief. It may have been the war that saved American Jewry, for the time being.

America is a young country, and a nation that came into existence with the good fortune to be sheltered by oceans from external attack; to be blessed with an abundance of natural resources; to have wide frontiers for expansion and economic opportunity for all who came to these shores; to have been born of a successful revolt from tyranny, and, hence, given an understanding of the precious benefits of liberty and tolerance. With all that, the Jew has seen—with his own increase in population, wealth, power, and visibility—that Jew-hatred has escalated. At the same time he has watched as the democratic process and the pride in the American dream slowly vanish in the face of crises and a growing moral weakness and inability to meet those crises. America has a heritage of violence and is a violent country populated by violent people prone to violence, swiftly and frighteningly. It is not immune to horror against the Jew. Jew-hatred has taken root here in the past, it exists today, and is growing swiftly nurtured by the germ-culture of American crisis and readiness to react to that crisis violently.

The incredible phenomenon of Jew-hatred has been the subject of countless historical studies on the part of learned and analytical scholars. There have been almost as many reasons advanced for the disease as there have been studies made of it. In the end, each partakes of a bit of the truth and, at the same time, none is nearer a totally definitive solution than before. It is a disease that partakes of religious, economic, social, racial, and psychological hatred; of anger, bitterness, frustration, envy, fear, ignorance, and of objective forces that lead, eventually, to the Jew. One thing is clear. It is universal, transcending time and geography. The rabbis knew of its existence and had this to say about it:

It is an indisputable rule: it is clear that Esau hates Jacob.

And elsewhere they stated:

Why was (the mountain) called Sinai? Because, from there, came forth hatred (*sinah*-Heb.) to the world.

What the rabbis referred to was the indisputable fact that it was at Sinai that the creation of a peculiar and separate Jewish people took place, having a unique and different way of life; that there was an inevitable cultural clash with their neighbors and with those conquerors who attempted to impose a different way of life upon them; and, most important, that expulsion from their land and their subsequent dispersion as a tiny, weak, but obstinate and stubbornly different minority among the nations of the world, the Jew became—for many reasons, some universal and some peculiar to the particular locale—a target for mistrust, suspicion, fear, and hate.

In short, hatred of the Jew emerges from both objective and subjective factors. The first implies that if a society beset by crisis would have had no Jew in its midst—it would have invented one and persecuted him. The second postulates that when a society is given a Jew, he becomes a particular target for the mob. For, aside from all the objective factors that make a society turn upon a weak and defenseless minority, there is a special hatred in the desire to turn on the Jew. This subjective hatred is what makes the Jew like all other minorities—but more so. America is not immune to Jew-hatred. It exists here today; it is growing, and it is nurtured in the germ culture of violence and crisis.

There is no society in which it cannot happen. The mistake of believing in the immunity of certain countries from the disease of Jew-hatred was a contributory factor in the refusal of Jews to consider the possibility in Weimar Germany and in their failure to get out in time. They may be partially excused for their blindness since there was no precedent to guide them. One must really forgive a child of the twentieth century with his blind and touching faith in the new era of enlightenment, science and progress, culture, democracy, and tolerance, who stared in disbelief at people who spoke of that ancient and dying disease known as Jew-hatred. One may excuse the mistake, but never let him forget that it was a terrible one. It was an error that misjudged man's animal capacity, his brutal, sadistic, and weak nature and, in particular, his atavistic and basic hatred of the Jew.

Jew-hatred is not a dying thing. In no way does it grow weaker in democracies. In no way does it pass away with the rise of an educated class. It is not merely a religious phenomenon; it does not disappear as the Jew assimilates or integrates or intermarries, or tries to pass into the crowd. It is not solved by proletarian revolutions and classless societies. It does not disappear in the wake of culture, art, and civilization. Hatred of the Jew is an irrational and permanent thing. It follows the Jew in all his wanderings, cleaving to him wherever he goes. The Jew in exile, is that disturbingly permanent minority. He is the one who is stubbornly different, strange in his ways, different in his faith, too clever for his own good, too clannish and too arrogant as well. He is the one who cheats—else how does he prosper when other immigrants do not? He is the one who exploits—else how did he accumulate so much money when others did not? He is the target of all primitive emotions of avarice, jealousy, greed, and envy. He is the target of all the frustrations and rage because he is so small and weak. His weakness, and his reputation for weakness and pacifism, assure even bolder and more regular assaults. He is the weak link in the democratic process because his attackers know that others will not go out of their way to defend him. He is the classically different and hated minority who can never find peace in any foreign land.

Let it be made clear that it is an abnormality to live in a strange land—to be a minority is, de facto, to be a stranger. No minority is ever at home in a house that is not its home. To the extent that that minority is small in numbers, poor in influence and talent, impoverished materially, and no threat to the majority in any meaningful way—economically, politically, religiously, socially, or psychologically—it is tolerated, and hardly even thought about by the majority, as if it does not exist; and, indeed, in time it will simply disappear, assimilated into the mainstream, leaving hardly a trace.

But to the extent that it is numerically large, that it obtrudes upon the public scene, that it is extremely talented, and that it grows and prospers; to the extent that it makes itself and its different ways known and seen and felt and that it competes with and threatens the majority politically or in the economic sector (be it in the area of jobs or other yearned for things that the minority enjoys at a time that large sections of the majority cannot achieve them); and to the extent that its religious and cultural habits are strange and inexplicable so that they frighten the majority and make it uneasy; to the extent that it competes socially and sexually with the majority and sometimes succeeds in winning the kinds of things that make life bearable and exciting; to the extent that its success galls and feeds the bitterness or envy of the failures within the majority, to that extent—*given the proper circumstances*—the minority will be rejected and turned upon.

In all cases the minority is a foreign body in a system that cannot tolerate it in its peculiar form. It is either allowed to assimilate (in the case of a small, untalented, and unthreatening group) or lashed out at (in the case of a large or talented and threatening minority). In no case, however, is it permanently accepted on the same terms as is the majority. By its very nature, the minority is not the majority—it is different and, thus, not one of the family. It may be treated for a long time as a guest, perhaps even an honored one, treated with courtesy and dignity, it may even be allowed to marry into the family and lose its identity, but in neither case is it permanently allowed to live equally but differently. It will either disappear as a meaningful minority or it will be cast out or mistreated.

Jews are that minority which can never find peace in any foreign land and, in every country where they grow affluent and large in numbers or power, they can expect to be singled out eventually for persecution. There are no exceptions—not Golden Spain, nor Weimar Germany, nor the United States of America.

Once upon a time there was a land with a Jewish Foreign Minister, and let us not deprecate such things for there has yet to be a Jewish Secretary of State in the United States. And the Jews of this country prospered and owned much of the business and the press of the country, were among the leaders in art, music, writing, and science, and were such an integral part of the country that they intermarried and assimilated at a rate that made it appear that soon the community itself would begin to vanish as a separate entity. Above all, the Jews of this land loved their country. They loved it with a deep patriotism that we, today, may find a bit touching, naive, and even embarrassing. They boasted of their service in the army during the war and proudly displayed the medals they had won in defense of the homeland. They had been residents of the land for many centuries—far longer than their presence in the United States—and there was no denying the impressive change for the better that had taken place in their position. Politically, there were no disabilities; economically they prospered mightily; culturally there were none more advanced than they; religiously they had all the freedom to observe and the immense desire not to see.

It could *not* happen there. Czarist Russia was a backward, barbaric state and the Slavs who erupted into pogroms every so often were an uncouth and primitive race. But this was not Russia. . . .

Indeed, it was not. It was Germany. Weimar Germany of the '20s, where culture was more advanced than in any other country. Where avant garde literature and art made it the most progressive, liberal, and exciting place in the world in which to live, and where a "new Periclean age" was being created. Consider how Walter Laqueur speaks of the Germany of those days:

These were the years of the revolutionary theater and the avant-garde cinema, of psychoanalysis and steel furniture, of modern sociology and sexual permissiveness. It was a time of exciting new ideas and cultural experimentation, of the youth movement and youth culture. German literature and the arts, the humanities and science, were generally considered the most advanced and authoritative in Europe. Christopher Isherwood's Berlin was the most exciting city in the world.

An uncanny similarity to the kind of cultural concepts and civilization that we find today in the United States, except that Germany's was so much more profound and creative. Nevertheless, as Laqueur points out, there was so much that was similar in the cultural realities and decadence of the two eras. The chic radicalism of America echoed the drawing-room communism of Berlin West; there is a similar abnormal interest in astrology and quasi-religious groups, in the spread of pornography and drugs, and in the enthusiastic welcome and support given charlatans of all descriptions. The decadence, rootlessness, pathetic search for reason and purpose, irrationality, self-hatred and flight from freedom—all were found in Weimar as all are found in America. All the things that so sapped the strength of character and moral fibre there, that collapse before firm and determined authoritarianism, were complete—all those things are doing the very same here.

But the Jew could not see this. He saw only that his level of progress had never been higher; that he was first and foremost a German, not a Jew (a German of Mosaic persuasion was how it was put); that his fatherland and the land which he loved and would die for was Germany; that wealth, prestige, progress, and success were all his on terms of equality and acceptance on the part of his fellow German gentiles. It could not happen in Germany. Of all the countries in the world in which it could not happen, it was Germany. But it did.

The German Jew really believed that Weimar Germany was his homeland. He really believed that he was a part of the fatherland, and he really loved it and believed in it—to an extent that the American Jew cannot understand. He really believed that the comic figure, the ex-corporal named Hitler, could never succeed in turning his neighbors and fellow citizens against him. He really believed that Hitler could not possibly mean him, that he referred only to the Oest Juden—the Eastern Jews of Poland—whom he himself despised and who embarrassed him so with their outlandish long black frocks and beards, a humiliating reminder to the gentile German of his kinship to such barbarians.

He really believed that the phenomenal rise of Germany from the depths of military humiliation and economic disaster—a miracle that took place in the middle '20s and that saw Germany rise once again and take its place in the ranks of the world's leading nations—had forever buried whatever hopes the National Socialists had. And, indeed, the illusion of German economic revival was impressive. The land hummed with employment and business. People were happy and satisfied and great public works went up all over the land. The decline of the Right haters was dramatic and the 1928 elections to the Reichstag saw Hitler's party poll a pathetic twelve seats. The rise of civilized and cultured man, with the German as the paragon of the virtues, assured the continuing decline and death of Jew-hatred. The German Jew plunged eagerly and ever deeper into the business of life. He intermarried, assimilated, converted and went about his business of committing Jewish suicide so that he could be reborn as a German.

And then, suddenly, the world turned upside down. In the brief span of *five* years the German-Jewish world fell apart and its speed was such that even after it happened the German Jew did not believe it, and persuaded himself that that which Adolph Hitler had written, spoken of a thousand times, had sworn that he would do—would not really happen. But it did and we must try to understand why.

In the space of *two* years Hitler's Reichstag strength leaped from 12 to 107, placing him second among the parties in parliament. In two more years his became the largest party in Germany as nearly 38 percent of all German voters chose the Nazis. Millions of Germans voted for national socialism with all its abominations and tyranny. These were not Gestapo men nor Prussian Junkers. They were laborers and housewives, lawyers and small businessmen, clerks and shopkeepers. They were ordinary Germans who lived next door to Jews and who had smiled and associated with them for years. They were ordinary Germans so very similar to ordinary Americans. And they, voluntarily and knowingly, voted for the man who had said that he would destroy democracy, and eliminate the Jews. . . .

Let no one deceive us. The German was no more and probably much less of a Jew-hater than the Pole, the Lithuanian, the Ukrainian, the Slovak, the Hungarian, and the Rumanian under whom life for the Jew was infinitely worse. When German troops, during World War I, conquered Czarist Russian territory most Jews greeted them with joy as liberators and they, in turn, were treated with kindness and correctness. It was no accident that Auschwitz was built in Poland. The German was not a devil, had no horns or tails, was not some aberrant form. He was a man and woman like all others, just as decent or indecent, just as strong or weak, and that is the terrible and frightening thing about the entire Weimar affair.

There was no abnormal civilization here. There was no coup and takeover against the will of the vast majority of the people. There was nothing to give us some small comfort and some reason to believe that Weimar was an unnatural phenomenon, a thing that we might safely assume could never happen again. Rather there is the awful, normal spectre of ordinary people knowing what they were doing, knowing what Hitler represented, knowing what he would do to the Jews, stifling that knowledge and voting for him.

All that could happen anywhere, and in America, too. Consider the conditions of similarity: a cultural avant-garde decadence that masqueraded under the title of experimental or revolutionary theater; a sociological and sexual permissiveness that permitted nightclub orgies and pornography, and saw Berlin as the prostitution capital of the world; a bizarre interest in the mad and irrational that spurred a Berlin studio to produce *The Cabinet of Caligari,* a horror masterpiece that is a classic still; an abnormal interest in the illegal, the perverted, and the strange; an obsession with psychotherapy, astrology, and drugs; a hedonism that was almost a frantic search to burn oneself out to escape from life as quickly as possible, a youth culture and movement that respected nothing and that worshipped "life" and the "people folk"; a contempt for and loss of confidence in government and politicians; a monotonous and fanatical repetition of attacks upon the system and the establishment; a retreat from reason and rationalism to irrational romanticism; youthful cries for revolution and a love of violence that frightened a Thomas Mann, who warned against the "foaming at the mouth"; the alienation of youth from adults and the negative demands for destruction of the old without any rational substitute for it; the disintegration of authority and the loss of nerve in the face of extremist assaults; an inability to take decisive action; a country that had just emerged from a humiliating defeat and was being told that they had lost the war, not on the battlefront, but through treachery at home; a lumping together of all opponents of the Left as Fascists and a determination that Social Democrats and Nazis were basically not different; the emergence of the intelligentsia as a frustrated class with ambitions of its own, a contempt for all non-intellectuals and a desire for power; a breakdown in the moral fibre of the nation; growing fear on the part of millions of simple, normal, patriotic Germans of the rise of communism and revolution, the spread of chaos and anarchy and a desire to return to a normal, stable, and secure life. In all this, is there not some similarity to the America of today?

And more: The over-representation of Jews in the Marxist and revolutionary movements of the country; the anti-nationalism and pro-internationalist sentiment of certain visible Jews; the affluence and progress of Jews and the accompanying hate bred of greed and envy; the presence of a group that could be blamed for the "November criminals' stab in the back." Is there, again, not some similarity here? More than a little.

We must stop deceiving Jews—and ourselves. The hindsight of the '70s does nothing but cloud the realities of the '20s. We may tell ourselves, now, that the seeds of Holocaust were natural ones for Germany, but no one believed it then. We may speak eagerly and eruditely now about German militarism and barbarism that made killing natural and expected, but no one would have swallowed such nonsense then. No one believed that such a thing could happen in the advanced, progressive, cultured, and civilized twentieth-century Germany. But it did. And what happened in one place where it could not happen, can occur in America, too, where "it cannot happen."

To be sure there was also a terrible economic crisis in Weimar that was the spark that set off the social, political, and racial dynamite that so parallels conditions in America today. But there is no natural law that says that only an economic crisis can set off the madness in humanity, and certainly the American crisis of confidence, the frustrations of racial hostility, social decadence, military defeat, political hatred and fear, are powerful enough forces in a country that has certain aspects that are even more dangerous and more conducive to upheaval and tragedy than those of Weimar.

America is a far more violent country than Germany was. The everyday crime and brutality here is a thing unheard of in Weimar. Ours is a country where respect for authority at home, in school, and in government is far less than in Weimar and where drugs, anarchy, and nihilism are far more extensive and widespread. It is a country stricken with a clear and present racial problem—far more dangerous for the ruling majority than anything Germany had. Germany was basically a homogeneous country with Jews making up a pitifully small percentage. Nor did Jews pose any daily danger to the majority by threats of Jewish Power, takeovers, crime, and racial revolution. All these things *do* afflict America which is not homogeneous, which is much more divided, and whose varied cultures and ethnic groups do not, as so many liberals claim, stand as a bulwark against hate but rather as a guarantee of that hate, as each group angrily and snarlingly wants as large a share of the "pie" as possible and may join together only to eliminate the weakest of their rivals. The weakest is, of course, always the Jew who is a minority, but different from all the others, and whom the others quite correctly see as the weakest link in the chain and the one that the majority is least afraid of or interested in protecting.

Nor was Germany posed with such a threat to its freedom and existence as a free country as is America today. Germany may have brooded over past defeats, but its present was free and unthreatened. Indeed, if there was any fear in Europe, it was not Weimar's worry that it would be attacked but the fear of France and others of a revanchist Germany. The United States, on the other hand, is peopled with many millions who correctly fear a Soviet or Chinese plan to bring America down as soon as they feel that this will be possible. Such a fear creates a far greater crisis and desperation in the hearts of people than anything in Weimar.

And there is one other great difference that makes the outlook for the American Jew today so much more disturbing than the prognosis for his Weimar counterpart. Germany, the Jew, and the world of forty years ago had no precedent of holocaust from which to draw a lesson. No one could seriously believe that in our time such a thing could happen, and the thought of being the first to commit such horrors was enough to horrify and disgust most decent people. However, once an aberration—even the most obscene and unspeakable—has occurred, it is much easier and infinitely more palatable the next time. Repetition creates acceptance and it is the first step that is the most difficult. The second time there is not nearly the same degree of shock, horror, and repugnance.

On the other hand, who is there today who is so bold as to predict that America will be free of a devastating economic crisis? Are our markets, employment, and fiscal dollar conditions so vigorous and hopeful today? Are the basic conditions of American productivity and prices so healthy that we can blithely write off any kind of economic crisis? And in our times, with the rising expectations of Americans, revolution and holocaust need not wait for a massive depression of the size of 1929-39. A far lesser catastrophe can set off the explosion.

There are certainly differences between Weimar and the United States, and there are certainly more terrifying similarities. As to the differences, the real question is: Are they really relevant to the argument that it cannot happen here? Are those differences so fundamental as to make a difference? I fear not. The America of our day is certainly not Germany of 1932, but it bears an uncanny resemblance to Weimar of the late '20s, the Weimar that could never fall into Hitler's hand—but did.

Given the proper time and combination of circumstances, Jew-hatred comes to America as well as anywhere else—and perhaps more easily. The question only remains: Understanding the nature of man, knowing the weakness and violence of American society, recognizing the history of the latent Jew-hatred here, what are the conditions that exist today in the United States that give rise to fear of a true crisis? What is happening that gives one reason to believe that the climate is changing and that Jew-hatred is indeed an immediate threat? What is there in the country and within the American society to-day that suddenly makes Jew-hatred a clear and present danger, and massive persecution and holocaust a real possibility?

There is no one particular thing or reason but rather a whole series of them. We are dealing with a series of crises which will give forth fruits of Jew-hatred both because of hatred of the Jew per se and hatred of the Jew as a convenient target for frustration and bitterness.

These factors taken together, add up to a society in ferment and revolt, a nation in deep general national crisis, and a possible solution that may spell disaster for the present society as we know it, for the democratic political and socioeconomic form of American life, and for Jewish rights and life in particular. It is an honest and courageous willingness to look at the reality that will save the Jew by convincing him that it is time to return, time to go home.

PART II CRISES IN AMERICA: INGREDIENTS FOR TRAGEDY

CHAPTER 6: THE PSYCHOLOGICAL CRISIS

America's greatest strength always lay in something far less tangible than its immense material wealth. Neither the wheat fields of Kansas, nor the oil of Texas and Oklahoma, not the steel mills of Pittsburgh, nor the iron ore of Minnesota, nor scientific and technological inventiveness and technology constitute its true power. What made the nation unique and invincible was the conviction of its people that it was indeed unique and invincible. From all over the world eyes turned to America; the New World was more than a geographical term, it became an emotional ideal. Here was, indeed, a world that was new and fresh, where men could dream their dreams and see them come to fruition; a new world where men were judged on their merits and not their status; indeed, a new world where freedom and democracy were meaningful terms, where one could really speak his mind, write his thoughts, and breathe sweet freedom.

And the people who lived in this New World, and who had come from the Old, understood what they possessed and what few others did. They loved their country because they appreciated it; they knew that there was none better, and their love guaranteed a fierce devotion and dedication. They knew what life was *there,* and how much sweeter it was here. Because of this dedication there arose a real feeling of invincibility. America was not only the greatest country in their eyes, it was also the strongest, the country that had never lost a war and never would.

Such a feeling among its citizens gives the state tremendous strength. Confidence breeds confidence, pride begets pride. This inner strength guaranteed the kind of stability that helps nations overcome internal crises of the kind that tears other states that lack it apart. When a people believes that its foreign policy is always on the side of heaven, and that justice, morality, and righteousness, and freedom are allies of American might and strength, it will battle fiercely in wars, strive, and sacrifice and give willingly of itself.

When there is a psychological belief in the inherent correctness and goodness of one's nation and government, the problems that arise are met with more restraint and discipline, and extremism gives way to moderate and broad consensus. The individual learns to restrain his own desires and limit his own interests because of this confidence in his government. When people speak of the "manifest destiny" of their nation, they do not easily turn to depressing thoughts of the future, morbid national self-criticism and self-hate, and delusions about the greener grass in foreign pastures. There is a healthy self-confidence and inner strength that, in itself, is a powerful thrust toward victory abroad and growth and stability at home.

The American, until recent times, was convinced that his country was the best, the most just, the strongest, and the happiest in the world. Today that is no longer true: the sure confidence has been replaced by doubt, insecurity, deep self-criticism that borders on a neurotic self-hate, instability, and an unsureness as to where the country is going. This self-doubt is a contagious thing. Foreign nations and people sense it and treat America with a growing boldness and contempt. Americans at home feel the contempt and grow even less sure of themselves.

Within the brief span of twenty-five years, the America that helped to save the world from the nightmare of Hitlerism, that was peopled by citizens imbued with a deep sense of patriotism and love of country, whose armed forces were deeply respected and admired as the most powerful in the world, that was the envy and hope of people all over the earth, has undergone a complete change.

America has become a hated symbol for tens of millions of foreigners; it has also become the major enemy of humanity in the minds of millions of befogged and naive Americans. There is a wave of national masochism and self-hate, breast-beating and self-flagellation, that are psychological phenomena of unprecedented proportions. Millions of Americans simply hate their country. There has been a massive loss of confidence in its leadership, in its structure, and in its ability to bring happiness to its citizens. America has turned into a bitter, sullen, and unhappy country. Many millions of other Americans have responded to this self-hate with an anger whose backlash we will yet see explode into the open.

The bitterness and anger of most Americans over the wave of national self-hate and the deprecation of America and all that it does and has done, was clearly enunciated in an editorial printed in a right-of-center chain of newspapers on May 23, 1971. It should be read carefully as a classic example of the way tens of millions of Americans feel, and for an understanding that this kind of patriotic feeling can erupt into a massive reaction of violence and hate:

> Stop it, you anti-Americans! Stop criticizing everything and everybody and every motive and every action except your own. Stop constantly sniping at your government. What in the world is the matter with you? You have the most wonderful nation on earth, a nation that has gone to extraordinary lengths

to uplift the poor, feed the hungry, comfort the afflicted and extend justice to everyone. Yet here you are, applauding the very people who degrade and mock America, who tell you how selfish and corrupt Americans are. . . .

For the last couple of years you have allowed a small handful of hypocritical critics to flagellate us and our government . . . this anti-Americanism is corrupting our national soul. It's having a harmful effect on our children who are beginning to believe it. This false picture is making it easier for the haters and doomsayers and the malcontents to mislead and confuse us. It is twisting our values, making it difficult for our children to know right from wrong.

It is unbelievable that so small a minority of Americans, these loudmouths, could create such a terrible atmosphere here in this country. . . . Stop this anti-American rot. Because of you America's youth will be consumed by the stench of this hypocritical rhetoric. Stop it America, before it's too late.

A policeman from Garden Grove, California, moving with his family to England, was quoted as saying: "I am quitting America for good because I am tired of being called a pig, kicked, spat on, sneered at and having my wife and family insulted." The police officer had a tangible and personal reason for leaving. Millions of others have a much more general and basic desire to get out—they have given up on the country.

We are suddenly afflicted with a mass epidemic of national self-hatred, as in the minds of too many, America becomes the cause and repository of all that is evil and rapacious. The most incredible and exaggerated comparisons are made, wherein Washington becomes equated with nazi-fascist abominations; discrimination along social and economic lines is transformed into genocide; business corporations and their quest for profits are translated into parity with the Mafia; military leadership is pictured as a Wehrmacht, eager to kill and plunder. Every action is translated into a crime, and an evil motive is read into each word and thought. America becomes "Amerika" to the clever and foolish practicioners of the art of mass defamation, regardless of truth, and whole hosts of Americans join in the game of masochistic, national self-flagellation. The radical chic, from the tops of penthouses and the midst of the good life granted them by the "Amerika" they so glibly despise, lash out at their country; the bright young students, from homes that prosper because of the very system they would so blithely destroy, bask in the opportunities granted them by society and by their parents whom they hate and wish to hurt, and speak of the horrors of the Establishment that must be overthrown; radicals from middle- and upper-class homes blandly ignore every abomination in the Third World and traipse, with intellectual and historical blinders, through the realities of Marxism-Leninism, proclaiming their fealty to the death of imperialist Amerika.

With an intellectual microscope they would never use to study their own behavior, the nation is subjected to an agonizing scrutiny by self-appointed judges whose verdict is preordained. American guilt is assumed and history rewritten so that every past act is interpreted in terms of greed, imperialism, oppression, and hatred. Propelled by boredom, hostility to parents and a desire to hurt them, confusion and instability, and, above all, by self-hate—large numbers of Americans proclaim their undying enmity to the system and the Establishment, to America the nation and state—and pledge allegiance to the defeat of the United States and the triumph of they-know-not-what.

In concrete terms, the death of nationalism and patriotism results in a refusal to pledge allegiance to the state; the burning and desecration of the flag; alignment with the enemies of America both overseas and at home; the joining of groups dedicated to the violent overthrow of democracy; flight from the draft, and, in some cases, aid to the enemy at war; the most vile and distasteful reviling of the president and the leaders of the country, vicious attacks upon the military leadership, and the disparagement of the concepts of patriotism, love of country, and national feeling.

The spread and growth, in universities and high schools, of groups that are dedicated to the overthrow of the United States government as well as of its democratic system, is shocking. It is not only the actual members that have been bold enough to openly and formally join, but the very massive numbers of young people and intellectuals, nonmembers, who are poisoned by the Marxist-Leninist and revolutionary ideas, and who are prepared to take part actively, or acquiesce passively in the destruction of the American concept of liberty and democracy. Groups of the old Left, long thought dead, have been resurrected: Trotskyites, Moscovites, Maoists, all disciplined and ideologically strong, have come into the open. They run their own candidates and back selected others and form groups on every major campus. They publish regular newspapers and literature; infiltrate and maneuver the left-of-center wings of legitimate groups and political parties, sowing their ideological seeds among the pliable and easily manipulated young. The latter, who have grown up in an ideological and philosophical vacuum and are searching for something more than bread, are easily impressed and convinced. "Amerika" becomes, for them, the symbol of evil; patriotism and love of country are mockingly derided, and the crumbling of society has begun.

Watching all this, in overwhelming, fist-clenching bitterness, stand huge numbers of simple, unsophisticated lower- and middle-class Americans. They look, see what is happening—and hate.

I do not believe that most people, and certainly not most intellectuals and middle-class suburbanites, have any true idea of the depth of the anger, frustration, and bitterness that afflict huge numbers of Americans today. It may appear to be a joke amongst certain people to mock the kind of patriotism that was accepted by all a generation ago, but to tens of millions of "unsophisticated" Americans the traditions of patriotism, the flag, and unswerving nationalism and loyalty to country are deadly serious, and make up a major part of their sense of values.

Mocking those values, even if groups do it out of a belief that the values are foolish and outdated concepts, or even because they are thought to be harmful to "progress," in no way changes the fact that huge numbers of Americans are deeply hurt, angered, and embittered, by the cavalier, irreverent and contemptuous attitude toward things that are sacred and hallowed to them.

It is not a small and insignificant thing, this loyalty to one's land. In it is embodied a concept of gratitude for that which it has given the individual—protection against enemies from without and an opportunity to live in peace within, to raise a family and see one's children and children's children grow to manhood.

The America that the simple citizen instinctively senses is not recognized or understood by the political "sophisticates." It is an America that—with all its frailties—took in the immigrants, the wanderers, poor and enslaved, and gave them an opportunity to build a new life and climb to greater heights. It gave of its money and the best of its young so that the tyranny of the Old World might be halted before it devoured innocent people in its path. It is a country which has always allowed people to do the foolish things that its detractors and revolutionaries do today. Above all, it gave this same workingman and simple American the liberties and material benefits that he knows the people of so many other lands do not have. He works hard for his modest home and car and resents those who do not. He speaks bitterly of youngsters from affluent homes who deride the nation that gave them that affluence, and he has deep feelings of gratitude to the American society that gave him what he struggled for.

These are the things that the ordinary American sees in the piece of cloth we call a flag. These are the reasons those who spit with contempt upon it and upon the government and the men within it, who deride the institutions that others have seen bring them hope and opportunity, very much underestimate and mistake the temper of the people and the times.

The average American loves his country. He is the product of a family and an environment that looks upon patriotism and deep love of country as natural and vital virtues. He was raised to respect authority and the leaders of his country. He was taught to rise before the symbol of the nation and state that gave him what he has and vow his allegiance to it. He thinks of America as the land that gave him freedom, his home, his lawn, his television set, and he is thankful.

We make a great mistake when we underestimate the power of nationalism and patriotism. In the end, it proves far more concrete and tangible than the more illusory and visionary universalism and internationalism. It is in the nature of man to look inward rather than outward, and the familiar things that make up his homeland are far stronger magnets for his creed and his heart than foreign and strange symbols. It is normal for him to love that which is close to him and to resent those who attack it.

The act of burning a flag and of refusing to pledge allegiance to it, of defying the draft laws and failing to serve in the armed forces, anger the average American deeply. The thought that such conduct is spreading and that the philosophy behind it is being taught the young of America—including, perhaps, his own children—not only embitters him but frightens him. He is not prepared to watch his country maligned and, in his own mind, betrayed, while he sits idly by. He cannot understand why the country allows these things to continue. He sits before his television set and watches what, in his mind, are the unwashed and the unthinking defame and destroy his flag and his nation and he seethes with anger. The common tendency of the masses to mistrust the intellectual, and to envy and hate the product of the university, is given free rein here as the natural objects of his resentment give him concrete cause to pour out his wrath upon them. Here, in his mind, is the enemy from within, ready to destroy all that he has always believed in; preparing to overturn the values that have held him secure and certain; preaching the death of the America he has always been taught to love and die for.

Others may deride the concept "my country, right or wrong," but for the average American that remains a call to arms, a discipline, a dogma that commands allegiance. He cannot understand why his country allows these things to continue. He has little patience with constitutional law and civil-rights guarantees to those whom he has emotionally certified as the enemy. He cannot fathom the tolerance of those in power for the revolutionaries and defamers of his America. He will not long continue passively to accept what he sees as an "America going to hell."

He is a prime candidate for those groups and philosophies that plead with him to join them and act before the America he has known "goes under." He is a natural ally of those who explain to him that Washington itself is in the hands of the subtle, hidden, enemy, that an invisible government exists that controls those whom he thinks he has elected. Heaped upon all the other problems, all the other demons that have appeared to rip the country apart in an agony of doubt, he begins to see this attack upon the very essence of America as a careful and cleverly planned drive to destroy his country.

And so his hatred, frustration, anger, and bitterness grow until they explode into a terrible hate. And that hate becomes channeled and directed toward a concrete and "logical" target—the Jew.

There is a terrible irony here, a bitter joke, and the American Jew may yet die laughing. The angry American looks around and sees individual Jews taking a prominent part in revolutionary movements. He sees their names and watches their actions and becomes an easy prey to those groups on the radical Right who tell him: You see, as always, here is the enemy. Every Jewish name is emphasized and every non-Jewish one relegated to the rear of his consciousness. Kissinger and every other past or future Kissinger, becomes the power behind the throne, the evil and satanic Jew manipulating events and lives. Radical students and teachers with Jewish names are presented as overwhelming evidence that the Jew is behind the plan to undermine and destroy America.

The average American sees a Jewish revolutionary and does not think: Look at the Communist. He seethes: Goddamn Jew.

The irony? That these radical Jews have denied their very

71

Jewishness; that these are Jews who have cut their ties with their own people and who—for various dark and subterranean reasons—are afflicted with an incurable self-hate and a desire to flee from their own past and their own traditions. They want no part in the heritage of Israel and no part in the House of David; they have cut the ties to their people and their community, and wander, rootless, confused, and directionless. Having cut themselves off from their heritage and community, but with the full knowledge that they are still different and not truly accepted by the non-Jew, they gravitate toward universalism and internationalism, they conceive of themselves as citizens of the world, for they have nothing else. It becomes easy—and necessary—for them to tear down the symbols of nationalism and nationhood, to attack and condemn the nation and state as parochial, chauvinistic, racist, and narrow. Having no community ties of their own, they cannot conceive of their meaning for others. More, they find it necessary to become the leaders in a movement that will assure that everyone else will also join in the struggle against these symbols of "reaction."

They are not in the slightest concerned that the philosophy they preach is one that is repugnant not only to most Jews, but is basically alien even to those non-Jews whom they consider to be fellow revolutionaries. They do not realize the depths of the anger, resentment, and horror of the great masses of Americans to whom the concepts of patriotism, the flag, and loyalty to a particular country are as elementary and basic as life itself. They lead, but have few real followers; they are generals whose army will melt away at the first confrontation. It is a bitter joke. The American Jews who love their country will yet pay dearly for the acts of the minority of intellectual apostates among them, whose hatred of their own Jewishness is unrivaled by any anti-Semite.

The non-Jew understands none of this. He only sees this handful of pathetic, disoriented, rootless, but highly vocal and visible radical Jews attacking America and patriotic values. He sees them, not as radicals, but as Jews. All Jews are made to pay for the acts of the apostate few; all the vast majority of Jews who are loyal to the real Jewish heritage will be held account-able for the stupidities of those who have fled from all contact and ties with Judaism, who have rejected all connection with the Jewish people and who, to speak the supreme irony, are as much the enemies of Jewish nationalism as they are of the American kind, as much dedicated to the destruction of Israel as the United States. If not more so.

It is all irrelevant; the non-Jew is not interested. He is frightened at what is happening. He is frustrated at the thought that nothing is being done to stop it. He is bitter at the arrogance and the success of the radicals; he seethes with anger and a desire to destroy. He hates.

The target of his hate is clear to him. In his own mind, the presence of conspicuous numbers of radical Jewish intellectuals and students is enough to set off the latent anti-Semitic time bomb that has been tickling away within him all of his life. It is enough to confirm his silent beliefs. The Jew is the natural target, the eternal scapegoat. All the other, the non-Jewish, names do not count. The gentile radical is not the main enemy. It is the Jew.

The haters continually remind him of that mythical inter-national Jew, the one who owes loyalty to no one but himself, who has no allegiance to any state but only to his own interests, the one who plots the destruction of national states so that he may dominate them and combine them into a universal one, a supra-Jewish world. All the tired and weary stupidities of the *Protocals of the Elders of Zion,* of a Henry Ford, of a Goebbels, all the things we tell ourselves have disappeared from rational view, come to life in an irrational man. The Jew can never escape them.

CHAPTER 7:
THE POLITICAL
CRISIS

The outburst of national self-hatred and masochistic breast-beating has created a great political crisis for America. Those who believe, and those who wish to believe, that America is evil and must be purged by radical revolution are joined by millions of others who wish to make major changes in the system and are prepared to work together with the revolutionaries. What emerges is a powerful Left, both revolutionary and democratic, that is deeply upset by the American system today and is determined to change it, profoundly and radically, democratically if possible—violently if necessary.

More and more Americans, for whatever the psychological or political or social reasons, are disenchanted with the system. More and more are disillusioned with both capitalism and democracy and wish to substitute a different system for them. More and more are deeply disturbed by social, economic, political and racial problems and are inclined to join Left, revolutionary, radical, groups dedicated to the violent overthrown of the American system of democracy. More and more openly identify with American democracy's enemies—with China, the USSR, North Vietnam. Particularly among the young, the intellectuals, the minorities, the radical chic, and the discontented, the thought of revolution is not only no longer anathema but a flag which is waved high, and an objective which is actively sought. The old and patient parties of the Marxist Left, experienced and long-suffering, bided their time for many years, stoically endured the expected and inevitable wave of anti-Communist feeling that was symbolized by the Cold War and the McCarthy era, and counted upon the materialistic decadence and psychological crisis they knew would inevitably appear.

Revolution is invariably led by the classes that are least oppressed. The exploited are either too numb to react or too dumb to succeed. It is not the peasant who creates a theory of revolutionary communism, but middle-class intellectuals named Marx and Engels. It is not a muzhik nor a prolitarian who create a Bolshevik revolution, but a middle-class intellectual named Lenin. And it was not the Blacks who created their own liberation, but the whites who funded, guided, and in most cases led the original Black nationalist movements until they were able to stand on their own feet.

Similarly, the growth of the American revolutionary Left is a tale of young students from middle- and upper-class families and wealthy suburban and upper-class neighborhoods, who had the leisure to examine the political scene; some who found it exciting and chic to be armchair and salon radicals; of professors and other intellectuals who saw in revolution an opportunity to manipulate and lead, a chance for power and prestige; and, largely, of people who were genuinely disturbed by what they believed to be injustice and imperialism.

Many of the people who are committed to hatred of the American system, to overthrow of the government and of democracy, to victory of foreign Marxist powers and to the dictatorship of the proletariat, have successfully propagandized and manipulated many others who are not revolutionists into marching with them to weaken America.

The revolutionary Left that has grown up in America has cleverly and successfully propagandized, infiltrated, coopted, and used, a far larger left-of-center camp that has grown up in the wake of the Vietnam war, the Black crisis, and the economic discontent. This group is democratic and liberal, non-revolutionary, but discontented, and controls a growing part of the Democratic party. It may, indeed, be large enough to capture it. It is composed for the most part, of decent, honest, and sincere individuals who have been brainwashed, duped, and infiltrated by revolutionaries. Events similar to what happened in the '30s have occurred again. Then, it was the success of the radical Left in gaining control of the American Labor Party and of large unions and sections of unions within the AFL and CIO. And the same cries of disbelief that were heard then are being heard again today.

But it is true. Anti-war marches, drives for Blacks, Chicanos, the poor, and anti abortion groups, are led by people whose organizations are fronts for radical-Left groups and are wholly controlled by them. Women join, and march for peace; students join, and mobilize for peace; congressmen join, and coalition for peace. The great hope of the radical Left is ideologically to infiltrate and control the Democratic party itself so as to paralyze it and move it into a policy of isolationism and neutralism. They have already succeeded to a great extent. It would not be surprising, in the months to come, to see the Democratic party take a sharp turn left-of-center, thus polarizing the electorate and eroding, still further, the consensus middle that is already so severely shaken. The radical Left goes about the job unceasingly.

Propaganda convinces millions that America is evil incarnate, that Blacks are the victims of racist oppression, women of sexists, and youth of adult tyranny: that the Marxist-Leninist and Third-World movements are movements for freedom, liberation, economic and social equality, and progress; that anti-communism is a relic of the Cold War and its cold warriors; that America has no business being the policeman of the world and that American money should be spent, not on foreign "adventures," but on domestic problems such as slums, poverty, and the like; that America should cut its defense spending, disarm, dismantle its military alliances; and that a Socialist (read: Marxist) society should come into being which will create a proletarian society that will guarantee workers, minorities, farmers, and poor people peace on earth and security to all men. They spread anger and hate in factories and tenements of major cities; discontent and envy are fostered and malcontents encouraged, and consensus and a coming together is deprecated.

The days to come will see a growth and spread of radical-Left thinking, organizations, and activities in the United States. Fueled by the psychological, economic, social, and racial problems of the country, aided by and aiding black revolutionary groups who want revolution for their own reasons, extremism and revolutionary violence will grow, causing more and greater anarchy, chaos, and breakdown in the order of society. Greater desperation on the part of those who are oppressed and exploited or who feel themselves oppressed and exploited will result in more desperate and violent measures. Greater irrationality on the part of students and intellectuals who are in the forefront of revolution, will lead to more revolutionary acts of violence. A growing inability to solve the basic racial, social, and economic problems of the country will lead to alliances between worker and student and cause more and more to opt for revolution as the only way out.

We will all see a greater number of more violent strikes, riots in the streets, and more deadly and killing explosions in buildings, offices, and homes. We will see shooting of police and soldiers, martial law, and states of emergency. We will see fires, looting, shooting, chaos—and fear.

We will see a massive growth of Soviet and other Communist influence, prestige, raw military power, and aggression, as America—under the influence of naive pacifism, fire-breathing radicals, and cynical Marxists—withdraws from the Free World and disarms. We will see America turn inward to isolationism, its allies rush to accommodation with the Communist world, and the slow descent of the United States to the role of a second-rate military power whose own security and freedom will be in ever growing doubt.

At home, this will encourage the belief of the radicals, still further, in the decadence and weakness of America and in their ultimate inevitable success. It will spur them on to even more revolutionary rhetoric and action. The results will be more violence—and more fear.

That fear will be a chilling one in the hearts of millions of angry, frustrated and terrified Americans. It will lead to a backlash that will exceed our most terrible nightmares. It will be a backlash supported by millions of Americans who want to save the America they love, by Americans who fear for their lives and property, and by demagogic haters who see in it an opportunity for power.

The great rise in revolutionary thinking, groups, and activity will inevitably throw deadly fear into large numbers of Americans and lead to a polarization that will effectively destroy the great American consensus that has always marked this country as different from the Old World. People will not be brought together but will drift apart and then fall away into two hostile and hating camps. The middle will be eroded as extremism on both poles grows in numbers and power. Every act of violence, every explosion and killing, will bring forth calls for repression and repressive laws. This, in turn, will erode still more of the middle as many Americans who had straddled the center position will be forced to make a choice.

The moderation and consensus that kept America at relative peace with itself will come apart at the seams, and violence and extremism will take their place. Not only hard-core revolutionaries, but larger and larger numbers of others who have seen violence bring rewards in the form of collapse of authority to extremist demands, will begin to use it to get their own wishes and desires. Democracy, a fragile and often mythical concept, is always at the mercy of the vested interests of society. When these place the national interest over their own petty, narrow, and sectarian and parochial ones, democracy and society are both saved. When, as is usually the case, they are unable to, and then insist upon letting selfish interests win out, society and democracy must both collapse. The reaction that will take place as society becomes the victim of chaos is predictable. There will be a chilling fear down the spines of tens of millions of Americans terrified of revolution and threats to their own freedom, property, and lives. There will be a desperate eagerness to return to an ordered society, to a world that was once peaceful and understandable. There will be a desire to go back to an America that was calm and ordered, strong and unafraid. The words of a man spoken forty years ago, a man who could never be accepted here with a philosophy that could never be victorious here, will suddenly acquire a great deal of attention and support:

> The streets of our country are in turmoil. The Universities are filled with students rebelling and rioting. Communists are seeking to destroy our country. Russia is threatening us with her might and the Republic is in danger. Yes, danger from within and without. We need law and order. Yes, without law and order our nation cannot survive. Elect us and we shall restore law and order.
>
> Adolf Hitler, Hamburg, Germany 1932

Fear of revolution at home and of Communist aggression from abroad: these are the ingredients that make up the food of fear that America swallows and will swallow even more of in the future. Fear will be the most powerful of all drives in pushing America to the side of the haters. It is the haters who will promise salvation through law and order, strength against the enemy at home and abroad, and a return to American values and traditions. They will promise an end to racial strife and black power; they will promise an end to rioting, bombing, campus disruptions, and sit-ins; they will promise an end to social, economic, political, and racial anarchy. They will promise Yesterday again.

And who will be blamed for the chaos, the anarchy, the revolutionary threats and acts, the descent of America from a powerful, stable, and ordered society into one that is threatened on the outside by powerful aggressors growing more powerful, and on the inside by extremists and political anarchy? Of course, the Jew. The haters will see to that.

The presence of visibly Jewish names and vocal Jewish Leftists will—as it did in Weimar Germany—prove to be a boon to the haters. They will never let the country forget a single Jewish radical. They will never tire of informing the American people that it is the Jew—foreign, different, internationalist, heathen, greedy, and disloyal—who drove America to the brink of destruction.

And all that I have written is not mere conjecture. The process has already begun.

What triggered the explosion of American self-hate and remained its most glaring manifestation is, of course, the war in Vietnam and southeast Asia. More astute observers would not hesitate to say that Vietnam is not important in itself; that had it not existed it would have been, eventually, invented. In the end, this is irrelevant to our discussion. Vietnam did come into being, it did create a terrible schism within American society, it did serve to poison the body politic and unravel the fabric of American democracy to a degree we do not even begin to really perceive: It is the war that is not a war; the conflict that is fought with hesitation, bungling, and political manipulation; the disaster that sees tens of thousands of American soldiers die without knowing why, sent into a situation in which they could not win; the fiasco of fighting with limited strength and with limited aims. These are the ingredients of a humiliating and infuriating defeat for the United States.

We have not yet begun to see the inevitable results. The rumblings that are there in alarming measure have really not yet been heard or felt by most of us. But they are there. The poison has infected the American body, and it will kill. When the last of the troops are home and the ultimate defeat for Saigon,

Cambodia, and Laos comes to pass, and the full realization of the wasted opportunities and the complete futility of years of efforts, billions of dollars, and tens of thousands of dead hit home—someone will be called upon to pay. A violently angry and frustrated people will demand blood for blood; it will seek a victim. A scapegoat will be sought; a scapegoat will be found. It will be the Jew.

Already, a myth is being forged with frightening echoes of Weimar Germany. Just as in those days bitter men spoke of the "stab in the back"—the ability of Germany to have won the Great War on the battlefield if not for the Jewish "traitors" who sabotaged her back home—so, today, a similar legend is being woven. Just as the haters and the demagogues spoke to the people of the "November criminals" and the need to punish and destroy them for their treachery to Germany, so, today, has there begun a demand to search out and destroy the "traitors" who prevented victory in Vietnam and bled our country in the process. Just as the Jew then was made to pay for Versailles, so also will, today, arise a demand for his blood over Saigon.

It is not important that it is illogical and lacking in truth and substance. For the bitter loser, facts are not relevant; an emotional need to lash out at some enemy is what is important. For the embittered demagogue, all that is important is that there be bitter losers for him to manipulate and further embitter. Iron-clad logic and documented briefs are not important. All that there need be are isolated particles of truth, huge areas of half-truths, and ample opportunity to logically include lies. The mob and its individual components are never shaken by appeal to fact and reason. All the statistics, argument, and documented research will prove unavailing for the simple reason that when a certain point has been reached, the angry mob does not *want* to hear. It is overcome by a need to hate; it harbors a need to find an enemy and a target at which to strike out. All that is required is an ostensibly important reason for bitterness, a time when that feeling overflows its emotional banks, a handful of facts and an abundance of half-truths, and a logical, natural, target to blame, attack, and destroy.

All this is found in the crisis of the military debacle in southeast Asia. It is a war that, perhaps, could have been won militarily had there not been political hesitation. It is a war that saw the enemy being inexorably driven back and pounded into a progressively weaker force until the massively loud and successful protests of the "peace movement" forced a halt to bombing and a withdrawal of American forces under an artificial save-facing device called Vietnamization. It is a war that saw a massive bleeding of this country, its money and bodies, with complete failure in the final analysis. It is a war that left huge numbers of Americans humiliated, furious, poisoned, and anxious for answers and vengeance.

It does not matter that the reasons for the disaster were not treachery and treason but sheer timidity, incompetence, political error and miscalculations, and failure of vision and courage. It does not matter that it was fear of Chinese actual intervention and massive world condemnation that paralyzed United States foreign policy and limited its options. It makes not the slightest bit of difference that the peace movement back home was composed, for the most part, not of traitors and cunning Communists, but of naive and disillusioned, politically ignorant, and easily manipulated youth fearful of being drawn into a war whose reasons they disowned, radicals, bored and seeking excitement, and foolish politicians. It does not matter that, except for a handful, the peace movement that did, indeed, help America head for peace had nothing to do with treason and that, difficult as it is for the average citizen to comprehend, a Harvard cloak often envelops a political misfit.

None of these things matter. At a time when social, racial, and economic problems have already driven millions of Americans to the brink of angry extremism, the humiliating debacle of southeast Asia demands its scapegoat. It is the Jew.

The people are confused and frustrated, and so is another sector of America—the military. The military is angry over its unprecedented defamation and libelling by huge sections of the American intellectual, student, and political communities. It boils over as it considers how politics tied its hands in two

83

consecutive wars. It knows, all too well, the progressive deterioration of the United States armed forces as a strong and effective military unit. It sees, daily, the breakdown in discipline and military elan. It notes the mutinies, the desertions, the "fraggings" of Vietnam. It notes the rapid elimination of ROTC on campuses all over the country due the campaign of vilification of the armed forces by small groups of antiwar and leftist groups. It understands clearly that for the vast majority of young Americans, the armed forces are becoming identified with fascism, militarism, bloodletting, atrocities, and aggression while their commanders are portrayed as arrogant, Prussiantype, neanderthal bunglers who relish the excitement of war at the expense of countless dead and maimed soldiers. Futilely, it protests a Defense department policy that has seen the United States' lead in military weapons disappear to the point where it is becoming a second-rate military power vis-à-vis the Soviet Union, and proposes to escalate this policy by dangerous and naive disarmament schemes. It chafes as it considers the security and the very existence of the United States as a free nation threatened by a mood of isolationism and antimilitary feeling. It notes the steady retreat of United States power and influence in the world and a convergent Soviet and Chinese gain, both in prestige and in military domination and control. It sees America losing ground throughout the world while the systems of alliances crumble, and allies fly to make their own accommodations with the enemy out of pragmatic realization of American weakness. It knows that the U.S. army is not a powerful fighting force and may be incapable or unwilling to fight a war.

Its officers are bitter and angry. They become ideal sources for the haters of the Right. They easily become convinced of the existence of an invisible government plotting to destroy America, and of the truth of the "stab-in-the-back" and the reemergence of the "November criminals." Whom is there to blame? Who is the treacherous enemy back home? The very same enemy that Adolph Hitler found—the Jew.

Forgotten, really, are all the non-Jewish names—the haters

see to that. Buried from consciousness are all the gentiles who led the struggle against the war, for an end to "military adventures," for cuts in military spending, for disengagement, and conclusion to the Cold War, for an end to anti-Communist "paranoia." The names McCarthy, McGovern, Kennedy, Spock, Fulbright, Gravel are hardly thought of by the angry Americans. But the Jews. . . .

The Jews are never forgotten; they are never overlooked. Indelibly burned into the memory of the bitter military man and his sympathetic fellow citizen, is the Jewish radical he has seen parading against the war; the Jewish radical sitting in the streets of Washington; the Jewish radical sewing the American flag to the bottom of his pants. Only the Jew—there was never anyone else. All the hundreds of thousands of non-Jews who marched, never existed. The wandering Jew—eternally wandering through the subconscious of the gentile's mind, waiting for the crisis that raises him to conscious memory. The angry American sees the enemy and he focuses upon the Jewish name—it is an atavistic reaction. All the rest are blotted from memory, erased from vision. Only the Jew remains—to pay the price of mob anger and hate.

Here is not the time to discuss the historical, socioeconomic and psychological reasons for the overrepresentation of Jews in the antiwar and leftist movements. It would not help to, either. The American is not interested, impressed or willing to understand. He is emotionally only prepared to see that which he wants to see—and demands blood. Jewish blood. Frightened people are not rational people and, today, the American is frightened. Angry men are not patient and understanding creatures, and America, today, is filled with angry and bitter people seeking a scapegoat. They will find one—many already have. He is a familiar friend—the Jew.

It is crisis that brings out the hate in man, and the United States has a surfeit of crises today. Crisis brings forth all the latent hate and fury that is smoldering and festering and allows the emotional cauldron to boil over. The threat of an ever stronger Soviet Union to a progressively weaker United States is clearly understood by the average American. The terrible internal threat to stability and order that is posed by radical revolutionaries and chaotic movements of all kinds is instinctively grasped by the masses. The direct threat to the country they love and respect and, above all, *to their own freedom and security* is more than clear.

Like any animal, the human kind is most dangerous when he senses danger to himself. Who knows what the military officers may do? Who knows what an embittered corps may plan? But there is no doubt concerning the possibilities of action on the part of the frightened, angry, and desperate American civilian. He will surely lash out at the "enemy"; he will surely be lured by the siren call of the haters. Frustration, fear, bewilderment, anger, and hatred—all breeding a mood of receptiveness, inclining the ear to words which would otherwise be rejected as lunacy. For evil is born among men who are afraid and tyranny accepted by those who are insecure.

There is a great shift taking place, in our times. It involves a mass ideological movement to the right. It may not show itself overnight in the voting patterns, though the impressive Wallace vote is a strong indication, but have no doubt that it is taking place. Large numbers of ordinary citizens who only yesterday were moderates, in the center of the political spectrum, little given to ideological thought, cautious and conservative in their inclinations, have begun mentally to swing to the right. Things he clearly would have rejected in the past become acceptable to him today; ideas he would have laughed at or ignored yesterday, he soberly and seriously considers today. Men of extremes, of violence, of hate, suddenly acquire a certain sense of credibility and prestige.

It is not that these millions of Americans are Fascists or Nazis. Those who think that all voters for the extreme can be easily identified and labeled make a great mistake and only succeed in driving them even deeper into the arms of the haters. The millions of Americans who see the debacle in Vietnam and the growth of revolutionary movements and the collapse of patriotic values are not vicious Fascist-types. They are frightened people and angry people who pave the way to power for the Fascists. They are fearful and bitter people who silently assent even to haters, in the hope and belief that they will restore America to its original stability and security. Having taken the first ideological steps to the right, the swing will escalate and grow. In times of crisis a certain numbness of conscience takes place and a dulling of the normal sense of decency. Those who are insecure seek strength, not morality, and those who feel lost seek safety, not righteousness. They listen to the haters and believe them because they wish to, and need to, believe them.

And so many in America listen to these arguments: it is the Jew whose invisible government manipulated us into the war and then conspired to bleed us to death in a no-win war. It is the Jewish radicals and their groups who snatched defeat from the jaws of victory and led the successful demand that we pull out of southeast Asia, allowing the Communists to win. It is the Jew who is a slacker—a cowardly draft-dodger. It is the Jew whose control of the newspaper and communications media leads the drive to villify the army and its commanders. It is the Jew who leads the drive against patriotism and national loyalty, pledges of allegiance, and loyalty oaths. It is the Jew whose contributions to Israel constitute dual loyalty and whose true allegiance is to a secret Jewish world-domination plot. It is the Jew who incites to riots here so as to weaken the American fabric and make it easier to overthrow the government. It is the Jew who is a dove on Vietnam and a hawk on Israel. It is the Jew who is the enemy at home and abroad. It is the Jew who must be eliminated if America is to save itself.

These are the arguments that the haters on the right pour forth, and it is only the naive who will stoutly maintain that they make little impression. Is it so inconceivable that angry Americans will be impressed by these arguments? Were frightened and desperate Germans any less astute and were they unimpressed? The construction workers who beat long-haired antiwar marchers showed, for just an instant, the potential violence and hatred that lies waiting to be unleashed. Those who saw them erupt in New York City also heard the shouts of "Get the Jews."

The place to hear the voice of America is not in the salons of the chic and the place to feel its pulse is not in the lecture halls of the universities. It is in the bars and taverns where middle America and its lower and middle classes gather, that the feelings that lie just below the surface emerge. It is there that one hears what angry and bitter Americans are saying. It is not pleasant. For the Jew it may be deadly.

CHAPTER 8: THE GREAT RACIAL CRISIS

Three hundred years ago, the white settlers of America brought the first black slaves to America from Africa. America is still paying its wages of sin.

The racial crisis that began to grip the United States in the late 1950s and early 1960s has grown into a massive confrontation and bitter hostility between black and white. Only the uncomprehending fail to look beneath the superficial, outward picture and believe that racial harmony and progress have been achieved. There are, indeed, those who look and see that large inner cities are no longer set on fire during long hot summers; that the black man has made phenomenal progress in opportunities for education, employment, and general advancement; that legal discrimination has been struck down in every conceivable area of life. They assume, therefore, that things are better for the black man, that he is happier and more satisfied and that it is only a matter of time before full harmony between the races will be achieved.

It is not true. Conditions for the blacks have, indeed, improved, but racial relations have not gotten better; they have grown worse. The white American has always feared blacks and does so still. The black man is not satisfied with what he has achieved and only the foolish and ignorant will ask: Why? What more does he want?

The answer is a simple one: More. It is a natural desire, one that is common to every human being regardless of color, and it is to be seen in the demands of tens of millions of white union workers every year.

There is a clear and immutable law in human relations. It is called rising expectations. The peasant, who has known nothing but misery and poverty all his life and who has not the slightest hope of rising above his station or of improving his lot, is a relatively "safe" creature. Few thoughts of rebellion go through his tired and beaten mind; hopelessness is a poor breeding place for expectations. Give him, however, the idea that it *is* possible to improve his lot; give him hope; indeed, raise his living standard a bit and improve his misery somewhat—and you will give birth, not to a grateful creature who will thank you and be overjoyed that he now lives better than he did yesterday, but a man who suddenly has come to realize that it is indeed possible to escape one's status and to rise from the peasant level. And if one can rise one notch, why not two or three or a hundred or more? Progress never leads to satisfaction, but to its opposite. It is salt water to a thirsty man, momentarily quenching his thirst and leaving him thirsting for more.

The black man was given an opportunity to be more equal than he had ever been, and it tasted good. Quite naturally, quite humanly, he wants more and more. He wants, at least, what the white man has. The latter would react in precisely the same way if their roles were reversed.

But knowing this does nothing to change the picture of an America that, with each year of apparent racial progress through minority gains, has in reality seen race relations grow worse, as tension, fear, and hate escalate on both sides. In the black camp it is clear for all who wish to see, that black nationalists and extremists have captured the minds and hearts of the youth. On university campuses, there is hardly a black student group that is not fiercely extremist and white-hating. The patient black moderates who, in reality, won the major battles on which all the later extremist victories were built, are no longer meaningful for young blacks. Those who are not called "Toms" are simply tolerated or ignored. Their places of leadership and influence have been taken by white-hating, fire-breathing, leaders who preach separatism, revolution, community domination, and quotas. Their words are cheered by young blacks from whom the future intellectual leadership will come, and they also strike fear into the hearts of the whites who hear them.

If cities no longer burn during the summer it is not because black anger has dwindled or been assuaged. It is rather because the militant has become wiser and more sophisticated. Why burn down the stores that the community needs, leaving it barren and empty? More, the flight of whites from the cities to the suburbs assures the militant that the city will be his anyway. There is no need to burn what one, tomorrow, will have in his hand.

On the other hand, white anger, fear, and frustration has grown into a smoldering hate. The great gains made by blacks in area after area leave him depressed and furious. The majority of Americans may have agreed in theory to equal rights and opportunity for the blacks, but never in practice. Whites retain their fear of blacks as violent criminals, as ignorant and dirty, and as people with whom they would rather not have close contact. They were never happy at the thought of blacks moving into their neighborhoods, going to school with their children, competing with them for jobs, and mingling with them socially. Now that it is actually happening, they are unhappier than ever. I wish it were not so, and that the world were a nicer place in which to live; but, unhappily, these are the true facts of life. To deny the truth merely because it is depressing is a sign

91

of intellectual cowardice and stupidity of the worse sort, and can only guarantee that the situation will deteriorate still further and that no solution will ever be found.

Hatred between the races has, thus, never been greater; mutual hostility, fear, and distrust never more widespread; daily acts of confrontation and hostility never more common. We sit on a potential powder keg, waiting for the massive explosion.

Not a week goes by that we do not read of clashes between whites and blacks in some school in the United States—and how much more of the problem we never hear about, as authorities try to bury or minimize the facts. The busing of blacks into white schools has led to continuous trouble, fights, assaults and robbery. Blacks and whites tend to sit in separate groups, and racial confrontations are commonplace. Schools are closed to cool tempers; parents learn to their horror that children refuse to go to the bathroom out of fear of what might happen there; lunch money is stolen, attempted and actual sexual attacks are commonplace. White parents complain that what was once a good school has degenerated into a mediocre one, and into a place of terror and hate.

Teachers are attacked and taunted. At times they fear going to school; almost always, they look forward with little anticipation to the coming day, to the practice of what was once an interesting and challenging profession which has come to be only a job, and not a pleasant one at that. Both teachers and supervisors count the days to vacation and the years to retirement.

The busing of white children to schools in black neighborhoods has triggered a bitter controversy, open rebellion, and a massive swing to the political right. White parents, hardly neo-Fascist types as so many foolish politicians cry, violently react to the thought of their children being driven into neighborhoods they know are filled with violence, crime, and drugs. They are pledged to fight, with all the means at their disposal, the placing of their children in schools located in neighborhoods where hatred of the white is tragically rooted. And so we find masses of ordinary white citizens banding together to defy busing rulings and to vote for candidates whose racism is obvious. On a less obvious but more dangerous level, they ideologically slide into the camp of the haters. When it comes to what he considers a threat to his children, the human animal is capable of the most violent and extreme measures. In this combat, the normally disinterested female comes alive and becomes a raging tiger.

Efforts to translate equality into concrete terms by allowing blacks to purchase and rent housing in predominantly or all-white neighborhoods have led to the bitterest kind of confrontation and hatred. Whites are convinced that blacks bring crime, slums, and lower property values. Their reaction has been to threaten blacks physically who attempt to move in, or else to flee the neighborhood themselves. The result of the latter is not only that the area deteriorates, eventually, into a slum, but that the bitter white "refugee" tends to lose money on the house he dreamed of for so many years and for which he worked so long and hard, saved so patiently, and sacrificed so much. (The fact that this is exactly what the black man has been doing and strives toward is of no matter to him.) On top of this, he is also forced to relocate to a suburbia which is far more expensive than he can afford and terribly inconvenient and far from his place of employment.

Regardless of reasons, the fact is clear. Huge numbers of whites do not wish to live with blacks, and they demonstrate their feelings by fleeing both city and neighborhood. The city is thus faced with a massive flight of whites to the surrounding suburbs together with their capital and tax dollars. Left behind is a city that becomes blacker and poorer with each passing year, more segregated as a city, less able to cope with inflationary and growing social and economic demands, more bitter against whites who fled, more radical in its approach to solutions, and closer to racial upheaval and civil war. Any effort by the courts or government to overcome this by grouping city and suburbs into a metropolitan area, will see busing back and forth across political boundaries—this time at truly insane distances—taxing of suburbia to subsidize the city, and elimination of zoning ordinances which at present work to keep out the blacks. It is totally irrelevant whether these moves are moral or immoral, socially desirable or not. What is indisputable and more important is that they will escalate the hatred between the races and bring closer the day when the huge mass of whites will lose patience with decency, moderation, and democracy and fall victim to the siren song of the haters.

The bleakness of the situation is underlined by the fact that leaving the situation as it is will, in the end, probably lead to the very same thing. Bankruptcy of cities and their inability adequately to care for the most basic needs of their predominantly black citizens must, eventually, lead to rioting against whites, fratricide, and the same polarization of the communities, with blacks flocking in droves to the camp of black racists and whites capitulating to insanity in kind.

In the armed forces we see, today, a social laboratory that gives some indication of the horror that lies ahead. Leaving aside the disintegration of the military as a truly effective fighting force, the extent of hostility between blacks and whites is alarming. For every race riot that has taken place there, there are many others that the command attempts to ignore or to bury: attacks upon whites and robberies that have become an open scandal, on the one hand; open organization of the Klan and other hate groups on the other. Which precipitated which is simply a matter of debate, nor is it important. The relevant fact is that hatred between blacks and whites is open, and within an army camp, all too often, there are two camps.

Extremists of both races return home with lethal skills acquired in services and, too often, with a readiness to use them on behalf of their political objectives. Haters openly boast of their efforts to recruit veterans into their groups and of the use they intend to make of them. It is not a comforting thought, particularly in view of the inability of so many returning veterans to find decent employment as well as great difficulties in adjusting to a "normal" non-military world. Many of these veterans, despite their outspoken hostility to the army and their commanding officers, nevertheless found a certain niche and security in the armed forces and a comforting lack of the need to make important decisions for themselves. Returning home, where they now have freedom to find a job, freedom to cope with a complex and difficult world, freedom to be bored, they will find many of them drawn to ideologies and persons who offer them the dogmatic ideology, intense discipline and order, as well as the excitement of hate, extremism, and violence.

Behind much of the fear and hatred of the black is the spectre of interracial marriage and miscegenation. This wildly atavistic and primitive kind of emotion is raised continually by the haters. There are also those who harp upon the supposed lower intelligence of blacks as shown by the results of IQ tests and studies made by a minority of various scientists and sociologists who contend that the Negro has, at this point, lower intellectual ability than the Caucasian. These studies, and many that are far less scientific, are continually brought up by the haters along with dire warnings that the nonwhites, who supposedly have never created a great civilization and never will, will pollute the white race and thus contribute to the "mongrelization" and the eventual decay of the entire human race.

Such rationalizations are excellent fuel to feed those fires of emotion and fear that are sexually oriented. The presence, even among otherwise decent and rational people, of a wild, irrational disgust at the thought of interracial marriage and certainly at the sight of a "mixed" couple embracing, is clear evidence of a deep, basic, and potentially violent response in time of racial crises.

Fueled by rising expectations, black demands will increase in the years ahead, narrowing the area of possible accommodation with whites. Many of these demands will be exaggerated and impossible ones hardening the differences between the races. In many cases, the exaggeration will come from black frustration at failures of past programs and an irrational rage and fear of inferiority. Riots may even be a subconscious wish—a death wish—on their part.

Relative passivity on the part of whites in reacting to black gains in the past decade was an indication, not so much of acceptance and tolerance, but of lack of incentive and a belief that the issue was a remote one. Because of this, there was a seeming acceptance of the notion of true, concrete, equality of opportunity. But the average American still did not like blacks; believed as firmly as ever in all the stereotypes, and in no way wanted to make room for him or give him a place in the sun so long as it meant that he would get less of a tan.

There was, it is true, a reluctant acquiescence. First, because so much of the civil rights battlefield was in the South and not in the backyards of the North, East, or West. It is always easier to be free with someone else's problems. Second, because there was not really any problem in the North—or so the Chicagoan, New Yorker, and Pittsburgher thought. There were no laws prohibiting blacks from sitting in the front of a bus; there were no laws prohibiting him from being served in places of accommodation along with whites; there were vague laws guaranteeing him equal opportunity.

But the non-Southerner was soon to realize that the civil rights movement meant far more than what he had believed, and that the courts, with the power of the government behind them, meant to enforce that enlarged concept. Suddenly, talk was heard, not only about de jure segregation, but also about the de facto kind. That meant that if a neighborhood was, in fact, segregated—regardless of the reasons—integration of schools would be imposed. Suddenly, Jackson, Mississippi, came home to Chicago, Illinois, and Pontiac, Michigan. The results, we have seen. Marches, riots, burning of buses, open hate, and defiance of the laws. Northerners tend to react precisely like Southerners. Efforts by the government to put teeth into housing laws that enabled blacks to move into decent dwellings in all-white areas met with the same kind of reaction; the kind one normally associates with Alabama red-necks. But the most emotional and basic area of all suddenly became the target of minority demands—jobs.

Most of the liberal leaders of the fight for integration, and nearly all of the intellectuals and radicals, are in no way threatened by black presence or competition. They tend to be wealthier than the norm and thus able to purchase housing beyond the means of the average black. They tend to be concentrated in professions and businesses that are basically free of competition from blacks. This always makes it easier to be liberal.

In any case, great numbers of whites are in quite a different position. For tens of millions of lower class white workers there is direct competition with blacks for jobs that are increasingly harder to find, and that finds the blacks, quite often, armed with government support. Thus, great numbers of blacks have bitterly, and rightly, complained about rank discrimination by unions against them. Only a liar would deny the existence of this bigotry, but the truth is that it is a policy that grows out of the demands of the union members themselves. If blacks cannot be union members they cannot work in the trade. If they cannot work in the trade there is less competition for jobs with the whites. The result is predictable.

Because of this, civil rights groups have turned to government and demanded action. Among the remedies suggested has been the setting of minimum quotas. Thus, construction projects would be obliged to have a defined percentage of minority workers, usually corresponding to their percentage in the population. In a number of cases when the government has agreed to such quotas, the reaction of white workers has been explosive. It will get worse as the general job picture grows worse. This is a bread-and-butter issue; it is the point at which the white worker sees his security and that of his family threatened. He will fight against blacks and be fought against by blacks, who see precisely the same issue for themselves and their families. In the end, it is self-interest that unhappily decides questions of morality.

The white worker who, himself, came from poverty and is still faced with a daily struggle against inflation and the threat of unemployment and underemployment, struggled long and hard for the home, neighborhood, and other comforts that he now possesses. He has neither the tolerance, patience, nor sensitivity to understand. They are luxuries that he cannot afford. Raised in an environment conducive to violence, clannishness, provincialism, and intolerance, he neither understands nor wishes to understand anyone who appears to be a direct threat to his security and safety. For him, life is a struggle whose signposts are "every man for himself," and part of a dog-eat-dog world. His first concern remains for himself and in moments of great desperation there is nothing that he will not be prepared to do to guarantee his own survival.

And the problem of the white lower class is compounded by the presence of huge numbers of white ethnics, people whose parents or grandparents arrived in this country as penniless foreigners, unable to speak the language, subjected to humiliating experiences and discrimination, products of an era when social and economic concepts were not the enlightened ones of today. For them there were not the wages-and-hours laws of today, the government protection against discrimination and exploitation, pensions and social security, unemployment compensation, generous welfare benefits, day centers and preferential treatment. They have no sympathy for blacks, clinging as they do to the axiom that, just as they and theirs did, so must every group "pull itself up by their bootstraps."

More, they feel a sullen and growing anger at what they consider governmental neglect of their own problems. The Italian, Irish and Slav ask why they, too, are not considered ethnic minorities to be granted the same kind of sympathetic and benign treatment that blacks and others are. They see themselves ineligible for welfare but unable to meet the growing cost-of-living and inflationary spiral. They find themselves working hard at one, two or three jobs and with little to show for their efforts.

Indeed, they complain that the governmental concern for blacks is at their expense. Programs to allow blacks to take their place in civil service ranks without the need to go through the same testing as others is viewed as a threat by the ethnic white. Similar programs aimed at getting young blacks into colleges and universities are likewise attacked. Government pressure on employers to hire some more blacks is viewed as a threat to white jobs. Most of all the question is asked by the white ethnic: What about similar programs for us? What about compensatory programs for my children? What about governmental concern for the lower class, poorer and struggling whites?

The growing white ethnic consciousness and identity will be one of the great waves of the future in the United States. For years, these groups have remained quiet, docile and passive, little realizing the latent power they possess. Today, they are awakening and they are angry. Tomorrow they may generate the kind of violent force that, fed by the anger and hate that is present in such great measure in their midst, can shatter the system. They are not prepared to accept that which others, who have less to lose, are demanding that they give up. The racial situation in the United States has particular meaning to the white lower and lower middle classes. It represents a threat to them and they will react violently.

The fact that crime and violence in the streets have grown to alarming proportions is, also, not divorced, in the minds of whites, from the racial problem. They look and see an inordinate amount of black crime, including the emotionally charged ones—rape and murder. Few consider the relationship between such acts and the socioeconomic lives of the perpetrators. Ordinary people instinctively feel for the victim, not the victimizer and—above all—feel a vicarious threat to their own lives, bodies and property. The black becomes associated with crime and violence and becomes an object of fear. Such fear can only go so long without evolving into hate and erupting into violent reaction.

In the light of all these areas of racial conflict—schools, housing, employment, the armed forces, crime—all the old stereotypes concerning the Negro will be revived from the inner recesses of consciousness where they never died. The Negro is violent, criminal, lazy, stupid, apathetic, living from moment to moment, sexually permissive and yearning for white women, irresponsible and decadent, dirty. All the hatreds that never passed away, but were reserved for moments of deep drinking in neighborhood bars, will come out.

The tragic truth is that large numbers of people who consider themselves liberals, who have higher education and who are basically tolerant and most decent people have, because of contact with black violence in schools, neighborhoods and jobs, turned into people who openly fear and dislike blacks. With the huge numbers of relatively unsophisticated and uneducated masses the reaction is far more serious and severe.

For them, life is composed of simple and simplistic questions and answers: they dislike blacks and want to know how to get rid of them.

In the country, today, with far keener understanding of the mentality and gut feelings of the American white lower and lower-middle classes stand the haters. With a truer perspective of America than that from Capitol Hill, an Ivy League university, or the National Conference of Christians and Jews, they sense the deep racial ferment and hatred within tens of millions of Americans. They also sense a golden opportunity.

And so, they appeal directly, without need to mask their true feelings and intentions, to this frustration, anger and hate.

Why do you sit passively by while your daughter is forced to go to school with blacks? Why don't you do something about blacks who threaten to move into your neighborhood and turn it into an area of crime and violence where you can die and your property plummet in value? Why do you sit idly by while your job is threatened by minority groups? Join us and we will help you. Join us and we will point out the real criminal.

The real criminal. The eternal scapegoat. The Jew.

'It is the Jew who is held up by the haters as the man behind the successful civil rights movements and black demands. It is the Jew who is portrayed as the evil genius behind the scenes. It is the Jew who uses the Negro to destroy America so that he can take it over.

This is the message of the haters. They go to great pains to underline and hammer home the name of each and every Jew within the civil rights movement. The fact that Jews played a major role in the fight for equality for blacks is underlined again and again. The fact that every president of the largest civil rights group—the National Association for the Advancement of Colored People—has been a Jew is never neglected. The role of

Jews in forming and advancing groups such as Congress of Racial Equality (CORE), .Student Nonviolent Coordinating Committee (SNCC); the active part of Jews in the American Civil Liberties Union; the large numbers of young Jews who took part in voter registration drives, including the martyred Goodman and Schwerner; every Jewish judge who rules on northern busing and who strikes down de facto neighborhood segregation.

A great "invisible" plot to destroy white America is presented to white Americans. Is it really so absurd to think that desperate, angry and bitter Americans will believe it? Is it so incredible that a man who sees blacks as a threat to him and who wonders how they achieved so much progress and power in such a short time will believe the story of a Jewish plot? Is it so unthinkable that the threatened non-Jew reads all the Jewish names in the fight for civil rights and sees a "Jewish" pattern and plot? Is not the civil rights role of major Jewish groups and countless Jewish individuals public record and is not, in the mind of the angry American, my enemy's friend my enemy?

What must be borne in mind here is the hater's thesis that the black problem is really a Jewish problem and that, in the drive for black power, it is the Jew—not the black—who is the real master. Logic, reason, sanity all fly away in the face of emotion and fear. The era in which we live today is precisely one which is enveloped in emotional fear. The Jew will be the major target of the hate and violence that are the inevitable products of this fear—of that, let there be no doubt. All the years of Jewish efforts, money and time spent—in sincere idealism and decency—on ploughing the fields of the minority groups in America have now borne bitter fruit. The black is neither thankful nor loving—to the contrary, he hates the Jew bitterly. The white American, on the other hand, resents Jewish efforts on behalf of the black whom he considers to be a danger and further, blames the Jew for the rise of Black Power. He, too, hates the Jew strongly.

We are beginning to reap the whirlwind. The Jew will be the first to go under in an explosion of racial passion and that explosion, in these days of multiple crises and American despair, is almost inevitable.

CHAPTER 9: THE SOCIAL CRISIS

America is wracked today by a social crisis that is alarming both in its intensity and in its swift spread to major parts of the country. A people that a short time ago prided itself upon its dedication to hard work, discipline, religion, individual responsibility, a sense of the value compromise and consensus and a respect for authority, has—in an incredibly short time—manifested a reversal of these concepts, and exhibits all the symptoms of moral decadence that historically marks the death of civilizations and cultures.

The revolutionary explosion of science and technological progress have created a world capable of untold wealth and luxury. Daily, the opportunity to live in a manner undreamt of by kings and emperors was and is being created. Along with this has come a natural desire to enjoy and participate in the fruits of man's progress, a desire that is supported and given impetus by a whole series of political, social, and economic philosophies. All are based upon a justification of materialism and material happiness and man's inalienable and undeniable right to them. The "good life" has been hoisted high; it is the new Holy Grail. Life has been given a new purpose. Its aim has become to escape from pain and to seek pleasure; to share in the material wealth that is being produced; and to acquire the good things of life—and then more.

Life, suddenly, no longer appears to be merely a difficult path filled with burdens and problems and broken, only occasionally, by a ray of light. It is no longer merely a corridor through which man must pass in order to gain entrance into the great world-to-come. It has now become an end in itself, and offers tantalizing pleasures, luxuries, and the promise of the good life of materialism. Enjoyment has become the new moral imperative.

Naturally, the old and traditional concepts, painfully developed, earnestly taught, and handed down through generations for millenia, began to come apart at the seams. Values that stress discipline and self-sacrifice, will power and abstention, the conscious commitment to the spirit rather than the demanding body, are always at the mercy of the tempting siren call of pleasure. The race, by its very nature, is an unfair one. Man does not really want to be noble and sacrificing, he wants to enjoy good times. He does not want to dedicate himself to difficult and self-sacrificing goals, he would rather satisfy the flesh. He chooses the tantalizing immediate moment of pleasure rather than the far-off satisfaction of goodness. Little wonder that all the concepts of the Protestant ethic of work discipline and responsibility—a social and religious creed of centuries that stressed the importance of man's soul rather than his body—of the values of abstinence, self-sacrifice, discipline, work, responsibilities; of bending one's parochial benefits beneath the greater good of society; of willingness to compromise one's one desire and goals to achieve a consensus; willingness to accept obedience on the part of the inexperienced before the authority of greater wisdom and experience—all these flew in disarray in the face of the powerful charge of scientific and technological advances, the brave new world of luxury and wealth.

It was the First World War that shook America from its isolation—both geographical and cultural. The physical transplanting of Americans overseas, where they came in contact with another world, helped destroy the old orders while laying the foundation for new ideas in politics, sciences, and technology. It was the Second World War and the incredible affluence that flooded America that finished the process, marking the end of an era and the beginning of another. The simple, unsophisticated, religious, concensus-prone, accepting, patriotic American passed forever away. Under the influence of a war that wrenched America forever from the isolationism that kept it relatively simple and free from outside influences, the American was now plunged into the world around him. Technology and wealth enabled him to travel, and he saw things that wiped away his provincialism. The astounding technological advances gave him things he had never dreamed were possible, and the affluence of an America that remained the only power untouched by the ravages of war, gave him money to acquire and enjoy these things.

It is not true that poverty is the main breeder of discontent, crime, and violence. Often, the one who has nothing learns to accept his lot. But the man who is suddenly plunged into the opportunity to acquire, who begins to swim about in the pleasures of the good life, acquires a taste for it that makes his mouth water and demand more; that changes, warps, and eventually reverses his former values. "He who has a hundred, wants two hundred." The words of the Talmudic sages are as correct as is their observation that no man dies having achieved even half of his passion. And the greater the passion the more consuming the desire to satisfy it.

Under the influence of science, technology, and an exploding wealth of goods and materials, a new philosophy of "enjoy" came into being. It was a philosophy that destroyed all thoughts of a world to come, and which demanded that enjoyment *now*. People could acquire pleasure and they did so. Discipline, willpower, restraint, and the thought of putting off the enjoyment of pleasure, were relegated to the junkheap of historical antiquity.

At the same time, man's old concepts and sense of values were shaken by his new sense of power as his intellect and mental ability lay open new scientific and technological worlds. Man's genius arrived at its full flowering, and the fear and awe that had given birth to respect for a Higher Power and obedience to church authority was shaken and, eventually, wounded fatally. Man's mind had given birth to a belief in himself and in his intrinsic ability to achieve great things for himself and by himself. Man's heart was captured by the tempting, overpowering lure of the good, beautiful, materialism he was creating. The combination produced a predictable result. Old values of authority and discipline and a contented acceptance of fate came crashing down. In their place were hoisted new gods—all dedicated to the glorification of now; to the pursuit of material happiness; to pleasure and good times.

The natural, almost human desire to flee from responsibility and travail to pleasure and instant gratification *now,* was abetted by countless philosophies that encouraged materialism and gave birth to new adherents. Liberals of the nineteenth century extolled man as the repository of reason and goodness. They believed that in his brain was to be found all the wisdom and rational thinking to enable him to climb the highest mountain, reach the farthest star, achieve the sublimest peace, create the most abundant wealth. It was not true that Heaven had created man; it was rather man who had conceived of Heaven. Aided by scientific concepts of natural evolution, a glorious future was painted for man if only he would free himself from the fetters of man-made authority and medieval, primitive, superstition and acquiescence; if he would inquire into and question everything.

What political liberalism and Darwinian science started, economic materialism finished. Karl Marx was a product of the rationalism of his times, of the liberal belief in an unbounded world of material progress, in the enjoyment of this world, rather than in the contemplation of the next, for others besides those few who had always enjoyed this world's luxuries. If materialism was the goal of man, why should not all people achieve it? Why should not the worker as well as the bourgeois and the aristocrat have the right to enjoy the fruits of material happiness? And so socialism and communism arose based on the pursuit of material happiness in this world and its acquirement by all men. It emerged not one whit different from the bourgoise liberalism and capitalism with which it is locked in mortal combat. Political combat it is, but not ideological: the struggle is now evolved over who shall enjoy the fruits of the abundant material life, not over the right of man to do so.

Marxism is merely an extension of the ideological and philosophical capitalism that emerged in the latter part of the medieval era and made its first breakthrough during the Renaissance; it sided with king against pope; supported merchants who favored Protestantism in the belief that the newly emerging values would allow for an enjoyment of life by more than the few in this world. Free yourself, it cried to the impoverished. Smash the chains that fetter you! Rise up from the oppression of authority and medievalism. Life is to be lived as you see fit! You are answerable to no one but yourself. Arise, O man, and crown yourself king!

It was a great success: the revolution of science and technology; the dawn of a potential for the enjoyment of material luxury; and the political and economic philosophies that urged all men, not only the privileged few, to set their sights on a full life in this world, and to bring down oppressive authority—all succeeded.

Idols and icons came crashing down; churches and Heavens were cast aside—parents and home; priest and church; teacher and school; leaders and government—all these and the authority, teachings, and commands that emanated from them were weakened, and, eventually, became irrelevant. In their place, men hoisted the new faith, the new religion, the new authority, the new life: man, his desires and pleasures, his instant gratification, his right to do his "thing."

The process has continued to the present day, and the results are there for all to see. The home has been torn apart as parental authority is smashed by youngsters who have been raised to question everything, and by parents whose own way of life has led to an abdication of responsibility. After all, if children desire only the good life and an escape from responsibilities, do they not merely reflect the ideas their parents generate? How many of their elders are people whose goal in life is merely to acquire material possessions and to attain a good life of luxury? How many of their parents secretly wish to acquire the life-style of the anarchists they unsuccessfully and unconvincingly denigrate? The home is under attack by forces that question its authority and, more and more, it loses the opportunity to instill its sense of authority in its children. It is a monotonous cycle: the home is attacked and authority diminished; the diminished authority loses its ability to instill discipline into the child, and respect for obedience and authority; in turn leading to further assaults upon it and less ability to withstand the assaults.

Schools are under attack by libertarians and are restrained from acting with authority. Students' rights are trumpeted as teachers and administrators are straightjacketed and paralyzed. The school is stifled in its efforts to create strength of character and self-discipline, and the child is the great loser. He joins the ranks of a generation that is weak and frightened, insecure and unsure, suffering from the pagan worship of self with neither love nor respect for the object of his adoration.

Government becomes a target of all the malcontents who are caught up in their own parochial and narrow interests, unconcerned with the larger good and unknowledgable concerning the complexities lying in the path of solutions to social and economic problems. They are unable to practice patience, austerity, and discipline. Their leaders have taught them well. The politicians who purchase elections with grandiose and impossible promises of instant Nirvana have sown the seeds of greed and desire all too well; the result has been a bumper crop of greedy, clutching and demanding hands, of envy, impatience, and immature demands for instant magical solutions. Everyone is promised everything and everyone expects someone else to pay for it. The outs are promised in and the masses of the less privileged guaranteed a better life at the expense of the rich. Democracy, infused with populist pandering to greed, envy, and instant gratification, turns more and more into mobacracy with demagogues ready to stand up and fuel that process with impossible promises and outrageous pledges they know will never be met. When, inevitably, promises are broken and pledges unredeemed, mob fury grows hot and its patience short. In the end, the mob breaks through the weakened dike, flooding democracy, stability, and civilization.

With the collapse of authority and restraint, long-accepted morals began to die in America. The traditional values that had been a permanent part of the America of old crumbled, first slowly and, then, faster and faster. With that collapse, an incredibly decadent society has been created, unable to discipline itself, its needs and desires, or to look beyond today; with a lack of identity and purpose and an irrational drive for pleasure to escape a terrible boredom it can no longer cope with. Irrational, too, are its attempted solutions to our loneliness and boredom; its desperate and frantic race for excitement and new fads. The new society suffers from rootlessness and cynicism, from self-hatred and its resultant expression in violence, a lashing out against the world to destroy it.

This terrible society that is being created is one in which flight from pain and race toward pleasure have been elevated to a principle of living. Sex for its own sake—in its most preverted forms—has gripped millions of Americans, driving out love, the most powerful of all human weapons against man's animal self. Men and women use each other rather than love each other, with an unprecedented immaturity and weakness.

Losing ourselves in the numerous pleasures of instant and loveless sex, we are ever more dissatisfied groping for something real. Sex becomes illicit, with prostitution and adultery and perversion and mass orgies and wife-swapping becoming more and more common. When he finds himself still unsatisfied, the most bizarre sex is accepted, and even homosexuality and every kind of aberration, defended and upheld as a proper and more beautiful kind of experience; millions of Americans turn to all that is unnatural and decadent—all the while defending, militantly, their own madness. Raised in a society thus committed to pleasure and gratification, America is becoming a nation ever more hooked, like some addict, to the goals of pleasure.

It is not strange or very difficult to explain. The key effect of the materialistic society that created this great pleasure imperative was to create, too, a society of weakness. Who is truly strong and courageous? ask the rabbis. One who is able to conquer his (evil) inclinations. American society is pathetically weak and fearful. It has become a society totally unable to conquer its passions, that collapses before desire, pleasure, and enjoyment without a struggle. It is this societal weakness that drives men and women to escape from the difficult task of creating mature and lasting relationships based upon mutual respect and honor. It is this weakness that leads to illicit relationships, to homosexuality, and aberrations; where there is no need for honor, there is no need to live with mutual compromise and respect. These relationships are the natural refuge for the weak.

It has caused a mass flight of Americans toward escape from hard and difficult reality. Whether through drugs, liquor, or entertainment, the average American—more than the average citizen of any people or society before—escapes daily from reality and its hardships. Strong men face up to the struggles and conflicts of life; weak ones ignore them by pretending that they are not there and expecting them to disappear of their own accord.

It is because of this that so few drug addicts are cured. For their addiction to a particular drug is merely a secondary reaction to a far more powerful and terrible addiction—escape from pain and reality. The need to flee from painful present to pleasure of some kind has driven a whole society to drugs, from the tranquilizers that housewives cannot survive without to heroin that is their children's recourse, and the drunken stupors of their husbands. It is this weakness and inability to cope that has seen an infinite increase in the psychiatrist's couch and the analyst's patients.

It is this weakness that sees a wholesale abdication of responsibilities, a flight from the difficult consequences of our own actions and a retreat from the hard obligations of life. Women reject motherhood, men their duties as fathers and husbands. Children are raised in homes where parents have lost their traditional roles and have not yet found their new ones. Rather than bear an unwanted child who gets in the way of their pleasure and freedom, women simply stop having children or limit their families to one or two. They idealize their actions in terms of the need to refrain from overpopulating the world, but the real reason is to avoid inconvenience.

People no longer want to work, no longer give an employer every minute he has a right to expect of them, and produce shoddy goods and shoddy services. There is no longer immediate contact between a man and the finished product of his work and no pleasure in a hard and productive day's labor; more time is spent dreaming of leisure than concentrating on the work one is paid to do.

In the affluent and presumably happy society that materialism built, the suicide rate is still disastrously high. We are an unhappy and a weak people.

Life appears to be too hard. It is easier to escape from our problems than cope with them. And so, how much easier it is to be a permissive than a disciplinary parent: how much less difficult to find an instant solution in allowing a child to do whatever he wants and in gratifying his whines, wails, and shouts. How much easier and less demanding. Because American parents are seekers after pleasure, they both understand what his child wants and also know the easy way to quiet his whining. They simply collapse before their child's selfishness and demands; they try to give the child everything—and destroy him in the process.

We see the results today in all their alarming aspects. The child who is given everything grows to demand and to expect everything. He becomes progressively weaker in character and unable to cope with adversity and refusal. Once outside the home and the artificial womb America has created for him, he faces, for the first time, the chilly and cold reality of the world. And he cannot cope with it. America is the land, par excellence, of men unable to cope. It is dotted with nervous breakdowns and psychiatric and mental clinics. It is filled with pill-popping housewives and their immature husbands. Difficult problems and admitted crises in life become unscalable mountains before which Americans collapse and go to pieces, rather than struggle tenaciously to overcome.

Although the American male complains about women's domination and demands for liberation, secretly, he welcomes it. When his wife takes over as master of the home he may lose her respect, but he also escapes from the responsibility that he feels is so awesome and difficult. In the end, the American man is no longer quite a husband, his woman not quite a wife. There is a great loss of identity which leaves everyone confused and uncertain, with the child the greatest loser of all. Raised in such an atmosphere, he becomes an adult who is destined to follow the path of weakness, decadence, and aberration.

A person who is weak and has lost the respect of those whom he most cares about and from whom he desperately needs respect, is a man who will never respect himself. He is a self-hater; such men are dangerous. For people who are filled with self-hate cannot love anyone else and will transfer their hate onto others. It leads them to their own destruction and, like Samson, to drag down with him as many Philistines as possible.

Thus, the social crisis in America has produced two terrible dangers to the continued stability of society, to the domestic process, and, ultimately, to the Jew. The first danger results from the outward effects of the crisis; the second, from what the crisis does to the character of the person whom it has affected.

The outward effects of the social crisis are to be seen from the reactions of people whom the crisis has hurt, or frightened as they watch its manifestations in terms of the problems it creates: a shocking rise in crime; a drugs disaster; a collapse of morals and authority; a denigration of traditional religion. These are problems that are the most dangerous of all because they affect people in their daily lives. They are not remote and theoretical; they hit home. The weakness and decadence of America has bought crime, drugs, and moral disaster into the home—and the backlash cannot be long in coming. The many millions of Americans who have retained a commitment to hard character values and discipline and who see the results of the Age of Weakness and the social crisis today, are frightened. They are frightened for the country, but mostly they are afraid for themselves and for their children. Such people are angry people and they hate. They hate those who are threatening them and they look for ways to stop them as well as for ways to return to that which they regard as sane and normal.

The social problems of America, which strike at the country as a whole and at individuals in their personal lives, are too serious and real to ignore as a potential for explosive backlash.

Crime explodes in America. People who never locked their doors now have bolts and locks of ingenious complexity. Fear keeps people inside their homes even as they became the targets of burglars. Muggings, rape, and armed robbery become commonplace, and crime and its partner—fear—grip the American scene.

Whole neighborhoods have become terror-ridden places of fear. An elevator no longer is merely a convenience, it now becomes a place of lurking danger. Streets are deserted after dark and organizations rarely hold meetings at night, if they can help it. Crime is exploding in the country and it is a fact that cannot be denied. People are afraid, and no problem is more meaningful to people. We talk of civil rights, and no civil right is more basic than the one of which so many are deprived—the right to normal safety and immunity from attack.

And, added to the staggering rise in the quantity of crime, is an even more disturbing change in its quality. Crime was once mainly the province of the poor; now middle-class youngsters indulge in it as well. Worse, the attacks have become tinged with a viciousness and sadism that was never seen before. People are killed for no rational reason; victims are brutally beaten even after they have turned over their money. Young children are more and more the perpetrators of vicious crimes, and people are afraid their own children will suffer—either as victim or victimizer.

People grow weary of violence and chaos; they long for safety and order. When that weariness is too much and the violence grows unbearable, people will exchange their freedom to walk the streets in fear for the safety of totalitarianism. That, in itself, raises a desperate challenge for democracy; but there is more.

No matter how painful it may be, the fact remains that a majority of visible crimes are committed by minority groups— by blacks in particular. The argument of liberals that these things occur because so many blacks are poor and deprived is not at issue here. People who dislike blacks to begin with, are not impressed with sociological explanations; they care only about their own bodies and the possibility of harm to their own persons.

Thus, the call for law and order and a hard-nosed demand for strong laws to stop crimes. Denizens of safe neighborhoods tend to take liberal and, what they choose to call, "humanitarian" and "progressive" views on such issues as capital punishment and treatment of criminals. The millions of largely blue-collar and lower-middle-class Americans who live in the urban centers are far less sophisticated and tolerant. Living in a danger zone has a most emphatic effect upon one's social and sociological views.

There is a demand for hard and fast action against crime and a bitter resentment and hatred of blacks for committing so many. But most of all, as with every other issue that touches on black-white relations, the racial antipathy toward blacks manifests itself in a primary hatred of Jews. Again, as in all other racial problems, the Jew is blamed for the black. Here, where the issue is such an immediate and intimate one for so many whites, the reactions are emotional. Hatred of blacks acquires greater intensity and tangibility, and hatred of the man who is looked upon as the power behind the blacks, the Jew, grows in equal proportion. The fact that so many Jewish liberals live in the suburbs and are relatively free of the problem adds to this hatred. The non-Jew in his latent hatred of the Jew under the best of circumstances, is not bothered by such facts as the large number of poor and middle-class Jews who live in urban areas under, perhaps, worse conditions of crime and fear than he. Facts that will exculpate the Jew from guilt are never popular with the Jew-hater. And so he concentrates only on the Jewish judge who may give a criminal a lenient sentence and the liberal Jewish politician who speaks out against harsh penalties for criminals. As in all other things, irrationality wins again and it is the Jew who is blamed because of his liberalism and support for the black—who is blamed by the haters for the upsurge in crime.

Shooting of policemen comes as a particular shock to the American. Not only does his first line of defense suddenly come under violent and audacious attack, threatening him with anarchy and the jungle; not only is there, in his mind, a planned, revolutionary, and, usually, black conspiracy to kill police, but authority in its most visible and powerful form is under the gun and the country's stability and actual existence are threatened. The average American is frightened and angry that these elements in society have become so bold, and is prepared to do anything to change the situation. More important, the police officer who has suddenly become the target of snipers and assassins reacts predictably. He moves sharply into the ideological camp of the haters. He is suddenly wide open to their blandishments, and the longtime prejudice, bigotry, and sadistic violence so often a part of the makeup of people who gravitate to the police force, are exacerbated. Who knows how many peace officers are members of hate and fringe groups? Who knows how many so sympathize that they would stand idly by and watch the haters come to power? Too many. For the Jews it is a shocking thing.

The terrible specter of drugs haunts millions of American

homes. The age of puberty, the beginning of their children's march into the world outside the home becomes, more and more, a terror for the parent. One cannot overestimate the feelings of dread that drugs have introduced into the hearts of parents in this country and the bitterness against those who refuse to join the battle for the harshest of penalties against drug sellers, the anger toward advocates of legalization of certain kinds of hard drugs; unimaginable are the feelings of many Americans who see, in this, part of the whole spectrum of permissiveness and liberalization of morals and standards. Their children are at stake and, like all animals, the human is most dangerous when protecting its young.

The collapse of authority and respect for home, school, and laws, and the social collapse of respect and honor for one's "elders" and those who "know better" is, to the average parent, nothing less than a challenge to save their children. In their own minds they lose not only the respect and love of their children, but the special, irreplaceable and unique relationship that makes the bond between parent and child so sacred. In effect, they lose the children themselves. It is too terrible to contemplate, and breeds a special kind of bitterness in the hearts of those who bring them into the world, nurse and care for them, weep and worry over them, dream their dreams for them and are now brought to the state where, figuratively, they bury him. The death of morals as understood by a generation of tens of millions of Americans, morals practiced and accepted as natural and immutable, morals that were part of the Christian heritage for centuries, leaves these millions angry, bewildered, and frustrated. It is not only that they see the country going to hell, but, much more important, they watch their own children becoming targets of new ideas, concepts, and values, and practitioners of the "new" morality—neither new nor moral, but as old as paganism.

The collapse of the kind of morals the American has always known is not a thing to be taken lightly. There may, indeed, be sophisticates whose progressivism is manifested by their gracious welcoming of a daughter and boy friend to sleep in the same bed, but for most Americans who are still gripped by the old morality, standards of sexuality remain as they always have been and the rise of promiscuity, permissiveness, premarital sex, homosexuality and other aberrations, are things that herald disaster for America and their own children. The new morality is represented by the incredible growth of pornography and sexual deviation, by books and films that openly portray the kind of decadent activities that no one in the not so distant past would ever have contemplated or condoned; it represents danger and fear to the average American. It is part of the whole cycle of decadence, moral decline, and the crumbling of American strength of character and discipline. The era of permissiveness, the intrusion of sex education into the schools, and studies in birth control is seen by millions as a disastrous, undermining of the American, Christian, moral fiber.

Again, the culprit in the minds of millions of frightened and concerned Americans is the Jew. Every Jewish name linked to sex education, pornography, or sensitivity training is carefully noted. Every absence of a Jewish name is forgotten. The fact is that liberals are in the forefront of drastic social change and a revolution in values and concepts, and in the minds of many non-Jews, all Jews are liberals.

Liberalism is synonymous with freedom in non-economic matters. Freedom to do whatever one wishes if it does not harm one's neighbor; freedom to go to hell if one so wishes. It is this that drives the liberal to the position that man has the right to do with his body what he wishes and there is no authority with the right to impose its standards upon him. And so it is the liberal who is in the forefront of abortion on demand; for the right to smoke marijuana; for the right to produce, read, and watch pornographic art; for the right to perversion in sex; for the right to have children exposed to explicit sex education; for all the things that tens of millions of Americans have been raised from childhood to look upon with horror, all the things that Christianity (and other major faiths) have long taught to be sinful and evil; all the things that simple and ordinary American parents instinctively and quite correctly sense are dangerous and disastrous to their children and to society as a whole.

Since liberalism is in the forefront of the new morality, it is the Jew who, over and over again, stands out as a spokesman for this morality. For it is the Jew who is overrepresented in the ranks of liberalism, and the latent hatred bursts forth and smolders. The Jew: he is to blame for the destruction of Christian morality and the death of our children and the society of America.

It is hopeless even to attempt to persuade such people of the strong and unflinching stand of traditional and genuine Judaism against all these things that Christianity condemns. (After all, it is embarrassing continually to point out that the values of Christianity were borrowed unquestioningly from its mother religion, Judaism.) The average American is not interested in the fact that the vast majority of liberal Jews who preach the new morality are ignorant of even the most basic concepts of Judaism. The troubled American is not interested in the fact that many believers in Judaism are even more upset at its ignorant members who preach so many things that negate their own faith. The latent dislike of Jews is far more powerful than reason or logic. When the issue is the future of the American child and society, the irrational refusal to be fair or to listen is reinforced. The Jew is the culprit. He is blamed for the death of morals, values, and concepts long held sacred by the majority of Americans.

Established religion that did not even realize it had begun to die was befogged by its statistics-oriented euphoria that, following the war, counted bodies at Sunday church services as true religion. It did not understand the superficiality of mere attendance, its *social* rather than religious motivation, the temporary symbolism of its opposition to communism in the days of the active cold war, and its lack of relevance for young people who were being brought up with contempt for the hypocrisy of a Sunday religion; its message made little impact where values were shaped by television, money in one's pocket, and the philosophy of "enjoy" that was encouraged by the weakness and permissiveness of parents.

It was only a matter of time before religion as it had been known by the majority of Americans, began to fade. Church attendance began to slip, with youngsters conspicuous by their absence and—the logical corollary—an attack on the basic and most sacred tenets and beliefs of the church. Youth questioned everything and adults could not give them answers. Worse, more and more churchmen—from priests and ministers to high officials—had their own doubts and problems. Rather than retiring to some quiet corner to solve them, they began, publicly, to deny and question hitherto fundamental beliefs. The result was a watering down of all uniqueness, an obliteration of all differences, and a social-justice concept that differed little, if at all, from humanism and secular social concepts.

The changes in traditional and familiar ritual—sometimes articulated in rock 'n' roll rituals—dismayed, bewildered, and angered millions of Americans whose long-held habit of acceptance of authority at first prevented vocal protest. But the anger and the bitterness were there—fed by fundamentalists of all sects—and it was not long before the anger gave rise to a sincere belief that there was some form of conspiracy to destroy the churches and the American Christian heritage.

Naturally, it was the Jew who was blamed, and the traditional hatred toward the Jew that is fed by New Testament teachings acquired reinforced strength. Not only were these the Jews that had crucified Jesus, but they were now attempting to subvert and destroy the churches that preached His gospel.

In the retreat of religion from the great power it once held, we tend to forget the powerful hatred and antipathy to Jews that traditional Christian teachings always contained—and still do. For centuries, when man lived in an age of faith and religion exerted the most powerful of all influences upon his thinking, Christianity pictured the Jew as a permanently treacherous villain who, for the sin of deicide, was permanently doomed to suffer exile and persecution. Christian children were taught this—directly or indirectly—in their religious schools and even in the most enlightened and well-meaning churches by the very nature of the New Testament story.

The efforts of churches in recent years to soften religious attacks upon the Jew and to absolve him of "blame," flounder in the face of continued teaching of the New Testament, which no rational person would ever expect to be stopped; by an unwillingness of masses of Christians to accept these efforts; and by the hostility of millions of angry Christians who see the church's attempts as only one part of a "new" church whose changes they resent intensely. There remains, therefore, a large reservoir of traditional church-taught Jew-hatred plus the added hatred that comes from the anger, frustration, and bitterness of Christians who believe that the explosion of atheism and alienation on the part of their youth as well as the fundamental changes that have taken place in their church, are the fault of liberal Jews and are, indeed, part of a conspiracy fostered by them. This is a terribly emotional issue that carries with it serious implications and a potential for disaster.

This religious disintegration and accompanying Jew-hatred is supplemented by rising clashes between churches and secularists over various issues that center around the constitutional question of separation of church and state. As the secularist age of materialism unfolded and the philosophical and ideological power of religion began to decline, the secularists of the country sensed unprecedented opportunities for the advancement of their cause. Court suits were brought challenging concepts that had long been traditional, accepted and considered to be permanent institutions.

Prayers in schools, despite their nondenominational quality, came under attack. Christmas pageants, Christmas trees in schools or on government property, were challenged. Government aid to struggling church schools that were being choked by inflation and rising costs, was fought. Under the banner of the First Amendment's separation of church and state as interpreted by the secularists, a whole array of challenges to religious aid and presence were thrown up, with some of the more extreme demanding such things as an end to armed forces, chaplains, and the tax-exempt status of religious institutions.

The reaction from the vast majority of Americans was one of revulsion and anger. There is no question that, if put to a referendum, the prayers, Christmas symbols, and government aid to private schools, would be overwhelmingly supported. The Christian could not understand the refusal of the Supreme Court to allow a simple prayer to the Deity to be said by kindergarten children. He was amazed at the protest over a Christmas play which to him was a fundamental part of his tradition. Above all, he remembered that, in *his* day, all these things had taken place without problems, and he assumed that these were their normalcy, naturalness, and vitality. Catholic parents, anxious to give their children a religious education and unable to meet spiraling costs, were bitter over the attacks on aid to even the secular aspects of their children's education.

The fact that in the majority of cases those who brought the suits in court or were amici curiae, friends of the court, were Jews or Jewish organizations, led to inevitable resentment, anger, and hatred of the Jew. The average Christian had no idea that the Jewish groups that came into court to attack the things he considered important, were not representative of the Jewish community, and that religious Jewry was as much for government aid to schools and nondenominational prayers as were religious Christians. The Christian—inherently antipathetic to the Jew to begin with—only saw the Jew, a minority in Christian America, blocking him from Christian values. Every victory won in court by a major American Jewish secularist group is in the end a disastrous defeat for the American Jew in terms of added resentment, rage and hatred on the part of the Christian. For, no matter how long we cherish the illusion that this is not a Christian country, we are wrong, for the simple reason that it is the faith of the majority. Thus, the results of the social crisis create a psychological climate of Jew-hatred, as the Jew is blamed for them. The haters know this and harp upon it. The hatred will yet explode into violence against the Jews.

But there is yet another, in the long run more dangerous, effect of the entire social crisis that has afflicted the America of our times. It consists of the effect that the degeneracy and decadence have upon the character of the people who live in its midst afflicted by its weaknesses and sicknesses. What kind of a man is produced by this society and how will he stand up to commitment for democracy, liberty, rights and responsibilities? Most to the point, what will be the relationship between ultimate Jew-hatred and the new-morality man?

What kind of man is produced by a society that undermines authority, discipline, self-denial, hard work, responsibilities, willpower, and respect for compromise and consensus?

What kind of a man emerges from beliefs, values, and concepts such as those that have captured America over the past few decades? What is the American that stands before us today, and what can we expect from him?

What emerges is a dangerous creature who is capable of any kind of action when driven by desperation, frustration, anger, and fear.

When society's values and concepts preach material happiness as the great goal of life and the overthrow of all restraint and authority that keep man from the freedom to pursue all that he cares to pursue; when he is unshackled from all moral restraint, he is a man cast adrift to flounder about in anarchy and chaos, lost in a freedom that has neither beginning nor end, nor real purpose nor meaning. Man is not an animal; he must have a purpose or he will go mad. Being told merely to enjoy the good life results in his trying every fad, joining every trend. Every luxury hungered for, tasted, enjoyed for a moment, turns to ashes of boredom and is discarded for a new plaything. He tries everything legal and, when that fails to satisfy him, he moves on to illegality. From there his discontent and restlessness lead him to perversion, madness, and a desire to escape from reality and from life itself. What emerges is a man who is restless, purposeless, bored and terribly, terribly weak.

The life that has been presented to modern man is a maze from which he can never escape, without beginning or end. He has no idea whence he came, and consequently, does not know where he is going. He has been presented with the fountain of the good life and, immersing himself in it, he finds that it quenches his thirst only momentarily, driving him, later, to a more terrible and burning craving, until he is no longer master of his own fate, but a pitiful creature at the mercy of his drives and emotions.

And this is exactly what has happened to America of today, the sophisticated, "hip" America that so scorns past values and authoritarian fetterings. It is a lost and frightened America and a lost, weak, and frightened American man. He runs to and from each new fad in a pathetic hope that here, at last, he may find an answer to his existence. There is precious little real difference between those who escape to beer or to heroin, to exotic political causes and religions or exotic sex. Their motivations are all too similar: not so much a desire to help others but a need to escape from the demons of purposelessness and rootlessness that pursue them, and a need to find some meaning in life.

Man becomes a captive of his own needs and desires. His rush to self-enjoyment—to freedom—brings him not the freedom he seeks but a tyranny and mastery that is imposed upon him by his own selfishness. The American has become a victim of a massive boredom and weakness that threaten his sanity. He no longer finds quiet satisfaction in family, job, obligations, and home. He has been told to enjoy, and he needs to enjoy, and his frantic search succeeds in uncovering vast areas of unenjoyment and discontent, but little else.

Boredom and weakness are potent and dangerous conditions. Bored and weak people are capable of committing all kinds of horrors. Life becomes an escalating search for adventure that will shake loose that boredom and weakness, and all manner of irrational acts may stem from it. There is a growing sense of irrationality and insanity about the actions of Americans, particularly the younger ones. Not only do we have more nervous breakdowns and psychiatric clients than ever before (there is indeed a mass mental breakdown and insanity in the air), senseless acts of violence occur more and more frequently; people from comfortable and even wealthy homes steal and rob looking for that ever demanding thrill; political attacks upon parents and country, both of which have given the attacker the kind of life billions hunger for, are made with a totally irrational desire to transform the freedom, which they demand for all, into slavery and tyranny for themselves. Devil cults with inevitably weird and irrational murders, spring up as a mad and frightening desire on the part of religious and political extremists to kill and destroy. Parents beat their children with a savagery that defies explanation. Irrational explosions occur that see mass killings of families, and political assassinations are perpetrated by faceless men who yearn to find themselves, for one moment, and to have the world notice them, if only for a grisly, passing instant.

This boredom, irrationality and violence are manifested clearly in rock music and the incredible, mass hypnotic and irrational displays of hysterical screaming, rioting, and anarchy that attend concerts of leading popular rock artists. The booming, deafening, beat of drums and the passionate throbbing of rhythm that drives those who are gathered to share the experience to an emotional eroticism and passion, reminiscent of the hysterical adulation and mass hypnotism that we saw yesterday in Hitler Germany and that can also be transferred, tomorrow, from music to politics in America.

The lashing out at a world which he hates, the brutal, sadistic violence and the stomping on a real or alleged enemy is the way out for those whose strength of character and sense of restraint and discipline have been eroded by the weakness and decadence of the new morality. Given nothing to live for but himself, given an ego and selfishness that sees himself as the center of the universe and, at the same time, bored, frustrated and without purpose because he cannot achieve the great things he has been given freedom to do, he is capable of taking out all his frustrations and inhibitions on those who are weaker than he. The parents who dominate, the teacher who dominates, the employer who dominates, the wife who dominates—all are explosively wiped away, as, at last, there is someone weaker and more unfortunate than he, whom he can dominate. All his dreams and passions for wealth, sex, power, that he was never able to realize, demand payment now—payment from the scapegoat, the weak and defenseless, and when that scapegoat superficially presents a justifiable excuse for attack; when he is stereotyped as wealthy, cunning, cheating, avaricious, different, clannish, and strange—then the perfect justification and rationalization makes that target an even more tempting one.

Given a crisis that threatens him, those around him, and that which he possesses, the new moralist will collapse beneath his own weaknesses, insecurities, and fears. His character and moral fiber have been rotting away for so long, leaving him far weaker and less able to stand up to challenge and moral responsibility than Americans of years past. The American who has been running from responsibility and difficult problems for so long is well known to his wife and children. The incredible rise in broken homes, separation, and divorce are a testimony to the immaturity, weakness and flight from responsibility of men in our times. There is hardly any reason to assume that in political, social, and economic crises, he will suddenly acquire greater courage and strength to do for others what he was too weak to do for his own kin.

To the contrary, it is clear that when threatened by crisis, the weakness and frailties of the modern American will—far more than in Germany—drive him to lash out at those who he feels are threatening him. He will, unhesitatingly, seek the support of a strong man who promises to save him. Weak people are rarely consistent ideologists. The very same hidden reasons that drive them, at certain times, loudly to support one end of the political spectrum will move them, overnight, to back the opposite. Self-interest is the only permanent yardstick.

Is not such a man perfectly capable tomorrow of turning, for the sake of his own security and sanity, to an authority infinitely more firm, demanding, and disciplined than the one from which he has escaped? When Erich Fromm speaks of "fear of freedom" he helps us understand that although man would dearly love to be free, he is unwilling to accept the responsibilities that come with freedom, once achieved, his life for the most part, becomes frighteningly purposeless and goaless. He is a ship anchored in a port that has become too oppressive. In great delight, the crew watches as the anchor is lifted, and the ship drifts into the wide ocean, free to do whatever they desire—without compass and without sense of direction. In the end, such people yearn for the safety of the harbor—any harbor. They trade their long-sought freedom for a totalitarian authority, infinitely more demanding and oppressive than the one they overthrew. This is true even in the absence of tangible crisis, how much more so when there is danger and threat to one's life, property, and one's little world. At such a time the weak and fragile product of the new morality will drop all pretensions to democracy and freedom, justice and tolerance. In self-preservation, he will throw the nearest and weakest scapegoat to the dogs. Even for a person strong in character and moral fiber, it takes courage to withstand the siren songs of hate and fascism when they promise safety and security. For the product of an era that has preached and practiced self-love, pursuit of the good life, fun, self-gratification and self-indulgence, screwing up courage and fortitude becomes infinitely more difficult. Perhaps impossible.

Nor should we delude ourselves into believing that the vast numbers of young people who apparently abhor the haters of the Right can be counted upon to stem the tide. In the proper time, the Left will also join in the crusade, as so many of the Left can switch their allegiance. The instability and passion that originally moved them can be guaranteed to move them yet again.

The target? The victim? Of course, the Jew. He is the weakest and the most logical. A minority—a small one—and one that has "made it." His relative prosperity and well-being mark him as a target for all the frustration, hate, envy, and jealousy of the weak new moralist who, weak in character and morality, will leap to destroy the weak in numbers and power. The savage outlet for their own weakness, boredom, fear, and facelessness is always the scapegoat—invariably the Jew.

It might very well be that a massive explosion of hate and a great flight to the haters of the Right will eventually come without a serious economic dislocation. The weaknesses of our times could very well see a more dangerous situation than that of Weimar Germany which needed an economic crisis to send hate crashing down on Jewish heads. It may very well be that the pressures and frustrations, complexities and facelessness of the modern world will themselves prove to be too much for a weakened man to cope with. It may very well be that all the social problems we have mentioned plus the growing specters of litter, pollution, poisoning of the environment, reliance on machines and mechanical gadgets whose breakdown leaves whole cities and millions of individuals helpless and hapless; overpopulation and crowding; urbanization and its dehumanization—all the tensions that afflict man in his daily rat race through traffic and nervous breakdown—will, indeed, lead to a breakdown of the human spirit and flight to the political psychiatrist whose remedy is totalitarianism; exchange of freedom for security, and elimination of the Jewish cause of all problems. It may well be that social tensions, breakdowns and weakness alone will yet bring the face of the Holocaust to America. But it is more probable that there will have to be some form of major economic dislocation and fear to spark all the other crises that make up our times. The ingredients for that kind of economic crisis are not lacking and they bode ill for the democratic process and the Jew.

CHAPTER 10: THE ECONOMIC CRISIS

Man does not live by bread alone and, in our times, that simply means that he also demands cake. We live in times and places far more dangerous and potentially more explosive than any previous. We live in a nation that for more than a quarter century, has lived a life undreamed of by kings and emperors in history. The vast majority of Americans have tasted the good life, have wined and dined at tables the likes of which potentates never sat down to. Never in history have so many people in one society owned so much that is material, luxurious, and comfortable. Homes, automobiles, television sets, indoor toilets and bathtubs, boats, appliances of all kinds, leisure, and assured employment and overtime in order to guarantee payment of all the loans and installments owed on the good life.

Such a people can be dangerous; far more so than peasants and beggars who have never enjoyed this life. The paupers and needy have little real or tangible concept of what they are missing. Their expectations are low, and hope for better things rarely rises in their breasts. A life that is complete misery seldom produces angry revolutionaries. It is, rather, conducive to apathy, hopelessness, and resignation.

When man, however, has tasted the good life and knows that there is more to existence than suffering, squalor and poverty, his expectations have been aroused, his appetite whetted. When he, himself, has reached a certain level of affluence he will not easily allow himself and his living standards to be lowered. When he acquires a certain stake in the good life he will not voluntarily agree to return to something less. He will rather become an angry and vicious opponent, a man ready to follow the most obnoxious, terrible, and extreme of men and groups if only they offer him a way to hold on to what he has. It is the one who once had little, later acquired a touch of the good life, and is now threatened with its loss and a return to his misery, who is the most dangerous of all men. He will do anything to hold on to what he has. That is exactly the problem of America today.

The Second World War marked the end of so many different things for the United States and the beginning of so many others. Among the things that ended as the war burst over Europe and then dragged America into the flames was the worst economic catastrophe ever to strike the country. Many millions of people were out of work for years, living on relief, at a time when that concept carried far more shame than it does today and when proud men accepted it only with the desperation of a last resort. The foundations of the country were shaken and talk of revolution swept the land as never before. Extremist groups surged forward and millions of men and women listened soberly to their words, words that they would have rejected out of hand only a few years before.

And then came the war, sweeping before it—from the face of the earth—decency and civilization, along with 30 million human beings. But in America it brought a strange blessing—the proverbial ill wind that always blows some good. While men and women died *there,* men and women worked *here* and accumulated money. There was full employment in the United States and the memories of the long soup lines and apple sellers of the previous decade slowly faded away in the full bloom of prosperity.

When the war ended and production turned to products of peace, American pockets were filled and people spent as they had never been able to in the past. America began to acquire all the luxuries and magic that modern technology and science began to produce and the factories could not keep up with the demand. This in turn produced more and more full employment and life was beautiful in the United States, land of freedom, wealth and envy of billions.

More, America emerged from the war as the one country unscathed and undamaged. Not a factory was destroyed and not a city leveled. Production was geared to an unlimited ceiling with not a serious competitor in view. All the rest—from Britain, France, and Germany in the West to the Soviet Union and Japan in the East—were in ruins. They were our markets, and the markets that had formerly been theirs were also ours. We stood alone, a monopolistic giant with no competition for the markets that our goods began to flood. Again, full employment was assured for us and America began to wallow in a luxury that would carry it for nearly twenty-five years.

Markets are the key to the prosperity of any country, and America is no exception, whether domestic or international; the main thing is to have markets for one's goods, and buyers to whom to sell one's products. If there are buyers, one makes profits. One is able to pay the workers who have produced for him and who depend upon the sales of his goods. Failure to find buyers means that production must be cut or discontinued. Such cuts mean that not all the workers and producers are needed and, consequently, staffs and working forces are laid off. These layoffs add up to unemployment for the workers, underemployment for professionals and executives, and a loss of the good life they have long enjoyed and upon which they depend in order to pay off the bills and installments on the individual items of the good life—home, appliances, automobile, college.

The destruction of American competitors, that took place during World War II, is now a thing of the past. One can walk through European cities that, in 1945, stood eerie and shattered, broken and battered, and not find a trace of war left. In place of the rubble and war-scarred structures, stand new buildings, shiny, bright, and modern. What has taken place in cities has also occurred in industry that, a quarter-century ago, lay devastated, crippled, and unproductive.

The Germany we pulverized with indescribable air raids and massive shelling has risen from the carnage. Thanks to the America that destroyed it, and that it now competes with in deadly fashion, its factories were rebuilt with the newest and most modern methods—far more modern and productive than our own. It pours forth its efficient and solid products that are at least as good, and certainly cheaper, than American ones.

The Japanese, pragmatic, efficient, and businesslike, used American money and knowhow and built themselves into an economic superpower. Their factories too are new—newer than many in America—and produce products that undercut ours to an extraordinary degree. In both cases, Germany and Japan, the differential in the price of the product is the result of the glaring difference in wages paid to workers there and here.

Consider the incredible difference between the wages paid to a Japanese or German steelworker and that paid to members of American steelworker unions. Is it any wonder that these competitors of America are able to sell their products at far lower prices and, consequently, win more and more customers and markets away from us? Industry after industry in America is hurting—seriously hurting—from this deadly and serious competition. Industries of all kinds are losing out on the world markets and selling fewer and fewer of their products. Indeed, the competition is so formidable, that even Americans in unprecedented numbers snub domestic goods and purchase foreign imports. Tape recorders, cameras, radios, sewing machines, glassware, automobiles, and textiles begin to bear foreign labels to an extraordinary degree.

The results are seen most dramatically in the shift from an America which, year after year, had a surplus of trade and basic balance of payments, to a country which in 1971 had its first trade deficit since 1896—a staggering $2.9 billion. They are reflected in the rising unemployment and layoffs as factories fall behind in the competitive race and have to cut back production.

All of this is the result of the lower wages of overseas workers; the sharp rise of wages in the United States due to workers' demands for higher wages (despite the fact that productivity not only did not increase but continued to decline); a selfish refusal on the part of employers in the huge, basic industries to cut back profits; the sharp lag in what was once a great American technological superiority; and a lazy and selfish attitude to one's employment that creates a general malaise and a refusal to care very much about one's work.

Perhaps the wages of overseas workers will rise in time, but they will be matched by new demands by United States workers and their union leaders, who must show that they are doing enough for the workers in order to keep their executive jobs. There is no sign of any change in the basic selfish and irresponsible attitude toward work or much hope of significantly higher productivity on the part of the workers. There is no sign that they care about the fact that only higher productivity—which will bring down the labor cost per unit of production—will enable their company to compete with foreign goods successfully and thus enable them to keep their jobs. There is no sign that workers' absenteeism on Friday and Monday is being reduced or that they will be more willing tomorrow to put in a complete day's work any more than they are today. On the contrary, there is every indication that workers will escalate their demands for more money, fewer hours and less productivity. They are, more and more, the subjects of interest of radical Left and Right groups who urge them to make more and more impossible demands. There is every indication of radical infiltration of unions, of sympathy on the part of younger workers who know about the Great Depression only from history books and who would rather have fun than eat, and of the displacement of more responsible union heads with younger, more demagogic ones who wish to take over unions with lavish and impossible promises.

There is no indication that the captains of industry are, in any way, prepared to cut profits in order to make the competitive battle an easier one. It is still simpler to lay off a worker than to cut corporate rewards. It is much easier to open a factory in Hong Kong or some other area of cheap labor, thus maximizing profits even though domestic workers lose their jobs. Employer and employee, both, share in the wave of the new selfishness and help each other to commit economic suicide.

There is no indication that the technology race will be dominated by the United States as in the "good old days." Vast amounts of money for civilian research and development are being spent in Japan and Western Europe. The rise of the Common Market with its great resources of workers, capital, and skill will be yet another formidable competitor for the United States.

Any tough efforts to meet this competition through trade barriers and tariffs is almost certain to bring about retaliation and a massive dislocation of international trade that has brought prosperity to the Free World through an unhampered flow of goods.

With a prognosis such as this, a decline in exports and in domestic selling, too, can only continue as higher prices and inflation drive both Americans and foreigners to buy the cheapest goods. In efforts to overcome the loss of market, industry will turn, more and more, to three tools: layoffs of workers, which will create dangerous unemployment; flight of investments overseas, which will do the same; and automation, which will do the same to an even greater degree.

Unemployment will reduce the purchasing power of the jobless worker who will be unable to buy, leading to the purchase of still fewer goods, the curtailment of production, still further, and a drop in profits and tax revenue that would ordinarily come from those wages and profits. It will increase unemployment still further with an attendant demand for unemployment compensation and a burdening of the dangerously overloaded social welfare machine of federal, state, and local governments at precisely the time when there is less money to feed that machine.

Still another worrisome factor that may seriously decrease tax revenue and economic growth is growing economic nationalism overseas. Not only are we faced with increasing nationalization and expropriation of industry by nationalistic and radical governments, but even friendly countries such as Canada, under pressure of nationalistic feeling, are beginning to put a priori limits on the amount of investment they will allow. This shrinking of investment opportunity decreases even more the amount of taxes available to pay for the important and growing social needs of the country, thus exacerbating an already dangerous situation.

What is happening, as productivity and competition fall behind, is growing unemployment, falling profits, falling tax revenue and soaring demands for social welfare and benefits at a time when they are impossible to fulfill—all combined by an implacable and stubborn inflation. For the average worker this means surging prices that wipe out any higher wages; growing difficulty in finding a job (at a time when social policies are increasing the labor force by making it easier for minority groups to compete with him); staggering federal, state, and local taxes that make it imperative for him to work at two jobs, and his wife at yet another—if they can be found; ballooning welfare and other social costs that compound his taxes even more; a cutback in public and private services as inflation and soaring prices destroy purchasing power and the dollar's value; naked crisis in city after city that finds the tax base shrinking as middle- and upper-middle-class families flee while demands for service grow as their places are taken by unskilled and unemployed minorities; friction and inefficiency building up in our ever more complex industrial machine that becomes more and more vulnerable to lack of skill and interest; an environment whose poisoning must be met with funds that are unavailable.

More and more lower-class, lower-middle-class and middle-class Americans see things they took for granted shrink or disappear from their grasp. Unemployment and inflation will decrease available money for mortgages and installment payments with foreclosures, and repossessions increasing. We will see more and more small businesses go bankrupt. We will see more people forced to live on the savings they had put away for their retirement; elderly pensioners and fixed-income people frustrated and alarmed as their monthly checks buy fewer and fewer of the necessities of life; and a forced cashing in of United States Savings Bonds until a critical moment is reached when the government may not be able to pay on demand.

Such an economic crisis that sees huge personal and governmental debt, and a cutback in the services and good life of many years, is a particularly dangerous thing for a people that has taken it for granted and that has been terribly weakened in its ability to accept adversity and a cut in its living standards. The fun-loving and pleasure-drugged American is not geared to accept drastic and serious cuts in the life to which he has become accustomed; certainly it is excruciatingly difficult for him to accept crisis and a personal economic crisis.

The kind of situation that transformed prosperous Weimar into depressed Weimar and eventually into a prosperous totalitarian Hitleriasm can easily develop here and its roots are clearly visible. Again the words of Nazi Rockwell:

> Our battle is not planned for today when the white man has two cars, a power lawnmower with a little seat for his lardy bottom, bathrooms with hi-fi and all the rest of the easy living of today's white American, but for the inevitable day when our phony, debt-ridden war-scare and "foreign aid" economy blows sky-high . . . when Americans have nothing, they have nothing to lose.

It is true that people who have nothing to lose are the most dangerous of all and the crises-laden American powder keg may await only a match of economic crisis, to explode. People are angry, frightened and frustrated by their economic problems.

Most Americans are in debt and many are without the jobs and wages they counted upon to pay those debts. There is a revolt against the oppressive taxes that saddle productive citizens and against welfare services where so much of those taxes go.

There is a feeling of frustration that is articulated in such words as: "You struggle and slave and have nothing to show for it." There is a Populist feeling that government and politicians are corrupt thieves and that the rich and swindlers are making money at the expense of the little American, the "people." There is a terrible fear among people on fixed incomes as to how they will be able to survive on their shrinking dollars. There is a gnawing fear that the civil service pensions that local and state governments owe may not be honored as these units face ever more real threats of bankruptcy. There is deep despair as local government runs out of money and services begin to be eliminated. Above all, there is a feeling of apprehension among people who sense the loss of a world they are not prepared to give up cheaply.

Nor should we overlook the continuing crisis of the dollar. The dollar, that since the agreement at the Bretton Woods conference in 1944, and through all the years of unchallenged American productive, technological, and trade superiority—if not monopoly—has stood as an unshakable rock and as the unofficial world currency, is under attack today as never before. The huge outflow of dollars from the United States, an outflow that was unchecked, brought with it increasing demands for gold payments as promised by the United States treasury. The reason that the dollar was accepted by the trading nations as the international currency was because the United States promised to redeem every dollar presented by foreign central banks with the gold that was the real world value. As long as United States gold deposits were sufficient to assure such exchange, the system worked magnificently. But with the passage of time and the unchecked flow of dollars out of the country, the amount of gold shrank to a point far below the amount of dollars that were theoretically able to call for that gold. When the demand for gold on the part of increasingly nervous central banks grew to a point where it appeared that U.S. gold reserves would be depleted; when the dollar began to take a buffeting of staggering proportions, America was forced to renege and to go back on its pledge to redeem dollars with gold. The credibility of the dollar is shaken to an extent we may not yet fully realize.

Thus, we stand today in an uncertain monetary world. The dollar continues to be weak and to be mistrusted. The price of gold zooms higher and higher. No one really knows what will happen as the world searches for a new international monetary system. The possibility certainly continues to exist, and with ever greater probability, of economic nationalism, protectionism, and breakdown of nearly three decades of limited free trade. Should the dollar or free trade break down, the United States will face a crisis of terrible magnitude, and certainly a crisis of confidence in the dollar and the men whose job it is to keep it strong. This crisis of confidence would merge with other crises and with a mistrust of government that already exists. It will feed the peoples' discontent and give birth to all the bizarre and strange monetary schemes of populism that seem invariably to precede mob rule and hate.

What happens when people see their economic life closing in on them, their dollar weakened, their standard of living threatened, unemployment, underemployment, and inflation squeezing them, crushing taxes, making life ever more intolerable and never seeming to make the quality of life better? What happens when the lower and upper lower classes, together with the middle level of society, feel themselves and their economic positions and status threatened? The answer is quite simple. Given enough desperation and fear for their own property and future, they are prepared to sell out freedom with its insecurities and to accept totalitarian security with all its lack of freedom. They look for swift and simple answers to the dilemma and—bewildered by the nebulous, unseeable economic forces that cause their plight—seek a concrete, tangible enemy against whom they can vent their spleen.

In Weimar Germany this is precisely what happened, as the same economic problems that plague America today worsened and exploded into depression. Many desperate Germans abandoned the centers of democracy, social democracy and democratic conservatism for the demagogic extremes that gave them simple answers and simplistic enemies. The Communists gained many of the workers, but so did the National Socialists, the Nazis. The latter, for the most part, did not appeal to the industrialists, Junkers, and upper-class and aristocrats middle classes as so many think. Hitler derived his strength from those who had been destroyed by inflation and depression and who writhed in agony at the fact of declassification. They, who looked with supreme contempt upon the lower class directly beneath them, were overjoyed to find a radical party that was nationalist rather than proletarian. The emotional insecurity which occurred because of the economic destruction of the middle classes brought in its wake a loss of faith in the values of the old order. Democracy and capitalism both came under suspicion and attack and the bitterness that arose from the feeling that the system had betrayed them, led the middle classes—the bulwark of liberalism and democracy—to abandon the system and to seek something else. They turned to the Nazis.

The farmers saw agricultural prices fall severely and farm income decline disastrously. Foreclosure of farms became commonplace and farmers who, only yesterday, had owned their own land were now tenants for large landowners or were driven into strange and hostile cities. They, too, became bitterly anti-capitalist centering their fire on the banks that foreclosed on them and the bankers who ran them. They turned to the Nazis.

The lower classes, the lumpenproletariat, showed a marked turn to Hitler as well as to the Communists. Their misery, unemployment, and despair led to a condition tailor-made for demogogues who knew that they were dealing with the most responsive material—men who had nothing to lose and who were prepared, therefore, to do anything to lift themselves from their misery. The Nazis promised them a new world, a new order.

The Nazis were able to promise all things to all men, and appealed to the most primitive and powerful instincts in those men. If the peasants sought the security of land tenure and protection against creditors, they would be given that. If the middle class wanted to fight the industrial monopolies' unstoppable competition against the little merchants and businessmen, their high price and low wages, the Nazis would oblige. Above all, the Nazis were prepared to pander to the frustration and dissatisfaction of the discontented—the new Populists of Weimar Germany.

The Nazis were radicals and their social and economic programs—though fraudulent and impossible to achieve—were catered to appeal to the radical, envious, and expropriative, drives of the malcontents. The Nazis railed against exploiting, parastic, finance capitalism which was opposed to the productive capital that could be used for the benefit of the people. They cursed the international bankers and speculators who were the cause of their economic misery. Both Marxism and capitalism came under Nazi fire as the Nazis preached a glorious national socialism that would give both national pride and social stability to the wandering and frightened masses.

Thus did the Nazis speak to the discontented populists of Germany:

> Let the victims of exploitation overthrow their tyrants! Let our comrades unite in an oath to the country; then socialism and nationalism will be united as Adolph Hitler demands. No reform will rebuild the house in which they must live united for life. Only the German revolution which fate calls for, will make the Third Reich a reality.

And:

> The Party is striving against the present system and against the "three hundred" international capitalists who govern the world.

The February 24, 1920 program of national socialism contained planks that were designed to appeal to the most excited emotions of the malcontents:

> We demand the suppression of all income acquired without labor, and trouble, the abolition of any domination by gold and money.

> We demand the uncompromising recovery of all war profits.

> We demand the state ownership of all businesses hitherto carried on in the form of trusts and cartels.

> We demand the workers' share in the profits of big business. . . .

There is more, but it is enough to see that the appeal of a Marxist of the Left and a Hitler on the Right are almost indistinguishable to the frustrated, frightened, and angry citizen who is the target of their promises and blandishments. He could not care less about the philosophical and ideological nuances. He only knows that now he has less than he had and that what he has is threatened. He only knows that the system in power is threatening him and that here is a group that promises him a New Order. Given the proper fear and desperation—just as in Weimar—he will move into its camp.

There remains only one indispensable ingredient. The enemy—concrete and real—must be found and identified. In Germany, the haters gave the German his devil. That devil, that enemy, was the Jew.

It was the Jew who was the parasite; it was the Jew who was the exploiter, the speculator, and the international finance capitalist. It was the Jew who was the cause of all the economic misery and it was the Jew who would be made to pay and whose elimination would bring a new era of prosperity and light into Germany.

All this happened in Germany. Economic misery moved a frightened and desperate people into the camp of Satan. Those who moved into the camp were not themselves devils; those who voted for Hitler were not cruel and evil—they were simply frightened and desperate, and such people will do the terrible things and say the terrible words they would never dream of doing or saying in better and less desperate times. But the times *were* desperate and the people did do what they did, and they did support a man who destroyed six million Jews.

What happened in Weimar is duplicated here, at least in its early economic stages. The same discontent and anger of economically unhappy people is manifesting itself in the rise of a Populism in which can easily be seen the seeds of neo-fasicsm. The haters of our time, the disciples of the National Socialists of forty years ago, the new Nazis, exacerbate the problem, exaggerate the fears, multiply the anger and frustrations and blame the Jews.

How easy it is to turn economically troubled people against Jews who appear to be affluent and comfortable. How easy it is to turn the mob against a people they fear in competition, envy, against whom they nurse grudges and whom they hate? Especially when that people is one against whom there is a natural, latent, hostility. . . . The Jew is such a classic target! How can people not see the similarities between now and then?

The true nature and character of a man, the rabbis tell us, is revealed in three ways: through his pocket, his cup, and his anger.

When a man's pocket is empty, his cup and his anger both come into play and the real beast within him, the real hostility, the real Jew-hatred that grips him, emerges.

The economic problems that grip America are real and basic to the structure and the system. They may improve temporarily and bring psychological relief to many, but, in the long run, they are dreadfully complex and much too difficult to solve without the patience, austerity, and sacrifice that most people in democracies do not possess. Even without all the other crises that grip America, the economic one would hold within it the potential for holocaust. Together with the others, it stands as an even more explosive danger. It stands as one more reason for immediate planning for the Jew to go home.

PART III
THE
HATERS

CHAPTER 11:
OBJECTIVE:
JEW HATRED

Hatred of the Jew, as a Jew, is a phenomenon dating back many ages. Again, the reasons postulated are legion and each carries a certain kernel of truth. But whatever the reason or reasons, none can doubt the existence of a deep, malignant, actual hatred and fear of the Jew that has transcended boundaries, people and time. He is hated more than others and by more than others. He is hated for himself, for what he is, or for what others think he is. In short, he is hated as a Jew; because he is a Jew. This hate is a problem without a solution. No matter what the Jew does or does not do, no matter how ingratiating or docile or innocuous or invisible he may try to be, it will not help. Persecution may abate, but hatred of him and for the Jew that he is will remain.

It is this kind of hatred that lies dormant in the hearts of people until it flames up for a thousand and one irrational reasons. This is an anti-Semitism whose followers hate the Jew subjectively and without a real or rational causal connection to problems or crises. It is the kind that searches out the Jew and blames him for all problems regardless of the absurdity of the charge because—in his subjectively blind hatred of the Jew—the accuser wants, specifically, to attack him rather than any other possible target. It is the Jew-hatred that Jabotinsky called "the Anti-Semitism of Men." We have dealt with this in previous chapters, but there is another aspect to hatred of the Jew that is less understood, that is more dispassionate and objective. It attaches to him not necessarily because he is a Jew, but because he is there—in the wrong place, at the wrong time. In a word, it is the hatred that attaches to the Jew who, if he did not exist, would have been someone else. The hatred that would have attached to anyone in a similar position to the one occupied by the Jews.

Jabotinsky, Borochov, and other Jewish thinkers of the late nineteenth and the early twentieth centuries, realized that aside from the hatred of the Jew as a Jew, there was also hatred of him because of objective political and socioeconomic factors. It was what Jabotinsky called "the Anti-Semitism of Things." This Jew-hatred, he maintained, was a product of peculiar political and socioeconomic changes in society that led, inexorably, to the Jew being driven from society—not because he was a Jew but because he had occupied a place in that society that the majority now desired.

Jabotinsky referred to Eastern Europe, and to Poland in particular, where Jews lived as a large minority amidst a hostile and frustrated majority. It was a society where equality for the Jew would have meant overwhelming competition for the Pole. Concentrated in cities, and the product of long generations of education, intellectual scholarship, and sharpened mind, the Jew posed a formidable challenge to the Polish peasant and urban dweller alike. In equal competition he was assured of capturing a large number of positions that were in short supply even without him.

It was clear to Jabotinsky that the competition for a relatively short supply of desirable positions would inevitably lead to hatred of the Jew and to efforts to push him out—not because he was a Jew but because he was a stranger who was taking things from Poles. The inevitable was a refusal of duality to the Jews, their being driven from the positions they already held, and the resultant probability of poverty and deprivation for the vast majority. The solution was evacuation from Poland and emigration to the Land of Israel.

What Jabotinsky wrote concerning Poland is, at least, as applicable to the United States. The laws of physics are clear. Two objects cannot occupy the same area at the same time. There is a similar social law in society and, especially, in the modern, complex world that has arisen in the twentieth century.

When the Jew arrived in America in large numbers, he came to an underdeveloped country that had vast space for tens of millions. He did not come to an economy that was advanced, mature, and stagnating, but to an economy operating in a vast country of seemingly limitless unsettled territory plentifully provided with natural resources, and a serious shortage of labor. There was room for all to come and live, without desperate competition for jobs that elsewhere were so few in number. And so all kinds of immigrants arrived with the Jew, but each tended to gravitate into different areas—all of which needed them.

The Italian became a laborer and builder, the Irishman a policeman, fireman, and minor politician, the Anglo-Saxon masses were largely rural farmers and dwellers; the blacks simply did not count. The Jew, blessed with talent, intellect, and skill went into other areas where he was unchallenged and, there, proceeded to prosper. He became a businessman, went to college and entered the professions. America was a big country with a ravenous appetite for all kinds of people to fill many different jobs.

For huge numbers of Americans the thought of competing with Jews was out of the question. The professions required college and university training, and tens of millions never remotely considered themselves suitable, either mentally or financially. In addition, the Jews were an urban people and thus completely without contact or collision with the half of the country that then dwelt in rural areas (never expecting that they would have to leave someday). Jews entered professions and areas of civil service that required the kind of training and mental capacity that both higher education as well as generations of devotion to mental discipline, study, and education had given them. They became teachers (in part, also, because they could not become the doctors and engineers that they would have preferred), social workers, attorneys, pharmacists and businessmen. As World War II ended, and a combination of more liberal feeling, affluence, and a desperate need for professionals arose, more schools dropped their quota systems and Jews filled the universities in incredible numbers. Their ranks swelled among doctors, engineers, lawyers and certified public accountants; they became prominent in artistic literary, and theatrical fields, in the news media, and the professorial positions in the universities.

It seemed as if the American dream had never been truer and sweeter, and that America was indeed the exception to the historical rule of "hate the Jew."

But times were already changing. The very same winds of change that had combined to make for a more liberal and democratic era opening wide the doors of opportunity; the same affluence that now enabled people to seek and achieve things formerly considered unreachable, were beginning to affect the non-Jew, too. In urban areas, the former immigrants had now settled and become an integral part of the American scene and began to dream of moving upwards. They began to see the possibilities of better things for their children. They did not want their sons to be the laborers or policemen or clerks that they were and the great clamor for universal education that began to arise was, for them, an opportunity never before contemplated.

The rural areas of the country, caught up in the wave of social change and urbanization, saw mass exoduses of young people to the cities. Again, opportunity was now sought and seen as possible. But the great catalyst for non-Jewish upward mobility and competition with the Jew came from the blacks who, for the first time, demanded their share of the opportunities of American life, as teaching jobs, civil service placement, entrance to universities and the professions. Led, ironically, by Jewish liberals, they fought the great battles of civil rights for equal opportunities. The government, battered, pressured, and fearful of massive riots and chaos, began to crumble and soon the tide had turned—completely. Not only was government no longer hostile or indifferent, but thanks to the pressure of liberals and Jews, now became a potent weapon on the side of the black community.

A whole series of government directives was issued by newly organized governmental agencies to speed the inclusion of blacks in the general "good life" of the nation. Orders to start hiring blacks became common in federal, state, and local governments. It was no longer a question of merely stopping discrimination; it went beyond that. What was desired now was a quick hiring of minorities in order to "compensate" for past inequities. This could only be done by setting up guidelines and targets for hiring large numbers of blacks. It meant preferential treatment whereby blacks were hired at the expense of whites with equal or superior ability. Governmental agencies were told to report regularly on the number of minority members they had hired. Public housing projects and poverty programs openly discriminated in favor of these minorities. Private business was under intense pressure to employ specified numbers of blacks. Universities were ordered to show a specific bias in favor of hiring minority faculty members and similar preference in admission of students, or face a loss of government aid. A campaign for control by ethnic groups of their communities and the jobs within them was launched.

What blacks and other minority groups were demanding was nothing less than preferential treatment, quotas and communities run by ethnics who were a majority of the residents. Instead of merit as a basis for hiring, there was now a demand for giving jobs, in all areas, on the basis of the percentage of the ethnic group in the population.

In the beginning this issue was a starkly simple one that had no necessary relation to Jews. In practice, it soon became clear that it was the Jew who would be disastrously threatened.

The Jews were the small businessmen and merchants in black areas, either having had families that had lived there when the ghettos were still white and Jewish, or because few others wished to open stores in areas with such problems of crime and violence. Community control meant that these people would be forced out and deprived of years of investment and work as well as future income.

Because of historical and socioeconomic conditions, Jews had turned to teaching in large numbers and, suddenly, there was a demand for black teachers in black areas and for hiring of teachers and supervisors on the basis of quotas, not merit. The civil service system, which gave both quality and fairness, was under attack and the Jew would suffer more than any other.

The entire civil service organization was under similar attack. The social services, the numerous federal, state, and local administrative bureaus, all with large numbers of Jews who had gotten there by studying hard to pass the required examinations, were suddenly threatened with demands for an end to the system and hiring on the basis of quotas.

Realizing full well that education was the ultimate key to upward mobility, minority groups demanded entrance into colleges and universities regardless of merit, grades or qualifications. While such a course, called "open admissions," opening university doors wide to everyone, was merely a disastrous guarantee of leveling the intellectual standards and the educational quality of the schools, they did not threaten any other meritorious group of students with exclusion. But as it became obvious that lack of the huge amount of funds that would be necessary for universal higher education made such a thing quite impossible, blacks and others demanded admission based upon quotas. This meant that merit was to go by the wayside as a yardstick for measuring who should be given the privilege of attending a university. Instead, again, the demand was made that the number of students in colleges from any ethnic group should roughly coincide with their percentage in the local or national population.

What started with students now spread to faculty as the same demand for percentage yardsticks was made there. Suddenly, a whole new concept began to emerge on the American scene. Quotas.

The American Jew had risen to success and progressed in America only because of his ability and the opportunity given him through the merit system, to reap the fruits of that ability. Under this concept all men were entitled to compete equally for positions and rewards. If they were talented enough, clever enough, industrious enough, persistent enough they stood a wonderful chance of rising to desirable positions. Not only was this system fair in that it awarded the prizes of life to the deserving, but it also guaranteed the society that used it the best and most talented of people. It guaranteed that the best and most suitable would be the doctors the country needed, the teachers for its children, the engineers, attorneys, and physicists. It was a guarantee of both logical progress and just reward.

The quota system on the other hand was nothing more than an American version and, eventually, a duplication of the old numerus clausas that the Jew of the Old World had escaped. In czarist Russia, beginning in 1888, Jews were not allowed to exceed 10 percent of the total high school and university student population in the Pale of Settlement, that part of the state that bulged with millions of Jews. In other parts of the Russian Empire their quota was set at 3-5 percent. Hungary of the post World War I era had a numerus clausus that was eminently simple. It limited its Jews in most professions to 6 percent, a figure that was exactly the proportion in the nations' population. It was grossly discriminatory and unjust as well as a stupid failure to take advantage of the best minds and talent for the good of the state. It was this—*it is this*—that has returned to the America of today.

What the black, the Puerto Rican, and the Chicano want today, the Italian, Irish, Anglo-Saxon, Slav, and German, will demand tomorrow. Already angered at what they feel is the lopsided amount of government attention to the problems of the colored minorities, these ethnic groups are furious at the contrasting lack of sympathy and aid for their own causes and problems. They have seen unified, strong black political pressure win huge benefits and they have learned a great lesson from it. They are beginning to awaken to their own identity and desires and will do the same.

In addition, they, like the blacks and other minorities, also have begun to hunger for upward mobility. They also want the better things of life, "the desirables." They want better jobs, better status, all the things they never believed they could get. The changing times—the black revolution—have taught them that they can be achieved. Once, all Jewish children planned and hoped, as a matter of course, to go to college in contrast to a startlingly lower percentage of non-Jews. Now, it is different; many, many, non-Jewish children of white ethnic and Anglo-Saxon groups, also want to receive the benefits of higher education, and are determined to get them; they want to become professional men—doctors and lawyers; they want to enter higher grades of civil service, social work, teaching; they want to become a part of the theater, the cultural arts, the news media. They intend to do so.

When one carefully considers it, the quota system—insofar as it pertains to universities, the arts, the professions, and all the more desirable institutions and areas of life—benefits almost every major group in America except the Jew. Why should all the masses not eventually desire it also? They will.

There is almost no major ethnic group that is represented in the desirable areas of life in proportion to its percentage of the population—except the Jew. Under merit, far fewer Italians, Irish, Slavs, and Anglo-Saxons attend universities than their ratio to the general population warrants. Why should they, as their appetites grow parallel to their realization of the benefits of quotas, not demand it for themselves? They will.

Just as the old numerus clausus was defended by its backers as being inherently fair—a proportional representation of peoples—so will quotas be rationalized. After all, what could be fairer than having all groups represented to the extent of their percentage of the population? If one group constitutes 10 percent of the people, surely it is not unrealistic or unjust to limit him or to grant him 10 percent of all the places in the universities, the medical field, the professions, the arts. Every incompetent individual and every group that senses or fears that it will not be able to compete adequately on the basis of merit raises high the banner of quotas, for the free ride that it assures him.

Non-Jewish whites, no less than blacks, will realize that they may very well have a stake in quotas and a great deal to gain from them. They may very well begin to experiment with community control of their own neighborhoods quotas to limit jobs, businesses, and political control in those areas to the ethnic group in control. Merit, it is already beginning to be believed, has created a situation where, many groups and vast numbers of Americans, have not gotten their proportional share of the "desirables." No less than the Pole, the Hungarian, the Rumanian, of forty years ago, non-Jewish Americans will move to quotas to protect their own interests.

All this has nothing to do with anti-Jewishness per se. The drive by blacks, white ethnic groups and other non-Jewish whites for proportional representation in the "desirables" stems from a growing sense of narrow group identity; a growing realization that life can be improved; a growing desire to escape one's present status and move upwards; a growing economic pinch that sees jobs on lower levels growing scarcer; growing automation that makes the jobs scarcer still; growing social unrest and discontent with menial and lower-class jobs; growing demand for education and an expanding perspective of life, thanks to television and the popular news media; growing urbanization which has made former rural dwellers more sophisticated at the very time it has dislocated them and changed their social and economic horizons. Quotas are being given strong impetus by the economic problems of America.

There are no longer enough places on the lower rungs of life's ladder thus impelling those who dwell there to move upwards. At the same time, there is a natural desire and a feeling that the time is propitious for a drive for more desirable rungs on the ladder at a time when there are not enough places there, either. And so, by the very nature of this shortage of desirable places, competition will take place between those who are already there, their intellectually natural heirs, and the great new class of discontents. We live in an era when the discontented, the mass of "outs" are beginning to sense their lack of participation—their being "out"—as well as their potential power. They are unhappy and they want "in." The "outs" want "in," and if this means displacing, to a great degree, those who are already "in"—so be it. This is the beginning of the great new class struggle—not proletariat vs. bourgeoisie—but "out" against "in." It is the era of the great discontented mass—the new resurgence of Populism.

The new Populism. How our intellectuals and liberals savor the name! The New Populism, the people. The harbingers of a new era.

All the rot and corruption, all the injustice and inequality, all that is venal, exploitative, and oppressive will be swept away as the New Populism—THE PEOPLE—take over the reins of power and control.

The people. How much faith we place in them and how we misjudge them. It has become an article of faith among liberals and radicals alike that the enemy lies above and not below. That those who occupy the higher rungs of the socioeconomic ladder are the evil ones while those below are the humble embodiers of all that is virtuous. The wealthy baron is to be leveled and the humble worker, far below, to be raised on high. Only thus will the messianic era be ushered in, the era of the New Populism.

What is this Populism that we are told is so beneficial and progressive? What is this Populism that lauds all the "underprivileged," all the poor, ignorant, deprived, blacks, chicanos, white Appalachians, Indians, Eskimos, ethnics, tax-intoxicated middle classes, angry farmers—all the masses and masses of "the people?" What is this Populism that has become so politically chic that everyone wishes to become part of it, that every politician pays homage to it, pandering to "the people," those masses who bask in the new-found knowledge that they are Populists and popular?

There are to be sure millions and millions of Americans who suffer the hunger, poverty and exploitation that since time immemorial has been visited upon man. There are the poor and the elderly and the migrant farmers and the racially discriminated against and the forgotten. And their suffering and their deprivation cries out for solution and redress and, surely, they are part of the New Populists.

But there are others who are not hungry nor poor nor elderly. There are the lower middle classes with their never-ending struggle against unemployment, inflation and oppressive taxation, and they, too, are brought under the great tent of New Populism. And there are all the contradictions and paradoxes.

There are farmers who want higher food prices and consumers who want lower ones; suburban whites who don't want blacks and blacks who want to escape the city for the suburbs; law and order whites who want safety and security and minorities who demand justice; union workers who want higher wages and elderly pensioners who want wages and prices frozen; white ethnics who seek new neighborhoods and blacks who want the same neighborhood. How to account for all these people in the same camp? What is the common denominator that makes them one and what unifies them so that we lump them all together in a term Populism?

There is only one common denominator in this motley camp of groups and classes and races and interest lobbys, so contradictory in much of what they want and, by all past standards, mutually antagonistic and at each others throats. That single, unifying factor is discontent, dissatisfaction, opposition to those above and beyond them and a desire to lash out at a system that, in some way, does not do their bidding.

We live in a time of revolution in the United States. Ours is an Age of Discontent and all the discontented, all the collected malcontents and dissatisfied are massed together in an infinite number of different interests, lobbies, demands, and ethnicities. Some share common grievances, some are mutually hostile, many are mutually contradictory. But all are bound together by a mutual discontent with their lot and with the present system that has decreed that lot. Born into an age of affluence in which some have no share at all, others only a tantalizing taste, and still others a large share which they fear they are on the verge of losing; born into materialistic times and a philosophy that sees the good life as the beginning and end of all that is important in this world; titillated and seduced by a television world of good and pleasure; a part of a society in which dissatisfaction and discontent are built-in emotions programmed into the nature of the citizen; the masses of unhappy members of the discontented age grow daily more restless, more demanding and impatient. Theirs is a dull, rumbling sound of anger and impatience that emerges louder and louder and which warns of latent violence and revolution.

This age of discontent with its potential for and its probable class struggle, revolutionary upheavals, and desperate clashes, is what we speak about when we speak of our days of New Populism. What liberals and radicals alike have so lauded and named the New Populism is nothing less than the foundation for a potential new fascism.

Of course there are legitimate grievances and issues, but under the cutting knife and criticisms of the old fascism of forty years ago there were also legitimate grievances and issues. To be sure there is poverty and discrimination, hopelessness and despair. Yes, there is injustice and corruption, tax inequity and abuse of power, poor housing and racism.

But the New Populism has not come to create a Brave New World for humanity. The New Populism, a phrase coined by some clever political writer, does not exist except insofar as there are groups and individuals who demand change and all kinds of concessions—*not because they give a fig about justice and right but because they want "theirs."* We are dealing with an assortment of individual interests and interest groups, each of which is increasingly self-centered and self-interested. There is no thought here of what is the best for the common good or what is best for the nation or for even the people who they are supposed to be. It is the selfishness, greed, and self-interest that created the hate and Jew-hatred of the Populism of eighty years ago and the demagoguery and neo-fascism of a Huey Long, forty years ago. A Tom Watson was spawned by Populism as was a Henry Ford; the Klanism isolationism and selfishness of the years preceding the Second World War were also part of Populism and "the people."

Yes, there is a great deal that must be changed in the social, political and economic fabric of the nation. There is much injustice that must be eliminated and much corruption to be swept away, but the New Populism is not a light for the future but rather a deadly barometer of the stormy times and a frightful harbinger of a worse future. It is a deadly thing, that is neither new nor progressive. It is the reincarnation of the mobs turning the French Revolution into a bloody aberration; the masses sweeping through Arab and Asian lands demanding blood and sensing the power of anarchy and confusion. There are legitimate grievances, but alongside the grievances is also the flood of more ignorant, less talented, and less meritorious people sweeping through the country and demanding their share of the wealth, affluence, and influence they could not gain through merit. It is all the "outs" with their pent-up envy, greed, frustration and jealousy demanding to move up the next rung of the political-social-economic ladder and their place in the sun.

Tomorrow, they will be at each others throats. All the antagonists and contradictory interests will clash for the largest share of the meat. Whites against blacks, blacks against Spanish, farmers against consumers, city against suburbia, union against employer, pensioner against worker, interest against interest, each man for himself and against society.

It is the mob of upheaval marching with terror and hate as their weapons against those who are more successful and more talented than they. They are not interested in justice or democracy. They care little about brotherhood and equality. They resent talent; they do not care about merit; intellect and intelligence are of no relevance to them. They are not interested in the complexity and difficulties of the problems and solutions. They only know that others have the jobs they would like to have, the homes they would like to own, the life they see dangled before them on television every night—and they want it.

There are no longer the kinds of psychological barriers that once stood before the mob. The awesome fear and respect for authority—church, home, government—have long been swept aside in our generations. There is a contempt for and loss of confidence in those who rule. The concepts of discipline and respect for talent and mind are no longer accepted. The freedom we have advocated and the equality we have told everyone they possess, the democracy we have given, lead naturally to demands to translate that freedom and equality into tangible, material terms. The "outs" want in and that is the beginning and the end of the entire mystery of Populism.

There is no one to care about the costs of the demands and out of whose pocket the money will come. The main thing is that someone else—not I—should pay. The politicians, captives of the occupational hazards that mark the insoluble weakness of the democratic process, praise their voting masses to the skies, encourage them in their impossible demands, propose absurd and irrational programs, promise all things to all men (and now, women, too) and hope against hope that they will have moved on before the inevitable deluge. Democracy is held captive by the selfishness and greed of Populism and it will eventually die because of the impossible demands placed on it, the chaos that must emerge from the inability to meet those demands and the fear and weariness of that chaos, anarchy and revolution that will lead to totalitarianism and a long night of tyranny.

What must emerge are even greater demagogues than the democratic politicians who pander to the emotions of the masses in hope of election to office. They, at least, are blessed with a certain amount of responsibility and honesty that limits their pandering to the impossible. But there are the demagogues of the extremes, the Right and Left, who, with the sublimest contempt for mass intelligence imaginable, praise, flatter, and cater to the emotions of the people in their professional use of them. They will make the final transition from democracy to totalitarian hate.

It is not a new thing. The Nazis of Weimar spoke in ringing terms of "the people" and denounced, in their own unique fashion, those who exploited them. The February 24, 1920, Nazi platform was filled with all kinds of socialist promises and pledges. No one was louder in denunciation of exploiters, parasites, finance capitalism, international bankers and speculators than the Hitlerites. Capitalism was attacked by the Nazis with as much gusto as by the Communists, and class warfare was held high—of the national "outs" against the bloodsucking "ins."

There is no contradiction between those who speak for the people, the poor and the oppressed, and the haters. Those who cry about soaking the rich may be found, in the next moment, speaking of eliminating the Jew. Hitler promised to do both; Tom Watson and Huey Long were as fine a pair of propagators of class war and hate as any Marxists, and Father Coughlin's movement was named, Social Justice.

Note the statement by the Grand Dragon of the Michigan Klan following his arrest in 1971 on charges of bombing ten buses to be used for school busing:

> The Klan has never been the tool of the wealthy. It's been a resistance movement of the poor white people. It's an association of left-outs, who have no power, political or social. They are like boxes up against the wall.

Not really very different from the statement made by the Klan Grand Wizard in 1926 when he said:

> We are a movement of plain people, very weak in the matter of culture, intellectual support and trained leadership. . . . This is undoubtedly a weakness. It lays us open to the charge of being "hicks" and "rubes" and "drivers of second-hand Fords." We admit it. Not very surprising from a movement whose members had such curious close links with the Socialist party in Wisconsin. Hardly occasion for astonishment in our own times when union members in one of the most powerful union states voted with such authority for George Wallace. It may be very true that Populism is a movement of "nobodies" who want to be somebody. We have seen what happens when individuals who are "nobodies," who are "losers," lash out in desperate effort to have the world know that they exist. Populism multiplies this by millions.

There is no ideology of Populism, there is only self-interest. All the young, idealistic Left radicals who idolize and idealize "the people" and hope to recruit them by praising them to the skies; all who place their Marxist faith in the proletariat and peasants of America, will be in for a rude and deadly shock.

The New Populism is a symptom of the end of ordered democracy and the merit system that made America great. The masses of "outs" understand very well that merit constitutes a roadblock for them and, consequently, we live in a time when, as never before, merit is scorned and under attack. The "outs" want in and the great leveling process has begun. Talent is denigrated, higher intelligence and intellect are under assault as standards and yardsticks, and equality has come to mean a mass attack on all who have managed to achieve degrees of knowledge, wealth, and success. All people are equal today to the extent that there is a demand that each be given the same rewards, success and affluence—regardless of ability. Indeed, ability, intellect, and merit have become code names for racism, "elitism," and fascism. All who hold positions of power and success are viewed as enemies of the masses precisely because they are more talented and successful than the masses. With cries of "Power to the People" we have been ushered into what liberals and radicals alike praise, the "golden age" of Populism.

In itself this mass rise of discontent, this demand to have a share of the "desirables" of life, this new Populism is not necessarily anti-Jewish. It is directed against all who are "in," it is aimed at the merit system as such and at those who defend and benefit from that system. If there were no Jews, this particular drive would be aimed at anyone else who would be in their position. In practice, however, there *are* Jews and they are, in great measure, "in." In practice, the attack on the merit system and the demands for a new yardstick for ascertaining who achieves the "desirables" will fall heaviest upon the Jew. It is the Jew, who, in the end will suffer most of all. It is the Jew who will suffer most of all and the threat is immeasurably grave. He has most to gain and has gained most from the traditional American devotion to the merit system. He has the most to lose by the new discontent and Populism. Because of his mental ability, dedication to learning, hard work, and intellect, he is overrepresented, proportionally, in institutions of higher learning. He is overrepresented in the professions. He is over-represented in the fields of teaching, social services, and higher positions of civil service. He is overrepresented in the arts and the news media. He has ridden merit to affluence and progress and has done far better, proportionally, than any other major group. In the battle for limited "desirables," he has won a great many victories. Time after time, he has been the person who has—through mental ability, education and intellectual skill —managed to occupy the space that others would have liked to.

Those who are "out," the new Populists, the huge numbers of discontented are not interested in merit if that is a roadblock in their drive to achieve the desirables. They are not concerned with the fact that the vast majority of those who have achieved the things they would like, did so because of merit, ability, intellect, and hard work. They care only about the fact that others have what they want and they blame the "system." That system must, in their minds, be changed and they mean to do so.

Thus, the rationalization of all means that will give them what, at present, they do not have. Thus a fierce defense of quotas as "proportional representation," a concept that appears to be fair and equitable. Now is not the time for debate on this point. What matters is that the Jew, under such a system, will be destroyed as a strong and viable economic, political, social, and cultural force.

He changes from a group that, through the merit system and the democratic commitment to opportunity for all to find their natural levels achieved great affluence and strength, to a group that will be, more or less, bounded by its less than 3 percent of the total population. All the things we see today within the American Jewish community are threatened; the large numbers of Jews in the universities—students and faculty; the preponderance of Jews in teaching, social service, welfare, and civil service jobs; the hefty chunk of Jews in the medical, law, and other professions. All victims of the natural desire of "outs" to get "in," their natural resentment of those who have achieved what they have not, the natural desire to put an end to the system that created such a situation.

And from it, from a movement that is totally divorced from Jewish targets per se, begin hesitantly to emerge the first specific references to Jews. There begins to evolve the "anti-Semitism of things" of which Jabotinsky spoke.

From the general discontent, the general attack on the system and those who are "in," who "exploit" and "exclude," there comes a particular focusing in upon a particular group. The fact is that the system has given the Jew opportunity and benefits. It is the Jew who is so overrepresented in the "desirables" of life. Time after time his intelligence and education have given him the spaces that can be occupied only by one and not by two. He is conspicuous in his merit and his success.

162

The non-Jew cannot help falling over him as he scans the world of the desirables.

The Jew is visibly successful as success usually is. The non-Jew does not think about the almost total absence of Jews in the decision-making corporate structures of banks, railroads, oil, steel, where the real money and power lie. These are relatively hidden areas. He does, however, see the areas of Jewish triumph because they are so constantly before his eyes. So many Jewish doctors; so many Jewish lawyers; so many Jewish judges; so many Jewish teachers; so many Jewish students; so many Jewish storekeepers; so many Jewish artists; so many Jewish newscasters; so many Jewish writers. So many Jewish "ins" enjoying the good life and the "desirables."

For so many years he noticed it, secretly resented and envied, but assumed that there was little or nothing he could do. Bound by a merit system that, he knew, guaranteed success to the intellectually capable—a system that he thought could not be changed—he accepted it, unhappily, but relatively calmly. Today, however, things have changed. There is suddenly an opportunity to change the system. The black revolution began it; the Leftists in the streets showed that things could be turned around; the growing tide of ethnic pride, the economic and social problems in the country, suddenly gave sharp impetus to possibilities of change. The masses of "outs," indeed, aim at all the "ins" but Jewishness is an added reason for attack. The latent, natural anti-Jewishness that exists within the masses of gentiles, suddenly finds its place in a Populist and generally discontented demand for a place in the sun of "desirables." The Jew is a stranger—he is not Christian. The Jew is an outsider—not quite like other Americans. Why should he get more than his "share?"

The melting pot is dead as a concept and a reality. America is not ever going to be a nation where all are blurred into "Americans" regardless of origin, faith, and ethnic background. Such a concept, never a reality, while it was still a legend that was propagated and believed, succeeded in making merit and opportunity of ability a viable thing. In the inevitable discontent of the "outs" and the rise of racial and ethnic consciousness we return to a "European" situation, a Balkinazation of peoples, each with a particular identity, each with a particular commitment to its own interests, but each of whom, in line with that interest, bands together with similar ethnic "outs" against the common enemy, the system. It does not matter who, in particular, is part of the system; any such a one would be the "enemy." But when the enemy happens to be a Jew there is a special quality to this Populism. The *objective* calls for a change in the system, for quotas, become specifically *subjective* anti-Jewish ones. In Poland, the Jew had to make way for the Pole; in Hungary for the Hungarian; in America, he will have to make way for the American, and all his anguished cries that he, too, is a citizen will be unavailing.

In the beginning there really is no anti-Jewish feeling per se. It is merely an irresistible drive for the good things of life on the part of people who have been excluded by a system that recognized only merit. Such a system can never survive the ruthless democratic mass which, with political power in its hands, will not accept economic and social impotence. The Jew, as one who is affluent and successful beyond his numbers, is a normal target of the discontented outs. That alone is sufficient to guarantee his being reduced and limited to his "share." But, being a Jew, he is an abnormal target of people whose latent anti-Semitism leads them never to consider him as really equal or an American like all others. They look upon him as a stranger who is enjoying the desirables of life at their expense. In the end he is still only a Jew, and that is sufficient to emotionalize their demands that he be reduced and limited—perhaps below his representation.

Make no mistake. It is not only the black ghetto resident that resents and hates Jewish success and merit. Resentment exists among whites, too, and probably to a greater extent in the cultural and art fields where the sophisticated, liberal, chic radical, non-Jewish minority envies and hates the Jewish majority for its talent, cleverness, domination, and arrogance. The Jewish dilemma is clear; we must escape non-Jewish envy and resentment by being failures or resign ourselves to that reaction.

All this, in itself, should be enough for the American Jew to realize that his future is bleak and to consider concrete measures for returning home to the Land of Israel. When a mature economy reaches the point where the majority—whether homogeneous or composed of different, powerful groups—feels itself excluded from the desirables of life it must lead to an attack upon the system that they feel is to blame and the people who support that system.

This is why the "anti-Semitism of things" that is emerging so clearly in the United States of America is such an impossible situation, one that cannot be halted. The people who are outside the system will settle for nothing less than the total overhauling of the system and the substituting of quota and numerus clausus for merit and opportunity of talent.

At best, the Jew will be dragged from his positions of influence and success because Jews are overrepresented as a group. But it will go beyond that, for he is—in the end—the Jew, and the deep wellsprings of hostility to him, envy, and a sense of his being a stranger and not really an equal citizen, will lead to specific demands for his leveling as a Jew. The Populists of the nineteenth century began as levelers of all the "ins" and evolved into levelers of all, and especially of the Jew.

Once the "anti-Semitism of things" enters the picture, once the Jew is singled out for identification as the stranger, the one who is different, the "anti-Semitism of men" comes into the picture with all its hate, violence, death, and destruction.

We have seen this clearly in the already thriving black drive against the merit system. There, the cry for quota system based upon percentage of the population as well as preferential treatment to enable blacks to reach their "allotted" figure, is already tinged with violent anti-Jewish feeling. The same will be seen in the budding ethnic consciousness and political power of Italians, Irish, Slavs, and Anglo-Saxons whose path to the desirables of life will come in conflict with the presence of large numbers of Jews. Blacks, who raised the cry that there are too many Jews, Jewish teachers, civil servants, and students in New York City and that there is a Jewish "merit plot" to keep blacks out—are only saying what whites have long, silently thought and will, in the future, say.

When a majority—however homogeneous or composed of different groups—feels itself excluded from the desirables of life and there is a minority that is small, weak, but affluent and "in"—that group normally becomes the target of attack, regardless of its name. When that minority is called "Jewish" the attack becomes easier, more vicious, more violent, more deadly, more hopeless for the victim, because of the primeval qualities of stigma that attach themselves to the Jew.

The drive for quotas and its attendant constant emphasis and reminder of ethnocentricity are well under way, and the opponents of merit have made great progress. The Jew can look for no help from a government which has clearly shown its willingness to avert trouble at the expense of merit and the Jew. Even if it wished it can no longer stem the irresistible tide of the hungry mob. Nor is it making very great efforts to do so.

Government on all levels, dominated, in most part, by the established and entrenched classes, has already shown what happens when it is threatened by demands on the part of masses of groups. New York City's mayor, head of a city with more than two million Jews, stood tepidly by as a massive open and violent anti-Jewish feeling erupted. With polite and cursory protestations his strongest reactions, the mayor stood by and watched Jewish teachers and civil servants threatened and, in some cases, physically beaten; anti-Semitic slogans, speeches and articles flood the city, many emanating directly from city employees; antipoverty programs fall into the hands of racial extremists with Jewish residents of poverty areas threatened and coerced. He began a clear program of preferential treatment which was only a prelude to a capitulation to demands for ethnic quotas in civil service and community control; watched and supported the elimination of the merit system from the schools and substitution for Jews who had passed examinations for supervisory posts, of blacks and Puerto Ricans who had not; remained incredibly silent as riots, both large and small, decimated Jewish stores and property.

What took place in New York City had been duplicated in others. In addition the federal government has capitulated to demands for preferential treatment and quotas. Agency after agency has been ordered to hire more blacks regardless of merit. The Department of Health Education and Welfare has made it clear that it expects institutions of higher learning to hire minority faculty members on the basis of quotas and to admit students on the same basis. There is a mass capitulation on the part of politicians and the White Anglo-Saxon Establishment to extremists, racists, preferential treatment and quotas. We will see much worse; we will see a collapse before the worst aspects of Populism by the same people and for the same reasons. It is merely one more vital reason for Jews to consider carefully the need to escape from a situation that will grow progressively worse and more tragic.

The white Anglo-Saxon Protestant establishment, the one that is the true holder of power, wealth, and prestige in the United States has watched with a wary and fearful eye the growth of extremist discontent, and the threat it poses to *it*. When black discontent exploded into rioting and violence the establishment hastily began to make concessions. For the most part those concessions were made at the expense of lower, lower middle-class people, and, particularly, Jews. When burning and looting of Jewish stores took place in many cities and when threats, extortion, and arson were committed against them, the establishment's failure to act strenuously and on behalf of the merchants was impressive. What was happening was simply that the power brokers of the establishment were scarcely heartbroken over the fact that black anger was being diverted away from its logical and real target—the establishment—to the descendants of immigrants who had had no hand in the slavery traffic and exploitation. How much better that a ghetto grocer be burned out than the Stock Exchange! Certainly, the time-honored effort to divert mob anger away from the seats of power to a scapegoat is one that—if not actively pursued—was certainly not avoided.

Concession after concession was made to minorities, not at the expense of the Establishment, but at the expense of others, so often Jews. When demands were made for preferential treatment in government hiring, it was realized that it was not the wealthy scion who would be bruised by government acquiescence. When quotas were demanded it was understood that political leaders' children would not be affected by this, either in schools or in employment. And so, the weaker—for the most part, Jews—were sacrificed on the altar of quotas and concessions to pacify the mob which might, otherwise, overthrow the establishment; to satisfy the dangerous rumblings and cravings of the masses of colored minorities, the power brokers were ready to sacrifice the Jew. This is the reason for their silence in the face of open anti-Semitism; this is the reason for their passive acquiescence in the face of threats to and destruction of Jewish property; this is the reason for their capitulation to quotas and preferential treatment. They hope to buy peace for themselves at the expense of the scapegoat—the Jew.

It will get worse. The politician who knows no principle except that of staying in office smells the political Populism that pervades every area of the country. He senses the rumblings of truly serious discontent and hears the violent cries of the "outs" against the "ins." He will not fight very hard on behalf of justice and merit for Jews in the face of tens of millions of discontented and angry non-Jewish Americans. The Jew is small and far weaker than the myths that have been built around him. He is no political match for blacks, white ethnic and Anglo Saxon groups when it comes to being weighed upon the political scales. He will be sacrificed by the politicians and establishment, not because they are anti-Jewish, but because he is expendable.

The masses are on the rise in search of satisfying their self-interest and the Jew will suffer at their hands. The government, in fear of the masses, will capitulate to them and allow the Jew to suffer. Yet another reason to understand that the sun is beginning to set for American Jewry.

Added to all his other problems, the Jew faces situations in the urban areas in which he is centered that, while they partake of general American problems, certainly add up to a life that is filled with fear, anguish, and insecurity. I refer to the Jewish neighborhoods that are terrorized by crime and violence, whose streets are filled with the fear of robbery, bodily attack, and killings. I refer to the fear that drives Jews to flee neighborhoods, leaving behind their homes and their institutions, to find new dwelling places and areas, many times at prices that are beyond their means and at great distances from their places of work. The institutions they leave behind—the synagogues, centers, and schools—are sold for a fraction of what the new ones in the new neighborhood will cost to build, and once again, Jewish money is unnecessarily wasted.

Certainly, the fear that grips neighborhoods, the crime and violence that plague them, the flight and mass exodus from them, are not specifically Jewish problems. But who is willing to vouch for the absence of a special feeling of hatred and contempt on the part of the hoodlums when it is known that the neighborhood is a Jewish one? And in the end, what does it really matter to the suffering Jew whether his miseries are exclusively his own or shared by others?

I refer, too, to the merchants burned out of their stores and threatened with violence until they flee from the inner city ghettos. They leave behind businesses that supported them, and added to the general Jewish welfare by way of contributions to the community. I refer to the landlords, whose property values have been leveled and destroyed, again a significant economic loss for them and the Jewish community. I refer to the merchants who live in constant terror, unsure whether the person at the door is a customer or a thief; whose wives watch them leave and daily pray that they will come home without mishap. Again, it is a problem that is not solely Jewish, but can anyone doubt that the militants who decry "Jew stores" are doing a bit more than merely attacking a white man? Is there anyone who will debate that there is something special about the Jewish store and that a vast reservoir of specifically anti-Jewish hate has been built against the merchants and landlords?

Open and direct, violent and irrational Jew-hatred. The irresistible pressure of an economic and social mass Populist movement that demands a place for itself at the expense of the Jews and other "ins." The misery and terror of crime and violence, changing neighborhoods and the destruction of businesses and livelihoods. This is the America that faces its Jews in the years to come. Is this what we want? Will we remain quietly as we are, agonizingly brutalized and then destroyed? Is it not time to consider going home?

CHAPTER 12: HATE GROUPS

There exist in the United States, today, hate groups dedicated to the overthrow of the democratic process and its replacement by a government that is totalitarian, racist, or both. There are groups in this country that preach hatred of class against class, race against race, group against group. They exist on the Right, the Left and among whites and minorities. They pose a clear and present danger to the continuance of the democratic process, freedom and justice—and the very survival of the Jew. Too few know of their existance and fewer yet appreciate their seriousness and their potential for fascism and totalitarianism. For every American they pose a threat to freedom. For the Jew they pose a threat to national and physical survival.

There are Nazi and Fascist groups in the United States whose antipathy to the Jew is not that of the genteel and "respectable" anti-Semite. The latter is interested for the most part in merely keeping Jews out of his cooperative, school, country or midtown club, hotel and away from the top executive echelons of his large corporations. Such people, certainly, are potential followers of the haters but, in themselves, they are not people who would advocate extermination and decimation. They are the kind of people for whom dislike of the Jew is not a sustantive obsession, is not based upon desperate and bitter personal crisis that finds them needing to lash out in frustration. Theirs is a quiet and genteel kind of dislike, the kind that major Jewish groups have generally, on the surface, successfully confronted and neutralized.

They are the kind of respectable and genteel Jew dislikers who can be confronted in courts, in dialogues, and through social and economic pressure. Their lack of desperation makes their dislike less intense and less vital than that of others. They may not like Jews, but given their general level of affluence and well-being, it is not all that important. Such people can be lived with.

But the haters are different. Theirs is not dislike of Jews—but *Jew-hatred*. More important, their feelings toward Jews is not a sometime thing. It is an obsession, a drive, a thing that fills their waking hours and that colors all their thinking on any subject. These are people and groups who are not potential products of crises. *They exist, today.* They exist and call for the elimination, the extermination of the Jew. They preach expropriation, gas chambers, and holocaust. And they mean every word they preach.

They are growing. Nurtured by the crises afflicting America, encouraged by the growth of anti-establishment and anti-system Populist discontent, they have spread outside of the traditional or "only-to-be-expected" areas to the Northeast, the Far West, the areas of liberalism and trade unionism with their traditional hostility to such groups. They openly preach fascism and nazism; openly praise Adolph Hitler, eulogize him and celebrate events that commemorate his memory; openly display the swastika and openly call for the elimination of the Jew and his influence from American life.

There is an unfortunate tendency—that stems from a deep-seated liberal arrogance and superficial understanding of what happens in most areas outside their own particular intellectual ghettos—to conceive of the Nazis and Fascists as being totally devoid of intelligence and skill. If this were true, I would rest a great deal easier; but it is not. That they are morally and spiritually sick people is beyond dispute, but this has nothing to do with intelligence, cunning, and capacity. Their spiritual sickness in no way makes them less dangerous, and labels are totally irrelevant to the menace they pose to the Jew.

The truth is that they understand the mind of the masses all too well; far better than most of the decent liberals who oppose them. They understand the mind and the *problems* of the masses. They understand the anger, frustration, bitterness, and hate. Most important, they understand the *causes* that give rise to these emotions. Above all, they have turned their propaganda and political sights, with all the attendant demagoguery, on precisely those issues. They do so in order to exacerbate them, to arouse rather than diminish the discontent, to create anger where none existed before and to increase it where it existed only in small quantities. They are vultures who have been provided with a treasury of ammunition. Like furtive jackals they creep into the areas of tension and grow fat upon its terrible fruits.

The names of these groups will not be mentioned both because new ones will grow tomorrow along with consolidation and change in the old ones and, also, because seeing their names in print tends to inspire and encourage their narcissistic tendencies. Their names, therefore, are not important. What is relevant is to know that they exist and to lay before the reader examples of the literature and propaganda that are so cleverly, and effectively, brought to bear on the critical issues of the day. Hate is a painful thing to face and is presented here only to make the reader aware of its existence and the danger it poses.

If the American crisis is made up of the death of patriotism and the military fiasco, the racial crisis, political danger, social problems, despair, and the economic situation, the haters deal with all of them daily. They are discussed, trumpeted, blown up, analyzed and the blame is invariably placed upon—the Jew.

The racial problem is never allowed to abate. Thousands of articles and countless words are devoted to it by the haters. Thus, they speak to America:

> The Communist enemy has gone too far in his plans for the destruction of the flower of America— our youth. There can be no doubt that our people are ready to stand up and fight for our children. One fundamental right that has become a time honored tradition in America is that of a parent to send his child to a neighborhood school. . . . The rage against busing is heard from every quarter of the nation. When people go out in the streets to fight busing in liberal Boston and San Francisco—then you know it has got to be unpopular everywhere!
>
> White man awake—your sons and daughters are being sacrificed on the altar of school race mixing just so the treasonous Jews and liberals can appease their black supporters. . . .

And, of course, this is the nub of the matter. Who are the ones to blame? Who are the subjects of the article headlined: "Traitors Behind Busing Named"? Of course, the Jews, as we learn:

> Back on June 30, 1963, a leading member of the U. S. Communist Party, a Jew named Mike Davidow, wrote in the Red paper, *The Worker,* that we must "struggle to bring about a school system that is racially balanced. . . ."
>
> All of the court suits to bring about racial balance and busing to mix the races have been brought by the

NAACP—this is a Jewish organization and not a Negro one. . . . Every single [president of NAACP] has been a Jew right down to its head today, Kivie Kaplan (a millionaire Boston shoe manufacturer). The head of the NAACP legal fund is the Jew Jack Greenberg . . . the most massive long distance busing program ever ordered was written by Jewish Judge Alfred Gitelson of Los Angeles. . . .

It is our belief that this busing issue is the final straw which is going to break the back of the White man's tolerance for race-mixing. It is becoming clear that the chief driving force in America today for the busing of children for racial balance is the Jewish race . . . wherever you look the real ruthless energy behind race mixing is the Jew!

And there is so much more. There is the leaflet put out by the haters, entitled "Special Rights For Black Savages?"

DO YOU BELIEVE that blacks are entitled to special consideration . . . that law enforcement should be relaxed so blacks can murder, rape, loot and burn without fear of punishment . . . that Negro loafers and their illegitimate offspring are entitled to 80% of the welfare money . . . that arrogant Negroes should get the jobs of better qualified Whites . . . that White children should be forced to go to integrated schools where they are shaken down, molested and assaulted . . .

If your answer is an emphatic NO, then contact____

Or yet another article:

Here is the problem. The Black plague is polluting our White race and taking away equal rights from White people. Forced school integration, the cause of violence in public schools. Forced housing, the cause of slums decaying the enter of our cities. Forced busing, to force race mixing. Forced Black employment, causing layoff of qualified White people to make room for Blacks who are lazy, indolent, filthy, immoral and dishonest . . . the Jews wish to keep the Blacks here in America in order to have them melt down the resistance of the White race. . . .

And so it goes. Is it really so inconceivable that such propaganda strikes the target directly in the minds of millions of ordinary Americans? Is it truly beyond belief that anxious and angry Americans are capable of being ideologically sympathetic to such thoughts? Is it too far-fetched to believe that all these words and the countless others in the same vein that are daily trumpeted are seeds that burrow into the minds of countless Americans and wait for the proper time of desperation to sprout?

And are we so positive that the following thinking will inevitably be rejected by masses of desperate American:

The White people face total destruction. Jews and Communists control much of the world posing such a terrifying threat that many good people are paralyzed. . . . We are forced to work with and live beside the subhuman Negro and more and more Jewish propaganda take its toll among our youth as interracial marriage increases. . . . Are we so far gone that we are content with slavery under our Jewish masters?

Each idea has its time. Given the constant propaganda and the unceasing, tireless efforts of the haters to provoke discontent and hatred; given the proper time of crisis and desperation, that which yesterday might have been ignored, scorned, and rejected is, today, given careful consideration and increasing agreement and adherence.

The haters zero in on the violent opposition of whites to having blacks move into their neighborhoods and the determination of those who have already fled one neighborhood not to move again. Above all, there is the grim refusal of suburbanites to allow their areas to become black. It is tailormade to haters' efforts to recruit support:

> The big metropolitan planners, whose chief aim is to protect the investments of a handful of multi-millionaire downtown property owners, have come up with two new plans to save their investments and keep business from fleeing the central city. One is to annex large areas where whites live without the vote of the people—but merely by a vote of the state legislature—a plan put forth by the Jewish mayor [of Atlanta]. The other scheme is to move in welfare blacks to the White suburban neighborhoods with scatter type public housing projects. . . .
>
> The American people are being kept in the dark about a series of moves made in Washington to move the Negroes out of the ghettoes and into White suburbs. Past experience has proven that crime and terror follow the Blacks into White areas and results in the deterioration of entire communities.
>
> All across the country, White people are standing up against this rotten plot on the part of the fuzzy-brained race mixers. Secretary of Housing and Urban Development (HUD) George Romney learned how White people feel when he visited Warren, Michigan. He was cursed, hissed, and booed out of town. Blacks have been burned out of the homes they recently purchased in White Chicago neighborhoods. Whites are fighting mad and the massive protests against building welfare housing for Blacks into White communities is going to bring on the most fierce resistance this nation has ever seen. The White people no longer give a damn what the self-appointed federal

judges order or what HUD does. They are going to do whatever is necessary to stop the Black plague from destroying their homes.

Today public housing is for undesirables—namely Negroes. These people are violently anti-White. They have driven most White people out of neighborhoods, public housing, the poor, the aged, the disabled. They are now forced to take refuge with friends or make their own way.

The time has come to end all public housing hand-outs. We propose the abolishment of all further spending of the tax payers' hard earned dollars on Negro public housing.

And, of course, it is the Jew who is singled out for blame as the cause of the problem:

Senator Abraham Ribicoff of Conn. has introduced a bill which would require integrated housing in every city of America . . . [his] bill has been endorsed by Sen. Walter Mondale of Minn. and the JEW Sen. Jacob K. Javits of New York. Sen. Ribicoff said: "We must allow the Negro to live in the suburbs otherwise the central cities are going to be destroyed."

Another radical Jew, Howard Glickstein who is staff director of the U. S. Civil Rights Commission said: "It is not only legally but morally wrong to expand federal funds to benefit communities that exclude individuals on the basis of race or income."

Political authorities all agree that a larger percentage of Jews are liberals or leftists than any other racial group in America. They have also been the largest contributors to race mixing organizations and have completely controlled and run the NAACP since its founding.

An accompanying cartoon shows a stunned white man watching as a truck, labeled "TRASH" dumps ape-looking blacks on his lawn while a hook-nosed Jew with a Star-of-David briefcase labeled "Real Estate" says: "Here's your new neighbors, courtesy-of the Federal Government."

The realities of our time are clear—no matter how contrary to decent liberal thinking and how painful to contemplate. The racial crisis has triggered all the primeval hatreds and passions that have long lurked within the breasts of large numbers of Americans. The haters know how to exploit them. It is this kind of propaganda and hateful ideas that we should realize are spread daily. It is the Jew who is continually upheld as the evil genius behind the racial crisis, and one should never underestimate the power of statements such as these taken from the pages of the haters, pages that reach millions of people:

> Baited on by the wicked promises of Jewish masters and white race-traitors the Negro in America today is like a dog gone mad. And so must he be dealt with. . . .

And:

> Here in the southeast the reds have another tool; they are using the Mexican mongrels. Yes, these mixed breed spics [Mexicans] have announced that New Mexico, Colorado, parts of Texas, Arizona and Utah belong to them. Therefore it should be apparent to every thinking person that the minorities (Negroes and Mexicans, in particular) are part of the Jew-communist conspiracy that is designed to destroy our way of life, our racial line, American heritages and our very lives. We must never surrender.
>
> Yes, the Niggers and Mexicans are our misfortune; for without them as puppets, the Jew communists would have very little material to work with in this

nation. May White Christian America wake up before it is too late.

And:

> The Zionist Predators are not conquerors, they are killers. They are impure; they are sneaks, liars, cheats, murderers, distorters, filled with hate, greed, evil. . . .
>
> The bugle blows only for the Mighty—the rugged, the intelligent, the determined, the pure, the good, the honest, and the spiritual. You and I see them every day—the workers pouring out of the factories, the ordinary people along the street, the farmers, the policemen, the soldiers, *the real Christian*—United they will triumph over the enemy.

Can anyone honestly doubt that such words are capable of swaying the minds of angry and frustrated men—exactly as they did in the democratic Weimar Republic of Germany?

One can hardly overestimate the anger and bitter opposition to the growth of welfare and its abuse. This anger stems for the most part from the lower middle-class and better off lower-class working whites. Ineligible for welfare themselves, they struggle desperately to make do working on two or three jobs, as they watch taxes and inflation eat away their earnings and savings. To such people this is surely the kind of language with which they can deeply sympathize:

> The truth is that Blacks are but 12% of the population, Mexicans 7% and other non-White Spanish are 3%—yet combined they constitute an intolerable at least 75% of the total welfare roll in America. This amounts to an intolerable burden on the hard working, over-taxed White American which must be stopped. We are opposed also to any Guaranteed Annual Wage because it would double the number of parasites already on the public dole.

This is why large numbers of ordinary Americans are already in tragic sympathy with the following:

> And the first order of business will be to send the Negro back to his home in the jungles of Africa. It won't cost any more than it did to send millions of our boys all over the world to fight the Jews' last four or five meaningless wars. It will cost just a fraction of what it's now costing us for welfare, drugs, crime and all other benefits of Blacks and integration. So what are we waiting for? Let's get Blackie back to Africa! Boating not Busing!

The haters have a powerful weapon in their willingness openly to hate and be truthful about their aims and motivations. As opposed to the mass of white parents who have come out against busing, the haters say: "The big trouble is that they are not true believers in our cause—which is the preservation of the White Race. This is, of course, not the fault of the people, but of the 'clever brainwashers' who have infiltrated the cause to take the steam and will out of the people."

The haters mock the parents who rationalize their opposition to busing and mask it behind all manner of excuses:

> They promote the theme of: I am against busing because: "I don't like buses," or "My child has to get up too early," or "The long ride brings him home late," or "It's dangerous to ride so far in busy traffic."
>
> The correct response to why we are against busing is "because it mixes the races and leads to interracial unions which will result in the destruction of the White race and the end of Christianity."
>
> We are against busing only when it brings on integration. So let's be honest with ourselves, the public, the press and TV. Let's tell the world why we're against busing—Because we are against race mixing!

> American involvement in Asian conflicts must
> end.... [T]he end to our involvement must follow
> the immediate and total destruction of the Com-
> munist enemy using whatever means are necessary
> with minimum loss of American lives.... The
> treasonous system in this country responsible for the
> no-win policy which has wasted nearly 50,000
> American lives must be smashed and replaced by a
> National Socialism new order ... END THE BE-
> TRAYAL OF AMERICAN YOUTH!

Thus, at one and the same time the haters appeal to two contradictory trends among the vast majority of Americans. One: let us end our involvement in wars, internationalism, and all foreign things and concentrate on a strong and powerful America. Two: let us, however, not slink out as losers, but rather show the enemy that America is powerful, by exterminating them. The frustration will thus be released as American might lashes out at the enemy without restraint, following which we will allow the world to go to hell while America concentrates on its own self-interest. Is this truly not a thing calculated to appeal to the majority of Americans? Indeed, is not the clear ultimate aim of isolation and noninvolvement with other people's problems, a selfish turning inward, a return to Americans concentrating on its own problems and, in effect, "doing its own thing," something that is of immense appeal to American youth, even those who, today, may temporarily be on the Left?

The "treason" theme is reiterated constantly, as seen in yet another leaflet, this one aimed at White, non-Jewish servicemen:

> WHY TOLERATE TREASON?
> How long must White G.I.'s, Airmen, and Sailors
> die fighting Communism on a foreign shore while
> Black militants and arrogant Marxist Jews carry out
> Red demonstrations at home?
> Servicemen, better than most other White citizens,
> KNOW where our country is headed. You know the

Along with the article is a cartoon showing a group of terrified white children being bused by a hook-nosed driver to a school with a sign "Blackboard Jungle Schools." Outside the broken-windowed building stand scowling black youths with knives, hypodermic needles, guns, and one with a sweater on which is written "Black Power." Of such emotional things are angry haters born.

One of the great truths ignored and overlooked by so many commentators and intellectuals today is the genuine feeling of patriotism and love of country that exists among vast numbers of Americans. Far from being weakened, the foreign policy crises of our times and the continuous setbacks to American prestige tend to anger and frustrate such people and to strengthen within them a resolve to return to a bygone era of American strength and honor. Against the trends of today there is built up a massive backlash of violent nationalism. Where patriotism is scorned by some, superpatriotism becomes powerful among others.

This tendency is implanted, encouraged, and urged on by the haters. Their propaganda runs the gamut: Patriotism, the war in Vietnam, moves toward detente with the Soviet Union and Communist China, the weakening of the armed forces' military strength by cutbacks and disarmament talks, the breakdown of army morale and the racial crisis in the armed forces, the loss of prestige and honor for America throughout the world.

Thus, a leaflet by the haters reads:

Smash the No-Win System!

Why—after eight years and the sacrifice of nearly 50,000 American lives is the United States still bogged down in Vietnam. . . . Why is a first-rate military power like the United States unable to achieve victory over a tenth-rate power like North Vietnam?

The answer lies in a continuous policy of deliberate treason in the highest places. . . . *Of course,* it is impossible to win a war as long as the commander-in-chief is stabbing his own men in the back. . . .

TRUTH about the Negroes who are being crammed down your throats to the tune of hollow cliches about "human dignity" and "racial equality."

You know the reality of the Black jungle which our armed forces have become . . . you know whose side Black troops will be on in a race riot.

White servicemen must have REAL White leadership—not the self-hating White liberals and Marxist Jews of our present gutless political System—in the hell that's going to break loose in the next few years.

Our nation's dilemma requires a RADICAL SOLUTION—a National Socialist answer. . . . Join the White Servicemen's League. . . .

A strong and undeniably effective appeal to servicemen whose experience in the army has often been with racial conflict, rioting, and with racial separation by blacks. It is an appeal to people who have grown bitter and angry over demonstrations back home while they were at the front. The Weimar Nazi anti-Jewish shouts that Jews were slackers, had "cushy" jobs back home, were profiteering, and stabbed Germany in the back are all conjured up again. Worse, just as they were immensely effective fifty years ago so are they no less today.

Most important is the effort to gather together servicemen and ex-servicemen into a kind of elite corps of men trained and experienced in warfare and guns. This kind of a storm trooper corps *already* exists within some of the hate groups.

The intense frustration and fury at the decline of American prestige is a powerful weapon in the hands of the haters. Thus, they write in one of their newspapers:

An appeal to the world from the American People

To you, we Americans have become an object of contempt. Although you may still occasionally seek favors from us you laugh at us behind our backs . . . it is no wonder! For years you have watched our so-called "statesmen" almost deliberately undermining and destroying every basis on which we once claimed respect from the international community. Now you watch us behave without a shred of national dignity and honor.

You have seen us waste our blood and squander our national wealth in war after war, contrary to our own national interests. . . . [Y]ou saw us sponsor the bandit state of Israel which was created by dispossessing the inhabitants of Palestine at gunpoint and driving them into the desert to starve.

More recently you have seen us stab an ally of long standing [Nationalist China] in the back so that we could sponsor the membership of another bandit state which is our sworn mortal enemy.

And as you behold the insanity of the no-win policy in Indochina—my God, what you must think of us! Listen! Things are not as they seem. All that you have observed are not the doings of the American people. We are no longer acting through our own will, but through the will of an alien conspiracy which has fastened itself on the nerve centers of our nation, we have lost control of our national destiny.

But don't count us out yet. . . . There is still a glowing spark among the best of us and that spark is growing. One day it will burst into an unquenchable flame of rebellion and consume the evil which now grips us.

That evil, that hidden conspiracy, that invisible government is clearly the Jew—as the haters tirelessly point out. The charges made in the blatant forgery known as *Protocols of the Elders of Zion* and repeated by Henry Ford in his "International Jew" are repeated and underlined by the haters today. Thus:

We see daily that some sinister power is dragging our great nation down, down, down. . . . Who has decreed that the greatest people in the world should

just lie down and die? The reasons always stem ultimately from the same source, the fantastic conspiracy
of an alien minority to persuade the rest of humanity
to destroy each other. This exceedingly clever, dia-
bolical scheme is rapidly approaching complete
achievement and YOU are in dire peril. THIS IS
RACE WAR TO THE DEATH!

And in another diatribe:

Zionism is a dynamic ideology that gives passion,
energy and direction to its followers. It has dramatically mobilized world Jewry around its own political
state, built a complex propaganda machine and left a
trail of global tensions, international censures and
three wars. . . . Not Israel but the United States is the
true center of Zionist power. Their gifted leaders
control the major organizational, political and
financial leverage for directing the global aims of
Zionism. . . . We would like to explore further the
relationship between Zionism and American foreign
policy, censorship, spying, defamation and domestic
policy. . . .

According to the haters every disaster of modern times can
be laid to the Jewish conspiracy which seven presidents—Wilson,
Roosevelt, Truman, Eisenhower, Kennedy, Johnson and Nixon
—served "knowingly and willingly in effect and in fact
'poisoned the wells' of security and survival of the United
States."

In our times the haters have seized upon recent American
efforts at detente with Peking as "proof" of yet another Jewish
conspiracy, and the fact that President Nixon's chief advisor
and the man given the job by the president of working out the
rapprochment, was a Jew, Henry Kissinger, was leaped upon the
glee. Thus:

The motivation for the Kissinger policy of rapprochment with Red China lies, of course, in the Zionist. They are playing a clever, international balancing game with the world major powers—a game in which the moves are made on the basis of Zionist interests alone.

The names of Jewish radicals and their role in anti-Americanism are never forgotten. Thus:

If the radical, hippy, women's lib and other such subversive groups were stripped of their Jewish leadership most such causes would cease to exist. The Abbie Hoffman's, David Dellinger's, Jerry Rubin's, Bernadine Dohrn's, constitute the leadership of the movement. (Dellinger and Dohrn are not Jewish—ed.)
Of the radical underground newspapers throughout America, at least 80% of them are run by Jews.

The growing lag in military strength and preparedness, a growing weakness that many military men have warned is turning the United States into a second-rate power behind the Soviet Union, is a constant theme of the haters who sense that, in this way, they may gain powerful allies among the military. Thus:

The United States Congress is infiltrated with traitors, saboteurs, and stupid publicity hounds who consider it a brilliant exercise to undermine our national defense and force us into a position where the prophecy of General Curtis Le May could be fulfilled when he said: "Unless the trend is changed, Moscow and Peking will so far outdo us militaristically within a year and a half that they will be issuing ultimatums which we will be compelled to obey. . . ."

All this is coupled with the defeat and humiliation suffered by American foreign and military policy over the last twenty years. Thus:

> We lost face in Korea, we are losing face in Vietnam. . . . [T]he same hypnotic forces which led the late President Kennedy into perhaps the biggest blunder in American history is increasing our defenselessness in the world. . . . In the name of peace we are being asked to reduce our armanents and jeopardize our national self-defense and compromise our position of strength in the world. . . .
>
> Traitors are as common as flu germs in the United States. They have infiltrated our colleges, our church pulpits and our government agencies. The hypnotic influence of the mass media, operated under the direction of treasonable propagandists, has actually convinced millions of people that we have been engaging in an illegal, immoral conflict in the Far East even though the lives of 50,000 of our sons have been given to hold back the Red tide . . . the defenders of American moral responsibility are never quoted. Their statements are buried in the Jew-controlled press. . . .

The disintegration of the armed forces themselves is not neglected by the haters, who know how deeply troubled the military commanders are over a situation which they believe has made the United States armed forces unwilling if not incapable of fighting. And the haters write:

> Since Aryan youth has absolutely no stake in our Liberal Democratic society they simply withdraw from it by poisoning their minds and bodies with endless doses of drugs, alcohol, heroin. Entire U. S. combat units were high on marijuana before going into battle.

Another dangerous sign of rebellion in the ranks has been the practice of "fragging" or rolling fragmentation grenades under the beds of their commanding officers. This is usually done by niggers or hopped-up white soldiers. The rate of desertion by American troops is the most alarming factor of all; namely, the fact that the Pentagon officially reports that 52 out of every 1,000 G.I.'s deserted last year. The increasing number of semi-literate blacks inducted for military service has led to armed conflict between black and Aryan soldiers. Our military bases have been the scene of ever-increasing racial tensions, thefts and muggings. Even greater numbers of Black officers are being produced under the prodding of integrationist politicans. How many White boys want to trust their lives to a dumb "nigger" seeking to lord it over helpless Whitey? The Military Establishments are being filled with Negroes bent on the destruction of Western Civilization by Third World forces.

The real culprit? The one who is to blame for all this:

The Jew works as the Trojan Horse in our hallowed halls of government.

The present rapprochment with China is seen, in the eye of most haters, as simply a clever Jewish trick to link Washington and Peking against the Soviet Union. Thus, to masses that are at a certain point prepared to believe anything, the haters can blandly write:

The American Zionist Establishment has always supported Chinese communism. Russia always fought Chinese communism tooth and nail.

Under a headline that reads:

Who were Architects of Insane U.S. Policy that Betrayed U.S.A., China and World into Marxism?
Why Is It That the Man Closest to Every President since 1914 Has Been Always Jew?

Beneath are pictures of Sidney Hillman and David Niles, advisors to Roosevelt and Truman; Maxwell Raab and Roger Hilsman, who served under Presidents Eisenhower and Kennedy; Walt Rostow and Henry Kissinger, advisors to Lyndon Johnson and Richard Nixon. Each one is accused of treason and treachery. The implications are clear. It is the Jew who, for decades, has run America. He is to blame for all of its problems. It was the Jews who dragged America into World War II for their own sakes and in the final words of one of the hate leaflets that describes secret British papers indicating a Roosevelt desire to aid the fight against Hitler:

. . . And a quarter-million American men marched to their deaths.

The conspiracy theme is further boosted by continuous references to Jewish power over and control of the news media. Thus:

The American people have no regular systematic access to reliable truth. The news media is controlled directly by the Jews in a large portion and that which is not controlled directly by the Jews is subject to the veto of the Jews. The result is that the United States is now the victim of a blanket of smothering propaganda which approaches the nature of hypnotism. . . . The Jew-controlled press, the Jew-controlled television and the Jew-controlled radio have hypnotized the American public to the point where they have given consent to the depravity which is upon us.

In more specific terms the haters never tire of asking the question: "Who Runs TV Networks?" Their answer, and their reason for the success of the "Jewish conspiracy" is:

> The heads of all three TV networks are Jews. . . . Likewise they have installed Jews as directors and producers all down the line. This includes the movies selected for TV, situation programs and news shows. Jews have the final say on every news item that is cleared for TV.

Or to quote a different hate group:

> As we developed new media of communications as radio, motion pictures and television, the Jews stepped in with their superior financing, their ruthless piracy and Jewish discipline and took possession of all means of mass communications. They proceed in deadly earnest to scramble our brains, corrupt our morals and prepare us for slavery.

The "conspiracy of the Jew" is laid bare as the "answer" to the decline of America, to all its problems, to its inability to solve its crises. Thus:

> Truth has been kept from the American people by a secret, satanic force dedicated to one major objective: namely the complete destruction of Christian civilization. . . . This conspiracy has infiltrated every segment of our society whether it be labor, the pulpit, the right wing, the left wing, the middle, "patriots" or the traitors. When people in positions of leadership put their finger on the real enemy of civilization, the organized Christ-hating Jew, the wolf pack moves in. . . .

Nowhere is the danger to the Jew that is enclosed within the Vietnamese military fiasco and defeat, put more chillingly and succinctly than by the following comment by one of the Haters:

> As American troop strength diminishes in Vietnam a grave day of reckoning faces the leaders of both the Democratic and Republican Parties. They got this nation into this no-win war. They deliberately tied the hands of our military leaders who easily had the might to obliterate North Vietnam and win the war. What will happen if after our forces withdraw, the North Vietnamese with Red China's help invade the South and take power? Hundreds of thousands of South Vietnamese Christians and friends of the U.S.A. have been marked for liquidation!
>
> Over 50,000 of our boys will have died in vain. THIS WILL BE THE GREATEST NATIONAL DEFEAT IN OUR HISTORY! What will the rest of the free world think of the once mighty America defeated by a fifth-rate power? There is going to be a reaction the likes of which has never been seen before in America. . . .
>
> The New York Times let the "cat out of the bag" on May 10, 1971, when they quoted our Zionist Jew National Security Chief Henry Kissinger as saying:
>
> "With the fate of Weimar in mind [we must] avoid a sense of defeat at home that could swing America disastrously to the Right."
>
> The day of reckoning is near at hand. Our people know that something is terribly wrong in Washington. They do not yet fully realize the gravity of the problem because the full shock of defeat has not yet been driven home.

The terrible feeling of frustration engendered by the Vietnam fiasco, and the loss of United States prestige throughout the world is bitterly emphasized by the Haters who write:

> The great "slum" of the world is none other than
> the vast Jewish colony and hot-bed of culture distor-
> tion that the United States has long since become . . .
> the mighty structure of world power that the Jewish
> termites usurped and converted into the sty where
> now wallows the subbeastial, miscegenated mob
> which the Jews so profitably "farm." We speak of
> America's greatness in the past tense, for this great
> nation and its doughty builders are no more as a
> glance at the "American scene" today will show.

These are words that echo and reinforce the latent feelings of
many, many Americans. They *do* indeed sense the swift decline
of the America they once knew to be the greatest and most
powerful country in the world. The military and international
decline is frightening to them and inexplicable. The haters
"help" them in understanding. Only a fool would claim that
their arguments and answers fall on deaf ears.

This military and international decline is accompanied, in the
chilling words of the haters, by a social and moral decay at
home. And once again, they never tire of wringing their hands
over the "death" of American morals and internal strength and
predict ultimate, total disaster unless it is halted. They proceed
to name the culprit. In choosing the morals and social decline
the haters know that they have hit home at areas that deeply
disturb Americans from both traditional and personal stand-
points. They sow their seed in fertile fields.

Thus, the revolution in morals and sexual standards is the
subject of the following article by one of the more prominent
hate groups:

> One particularly heinous aspect of the corruption
> in our current civilization is the malicious degradation
> of our girls and women. . . . We should hold the
> honor of our girls and women inviolable. Yet what
> have we done? We have allowed the oriental rapist to
> tear the veil of natural decency from the chaste

bodies of our women. Our own daughters, sisters and mothers are the objects of innumerable lewd and obscene "jokes." Shameless exhibits of erotic under-garments fill our fashion magazines and our shopping windows. Our bookstores are crowded with sensual and profane books and periodicals, and our movie screens demonstrate in flesh color what to do with a girl: nothing can be too humiliating, too perverse, too swinish, for the "entertainment" of our youth.

The continuous attacks on the decline in morals is not a chance thing. The haters know that this is a legitimate area of concern and that linking Jews with it is a powerful weapon in their arsenal. Thus, another article is headed:

Jews Run Porno Rackets—The Pornographers:
A Cancer eating at the Heart of America.

The article was liberally sprinkled with the names and photo-graphs of Jews involved or arrested in connection with porno-graphy and alleged pornography and included a comment: "Smut: A great Jewish tradition."

The Nazi line is clearly seen in this effective leaflet:

Nazis Declare: Race Mixing Stinks. . . .

But not half as bad as the pornographic Jews who promote it. The sick, depraved Jews who monopolize the motion picture industry can barely wait to turn America into a mongrel cesspool. They are busy grinding out one obscene movie after another with race mixing as the principal theme.

Wouldn't you like to do something about it?

If you've had enough filth and degeneracy, if you're tired of seeing a bunch of rich Jews fatten their bankrolls on the proceeds of the legalized pornography racket and if you're fed up seeing your own race consistently downgraded, then contact us. WE'RE GOING TO DO SOMETHING ABOUT IT!

Indeed, they will, if ever they achieve power.

The emphasis upon pornography is only part of an attack by the haters upon the general decline of moral standards, upon sexual promiscuity, sex education, and the like. It is a splendid field of attack for the elementary reason that the overwhelming number of Americans—who have nothing remotely to do with nazism or fascism—are deeply troubled by it and are personally affected by it in the person of their own children. Many of these people read the Nazi-Fascist leaflets and the articles, and say: "I don't agree with everything they say, but in this case, they're right."

The whole gamut of social and moral decay is summed up and outlined by the haters in a long article under the heading:

> Formula for Destruction: Object—Liquidation of
> Christianity, Patriotism, Americanism.

Beginning by identifying "the real enemy of civilization, the organized Christ-hating Jew," the article warns against Communism's efforts to destroy America, saying:

> Communism is the politics of the antichrist originated by the Jew Karl Marx. . . . [W]hen the Soviet government was established it had approximately 325 commissars and 284 of them were Jews from America, mostly New York. This same enigmatic force is promoting and financing the destruction of America . . . because this is a Christian nation.

The Haters then proceed to sum up the social and moral decay of America, part of the Jewish "formula" for destruction:

> Atheism, cynicalism (sic), treason and sex depravity have enveloped our universities and our school system. Eight-year-old boys and girls are being taught the arts of sexual intercourse. It has been made illegal to honor God in a school room. . . .

195

Jew-controlled publishers are now having a holiday circulating thick books which profane the name of Jesus Christ and pronounce Him as a fraud and a hoax. Only those television programs and motion pictures that profane the name of Jesus Christ are built up, reviewed and advertised generously by the Jew-controlled news media. . . .

History has virtually been discarded in our school systems and we are raising a whole generation of people who do not honor the flag or the traditional principles on which this nation was built. They oppose pledging allegiance to the flag and they have been successful in many places. They insist that people come on the payroll of the Federal and State governments without pledging allegiance to our way of life. . . .

The Jew-controlled press, the Jew-controlled television and the Jew-controlled radio have hypnotized the American public to the point where they have given consent to the depravity which is upon us. . . .

The undeniably catastrophic problem of growing crime and violence in urban areas is a continuous subject of provocation by the haters. Knowing that every American resident of a city is deeply and emotionally involved with the problem and that it ranks among the most critical domestic issues for every American, the haters leap upon it. Invariably, they link it to blacks and the "real inciters"—the Jews. Thus:

Black crime against the U.S. White majority continues in a steadily mounting crescendo of horror. Meanwhile a White Power analysis of crime statistics shows that more than 50 times as many Whites have been killed by Blacks as Blacks by Whites since 1900.

Since it is the Jews who have been goading and inciting the mindless Negroes, with the communist-leaning "civil rights" movement, what we have here is another example of the Jews' secret race war (geno-cide) against the Aryan peoples. . . .

In the 20-year period (just passed) Blacks have killed far more than twice as many Whites as there were soldiers killed in battle on the American side in World War I. . . . Both wars, of course, were fo-mented by international finance for the purpose of killing off the Goyim. This was called for by ancient maxims in the Babylonian Talmud and Zohar. . . .

And yet another of the endless themes:

Street terror, rapes, knifings, robbery and murder have cleared White people out of vast areas. . . . Once the Black plague has devoured a neighborhood there is no turning back; to date no section of any city in America has been claimed or civilized once the Black Blight has taken root.

The emotional sensitivity and anger are well understood by the haters who appeal to that anger and potential violence in the following way:

Well, what are you going to do about it, Whitey? Are you just going to sit there and let your kids go down the drain, your boys ganged up on, knifed and forced to be servile to a bunch of moronic jungle bunnies, your girls tormented by hate filled she-niggers and seduced, or even raped, by gibbering he-niggers? Of course, you're not.

And the Nazis are right. There reaches a point where "of course" he will not. And perhaps he will leap at the answer given by the haters:

Or should we do some KILLING? Should we cut off, root and branch, the satanic Jews and all their

> lackeys who are stirring up the niggers after us? After all, they're trying to kill us. The Jews have secretly wanted to exterminate the White man for centuries? What's integration but the slow mass murder of our race?

The undeniable death of the American city is held up by the haters who know that they will find a vast reservoir of white approval from poorer and middle-class whites who cannot afford to move to the suburbs and who face the all-too-real problems of modern day urban America:

> Many great American cities now are about to be destroyed by this deadly disease—Black gangrene! Washington, Cleveland, Newark, and St. Louis are already dead. Soon to follow in its footsteps are Atlanta, Jacksonville, Richmond, Philadelphia, New York, Dallas, Nashville, Little Rock, Chicago, Detroit. If these great cities are destroyed—then the prediction of Boston's Mayor Kevin White (after visiting New York's devastated Negro Brownsville area) will come true. He said: This could well be the first tangible signs of the destruction of our civilization.

The haters mock the apathy and passivity of Whites, knowing that this is the best way to goad them to anger, reaction and violence. Thus a cartoon with the caption "Typical Average American," shows a scene with blacks pictured as wild, African savages looting, robbing and attacking, while a pathetic looking white man, holds up his hands and says:
"So what if they loot, burn, riot, murder, maim, rob and rape: no one has bothered me yet!"
Is there any need to argue the efficacy of the haters use of the emotional crime problem? And when the particular crime is *rape,* American blood is sure to boil in clenched-fist fury. It is not for nothing that the major headline of one of hater's issues reads in bold letters:

BLACK RAPE OF WHITE WOMEN GROWS

And the incitement that follows below the headlines:

> The crime of rape has jumped some 93% over the last 10 years. A woman is being attacked and raped every three minutes somewhere in the United States. The crime of rape is by far the fastest growing crime in violence in America. The brutal lust of Black men for White women is one of the chief reasons for this alarming trend.

Nor is black rape merely an unplanned thing. According to the haters, who quote Black Panther leader Eldridge Cleaver that there exists "ideological rape" with the desire to revenge themselves on whites by humiliating their women. The Haters supplement their articles with examples of black rapists. Needless to say, such inflammatory incitement works precisely along the lines that the haters desire and there is left only the need to bring in the *real* criminal, the Jew. Thus, if Jack Greenberg, the legal defense head of the NAACP, asks that the death penalty for rapists be abolished (on the basis of its swift use against blacks in southern states) one can be sure that the Haters pounce upon this and milk it for all the hate they can. The failure of the "system" to punish rape more severely is easily explained by the haters. They hasten to inform the American readers that the black man is only a tool in the hands of the Jews:

> Why this sudden Jewish interest in the Negro? Because they find the Negro a most useful tool to destroy us. They are using the Negro for two purposes: to degrade, corrupt and mongrelize you and your children, and to form a trained-ape Mau Mau Red Army to protect the Jews in case you wake up before it's too late.

There is no doubt that crime which involves sex is the kind of issue that triggers the most violent kind of emotions. Because of this the haters unceasingly emphasize it as well as the dangers of miscegenation, a topic that lurks behind many an ordinary American's fears and hatred of blacks. Such people empathize fully with statements as:

> This is what this entire struggle for the survival of the White race is all about. Are we going to allow our race to be outbred and downbred through the process of mongrelization?
>
> We are not going to sacrifice our wives and daughters on the Black-man's altar of rape just so the super-rich can keep the Negro happy.

Crime. Crime linked to blacks. Black crime linked to sex. A powder keg upon which America sits and to which the Haters are not afraid to light the match.

The haters understand full well that the general moral and social decline of American society which manifests itself in so many ways—anarchy, drugs, breakdown of family life, crime and sexual license—deeply disturbs millions of Americans. Consider and judge what kind of effect the following leaflet has on brooding Americans, gravely troubled at the gap in values between themselves and their own children:

> Did you know?
> That Anarchy, Nihilism and Bolshevism are Jewish weapons to sabotage and destroy everything that is not Jewish?
> That Jews are aware of their own vile, dirty, base and filthy low nature and that they suffer from that complex? They bring everyone else down to their sick level—hippies, yippies, creeps, encouraging others to dress like slobs and to be dirty and revolting?
> That Jews are promoting use of drugs among Gentile youths so as to destroy all resistance. LSD was first manufactured at the Weizman Institute in

Israel and Jews promote its use by their control of the 'hippie' movement. . . . All Jewish leftist propaganda glorifies use of 'pot,' 'hash,' 'acid' and all forms of dope.

Jews promote the "generation gap" among gentiles . . . the Jew family sticks together but Jew teachers and professors always encourage non-Jewish children to hate their own parents . . . another way of Jewish sabotage!

That Jews have a strict censorship over radio and TV? Everything done on TV must be approved by the Jew "committee." They bring ridicule to all non-Jews but never to Jews.

That Jews promote every type of pornography and filth in books and movies to sabotage normal instincts and feelings of non-Jews to create a lack of self-respect among non-Jews, to bring all society to the level of animals . . . that is what the Jew wants: a world state of animalistic, stupid, drugged slaves.

The Jews are the greatest threat in the world!

The lies, the foolishness, the ludicrousness are not relevant. Forget them. All that really matters for a thing to be believed is a time of crisis and a person caught up in that crisis who is desperate and weak enough to want to believe anything in which he sees a solution. That is precisely the kind of a time through which we are passing. That which seems laughable to us is heartily and monstrously agreed to by masses of others. That which is so obviously untrue to us is the essence of light and reason to others. The haters may be sick, but they are not fools. They know and understand the mind of the mass man.

Above and beyond all other problems looms the economic crisis and its attendant unemployment, underemployment and inflation. These, which were the soil from which Nazi Hitlerism drew its strength and achieved success, are continually exploited by the haters. In the words of George Lincoln Rockwell (the American Nazi leader who was killed by one of his own disgruntled followers):

> There are millions of Americans right this minute, who privately agree with us strongly, but dare not admit this even to you, their neighbor, for fear of the Jew. But let our phony economy "blow"—as it is doing with our gold pouring out—and these millions of secret Nazis will have nothing to lose when they are jobless and broke by coming out in the open.

The collapse of the economy and the attendant breakdown of society is, of course, exactly what the haters fervently desire. They realize that without such a thing their chances of achieving the power for which they crave are slim. One detects therefore not only a hammering away at certain truths in their analysis of the failing economy but a fervent desire, as well, that this failure accelerate.

Unemployment—the lack of jobs, the loss of jobs, the competition for scarce jobs—this is the gut issue among increasing numbers of Americans and the haters skillfully squeeze every drop of bitterness and hate they can from the situation.

It may be startling to many that many of the Nazi and Fascist groups are as vehemently opposed to the capitalist system of free enterprise and individual initiative as any radical Left group. Their attacks on capitalism and the system are derived from a demagogic effort to capitalize on discontent; on hopes of attracting the youth, and on the realization that there is a groundswell of Populism in the country, as well as on their natural desire to establish a centralized totalitarian regime in the country which is in direct contradiction to individual enterprise and freedom.

The unemployment problem is therefore immediate cause for an attack on the system and the "old order":

> By rejecting bourgeois-capitalist values, Adolph Hitler solved the unemployment problem in just two years after coming to power in Germany, while the Western democracies were still floundering in the Depression of the '30s. Unlike the capitalist regimes

in the U.S., Britain, and France, Hitler did not have to resort to war preparations to bring his country back to social and economic health.

And:

No totalitarian economic system has the problem of unemployment within its boundaries or requires constant war to supply the economic need of its citizens. Young people in Nazi Germany, Fascist Italy, Communist Russia or Red China were able to marry and raise healthy families without sending their wives out to work and slaving endless hours of overtime to keep a roof over their heads. American youth cannot do these elementary things because of hopeless inflated currency, impossible living costs, huge rents imposed by Jewish landlords and backbreaking taxation to keep the hordes of swindlers on the government payroll in the standard of luxury to which they have become accustomed.

What music to the ears of the discontented and frustrated masses of American workers and middle classes for whom life has become an economic drudgery and treadmill! The Populist urge within them is attuned perfectly to these kinds of words. America is today ready to accept the concept of a class struggle—not of upper and lower classes, but of those who are "out" against those who are "in." The atavistic urges and instincts—envy and jealousy, frustration and primitive hatred of those who are in power or successful. It is these urges that the haters feed and count upon to put them in power.

The attack on the system and the old order is part of the understanding of the temper of the times. It appeals to workers, farmers, youth, all the discontented and, because of this, uses all the arguments of the Left. In this war upon the System the Haters of Right and Left stand together in common demagoguery and pray for an opportunity to seize power:

Business profits and the massive employment of the American defense industry would suffer total collapse if brush fire wars in Asia were to cease. That is why our soldiers are utilized as cannon fodder to feed the bloody Moloch of American Capitalism, an economic system which must offer it up to its finest sons as a blood sacrifice on the altar of personal greed!

The American System is represented as offering no choice for the beleaguered "outs." In the words of the haters:

You have the privilege of voting for the Republican Tweedledum who aggressively represents the sublime interest of American Finance Capital ... and the profits running into stockholders' pockets down on Wall Street. Republican and Conservative Tweedledums will always speak in terms of business profits, property values and bank accounts. ... If you don't like Republican-Conservative Tweedledum we have Democratic Liberal Tweedledee who represents the big Labor Czars who work hand-in-hand with Tweedledum's Masters of Finance Capital in keeping no-win wars going so that they can promise full employment and higher wages to their dues paying membership.

The haters, with their Nazi philosophy, appeal to discontent and dissatisfaction by offering a Hitlerian vision of greatness and might. In particular, this kind of a thing appeals to the common, ordinary man, whose life is deadly dull and commonplace, whose days and nights are spent in the same monotonous and gray pattern. The increasing mechanization and automation of society with its attendant lack of meaning to life, comes in for sharp criticism by haters who understand the soul of the people very well, and its discontent. To the youth, in particular, they offer an idealistic, self-sacrificing, and valiant kind of vision:

In America's universities and colleges today, the leaders of tomorrow's world are being trained-oriented-molded. . . . We are living in critical times. The old, rotten order of things is coming apart at the seams. Born of the Industrial Revolution, it was nurtured on fratricidal wars which have been killing off the best and bravest of our race in the last 200 years. It is an order based on economic materialism, whether in its western version—democratic capitalism or its eastern version—Marxist communism. Its highest accomplishment has been the soul-killing proletarianization of our people, the reduction of our race to vast, blue-collared and white-collared armies, scrambling for economic sustenance in the neon and asphalt jungle which we call civilization today. It has crushed the spirit of our race, stifled our inner nature and poisoned the relationship of the individual with his community, his race and Nature.

The article is headed:

Build a New Order.

It would be more than foolish to believe that only concepts of peace, love, and brotherhood really appeal to men. There is at least as strong a pull on the part of hatred, violence, combat, and destruction. This is what Hitler understood and used and this is what his disciples repeat today. Their message has an appeal to a youth whose shift to the Left in recent years is not so much a permanent part of their stable thinking but a continuing search of a generation addicted to fads. The probability is great that many will be attracted to such concepts as the following:

Our people lack the "counting house mentality" of the Semite and were never meant to be a nation of petty desk clerks and merchant princes waxing fat on the misery of their own people. Our Aryan youth want their lives to have both meaning and purpose;

205

something which they can never attain in a Liberal-Democratic society. . . . Only autocracy can provide great statesmen who leave their mark on history. Democracy produces only collective mediocrities, swindlers and leadership of small mind and stature. People wish to live in a time of greatness when their sacrifices have meaning.

The growing unemployment problem is skillfully manipulated and played upon. As always, the culprits are found:

Black pressure upon the Nixon administration is creating a situation all over the United States which could boil up into a catastrophic reaction. In demanding increased numbers of blacks in various jobs, it is becoming necessary for employers to lay off white people deliberately, not because their work is unsatisfactory but merely because they are white in order that the political pressure may be satisfied and in order that the employer may avoid being indicted or embarrassed by a dictatorial bureaucracy. . . .

The Jew Robert L. Kunsig, head of the huge General Services Administration, arrogantly boasts that he has raised minority employment up to 40% of all available jobs and has raised their pay scale to an all-time high. He actually boasts of the number of whites who have been fired. . . . Leonard Bierman, also a Jew, is the senior compliance officer with authority all over organizations holding contracts with the federal government. He has been given a job seeing to it that every person doing business with the government puts on blacks and fires whites according to bureaucratic policy.

The Jew-controlled bureaus operating under the pressure of racist demagoguery are exercising the same type of pressure on the Navy Dept., the Treasury department, etc., etc.

The fact is that it is true that the government has pressured companies to hire more minorities and even attempted to set quotas. For the unemployed or underemployed white, this is the kind of situation that infuriates and drives him into the arms of the Haters. The Haters are well aware of it and make it their business to publicize the preferential treatment and quotas regularly. Thus, the lead story of a recent Hate newspaper carried the headline:

Blacks Taking Jobs From Whites
New Federal Job Rules Discriminate Against Whites

All across the nation the Nixon federal government is using the corrupt federal courts to force private business to discharge White employees and replace them with Blacks . . . more and more cities have been included in the federal government's "Philadelphia Plan." This requires racial quotas on all federally assisted construction projects.

The Haters go on to name city after city where the "Philadelphia Plan" was ordered put into effect. It is claimed that U.S. Steel of Birmingham had to fire "half its white clerical force"; that a New Orleans judge ordered half the workers of an asbestos union to be blacks; that a Newark judge ordered a local sheet-metal union to hire whites and blacks on a one-to-one basis, and a long list of others. Of course, the blame is put on the Jew:

The first federal judge to uphold the "Philadelphia Plan" was a Jew, Judge Charles R. Weiner of Eastern District of Pennsylvania. He held that discrimination against whites is constitutional for the purpose of achieving equality.

Thus, the great document, the U.S. Constitution, has been warped and subverted by ALIENS who are now using it as a means to enslave White People into a status of second-class citizenship. . . .

> Let's face it, the Black man wants your job—he does not want to work to earn it. We stand four square against special privileges for Blacks and the relegation of the White man to second-class citizenship in our own country. We stand for the rights of White people to run their own country and for the removal of the betrayers of the White man.

Preferential treatment and quotas are explosive issues at a time of unemployment and inflation. At a time when the economic situation is growing worse with a continuing loss of markets to cheaper Japanese, German, and Common Market goods; at a time when the dollar is buffeted and in serious trouble because of balance of payments deficits and the dollar drain, the Haters know how to inflame American minds and passions. Under a screaming headline: "Jew Fund Raising Perils America," the Haters attack the giving of money by American Jews to the United Jewish Appeal and Israel Bonds:

> The pouring of American dollars into Israel has reached the flood stage. This movement of American wealth out of this nation has had a severe effect on our growing balance of payment deficit. It is now at the critical stage. Zionist leaders continue to recklessly pressure Jews to give more and more money to Israel.
>
> Jews are by far the richest nationality group in America. They have the nation's largest secret businessman's fraternity with over 300,000 members. Here Jews are able to meet and agree on how to aid one another in business, force out Christian competition, gain monopolies over such lines as publishing, entertainment, garment and textile industries, etc. Jews are first in property, stock speculation and manipulation. . . .
>
> For this reason the wealth of America has moved into Jewish hands. Now they are pouring the wealth

our people created into Israel. At the same time they
are able to write it off their income taxes because our
government has granted the Jewish Agency tax
exemption despite the fact that they are easily proven
not to be qualified for such tax deductions. Israel is
the only foreign nation in the world allowed to sell
government bonds in the United States. No Jew
would ever consider buying an American government
bond. They all buy Israeli bonds. They are now
organizing a drive to force Christians to buy Israeli
bonds. . . .

The Jews can write their gifts off their taxes there-
by avoiding millions of dollars in taxes. We working
Christian people have to make up the difference! At
the same time the nation's deficit in balance of payments continue to zoom in large part due to the Jews
siphoning such huge sums out of America. The future
of the nation is at stake and these parasites are
bleeding our nation dry. How long can we continue
to stand for this TREASON? Are you fed up? Do you
want action to correct this outrage and many others
perpetrated by the same race of People? Then
join____.

In the same article and almost the same breath, the angry
reader is able to hate the Jew for his wealth; for the fact that
he, the gentile, is not as wealthy, and for the Jewish plan to
bleed America of its dollars.

The ever more unbearable tax burden that is being carried by
the lower middle and middle class is yet another powerful
weapon in the arsenal of the Haters. The eating away by
inflation of the savings of the frugal and the elderly pensioners,
the apparently unstoppable and ever-growing welfare burden,
are all things that the Haters exploit. Thus:

Millions of Americans are losing their homesteads
because property taxes are becoming confiscatory. . . .

Big industrial plants are closing down all over America because they cannot compete with slave-labor production of foreign nations. . . .

Most of the gold which evaporated out of Fort Knox has gravitated into the hands of the hidden personalities, mostly Jewish money-changers. They are holding this gold against the day when inflation will destroy values for America and they can come in as they did in Germany before World War II and buy valuable property for a little handful of gold. . . .

One of the chief reasons for the recent huge quarterly balance of payment deficits is the fact that Wall Street's financial manipulators have been shipping "tons" of cash to Europe. . . . After devaluation these 'gnomes of Manhattan' can be expected to take their profits by buying back their dollars at a cheaper rate than at which they sold them. . . . The profit made by the money changers must be over $3 billion. This money will come back and be used by the Rothschilds, Rockefellers, Kuhns, Loebs to purchase more property and business in America. You will work long and hard to pay for the vast profits reaped by these international bankers—who become superwealthy overnight without a day's labor. The same thing occurred in 1934 when Roosevelt devalued the dollar by a whopping 41%. Jewish international bankers reaped gigantic windfall profits and bought out much of U.S. industry which today has so many White Christian workers employed by Jews. . . .

The people will tolerate the trickery and deceit of the money changers for just so long. In the end they will reap the whirlwind when the people realize the extents to which they have been robbed. Then their pent-up fury will be fully unleashed.

We are ruled by a financial tyrant known as the Federal Reserve Bank. This little handful of money-changers has more power than the President. . . . The

Jew head of this outfit, Mr. Burns is now showing his teeth to the point of defying the President. . . .

Welfare is Robbing Taxpayers. . . .

Burgeoning Welfare Rolls Bankrupting States

Jews, Wall Street Back Nixon 'Freeze'

Once again Americans were led down the primrose path to poverty by Tricky Dick and his star of David-studded coterie of "advisors." Names of the men who formulated and direct the current economic program read like a bar mitzvah guest roster. . . .

The Jews have gotten huge numbers of our people convinced it is their duty to love little Jews, niggers, Chinamen and anything else with two legs and we pay billions in taxes to nurture and feed billions of worthless human trash all over the world while millions of our own kids go hungry and in poverty. . . .

Jews are sending three out of four young Jews to colleges and universities while our own kids are lucky to make it through high school. They own more and more of our real wealth and are pushing in everywhere. Just take a look at the swarms of greasy, rich Jews rolling in their wealth in Miami Beach and in the Catskills. Then visit a hat or glove factory in Pennsylvania where the Jew owners pay the Gentiles by the piece.

Jews are notorious all over the earth for not working. A Jew farmer or day-laborer or sandhog or steel laborer—all of these sound almost funny because the Jews flock only to occupations where they can connive and outwit Gentiles for CASH.

Farmers are joining workers, students and all other segments of American society in crying: "A plague on both your houses!" The people are demanding an end to this oscillation between useless parties that secretly come together at the top in the Wall Street Jews who finance both of them. National Socialism will change all this overnight, by cutting out of the body politic the evil cancer of materialism Jewish materialism and exploitation.

Through their complete dominance of Wall Street, the Jews broke the Stock Market in October, 1929. By withholding billions of dollars from circulation, they threw the economy into utter chaos. As they have done often, they created a disaster and then obligingly offered to save us at the price of our constitutional government which they have completely destroyed.

We are now being taxed far past the point where all other people in the world have revolted. And we raise not a finger because we do not even know against whom to revolt! We let the Jew villify, slander and ridicule us daily while we are not allowed to even hint that any Jew can possibly do wrong. Has any Jew ever been sent to the penitentiary for the billions of dollars of income taxes we know they have evaded?

There is a fury and an angry frustration sweeping the land today. And the Haters understand its roots and symptoms well. Understanding the *real* motives and psychology of the New Populism and seeing in it the roots of a neofascism that they can nurture and guide, the Haters sense the yearning and eagerness on the part of the discontented for a *total* change and a sweeping elimination of the "rascals."

Thus, they openly decry any calls for "reform" and boldly declare that the only answer is to sweep away the entire System. With the same hatred and enmity of the Radical Left, the Haters attack the System, the democratic and capitalist framework and call for its total destructions:

> Richard Nixon is a criminal; a traitor to his race and his nation. But so were Johnson and John Kennedy and Eisenhower and Truman and Roosevelt.

Kicking Mr. Nixon off the top of the garbage heap and putting Mr. Wallace there will not change the basic values of the System.

Far more sweeping—far more profound—changes must be made in America than electing a right-wing president. . . . It requires building a whole new structure to replace the present, rotten structure from the ground up. If America is to survive and our race to survive the movement must one day sweep over the land like an irresistible flood which will wash away every trace of the present rottenness.

The Haters understand their Populism well, far better than the liberal and neoradical reformers. They sense perfectly the anger, bitterness, frustration and hate that yearn to explode in violent reaction against enemies, real and imagined.

And so, the attack on the system is total:

We do not want to restore America to the good old days of William McKinley. Our aim is to sink the dagger to the hilt in the corpse of the Jewish intellectual power system. We will not be swindled into tinhorn arguments about how the world ought to be run. If it is to be run by the Jews we definitely prefer that it not be run at all. . . .

A recent Gallup poll showed that 24,000,000 Americans, or one in eight, have given up on the U.S.A. They want to leave the country and are looking eagerly for a place to which they may emigrate. . . . They want to escape the rapacious tax collectors, the crooked politicians, the whole lying fraudulent structure of a capitalist establishment. . . .

We have one purpose only: to demolish the vile and perverted intellectual system which has enabled Jews to run the Western world for a hundred years. Jews, did we say? The racketeers of this system are as often Rich Goyim as rich Jews. The only race they really belong to is the rich race. We have no stake in their system; we cannot be swindled into believing that we have.

And, suddenly, from the Haters who wrap themselves in the mantle of love-of-country, loyalty and the flag we hear more and more talk of the only way left to eliminate the System. Revolution:

> It is time that those of us have thus far survived the virulent plague sweeping our country started seriously thinking about revolution. Yes, we have just uttered the word that has become, through long association with anarchism, anathema to the comfortable majority and all righteous and dutiful conservatives still living in the good old days. . . .
>
> In the full realization of the meaning and effect of the word revolution, lies the only hope of saving whatever is salvageable in this culturally and racially moribund nation of ours . . . the great slum of the world is none other than the vast Jewish colony and hotbed of culture distortion that the United States has long since become.
>
> The choice is quite clear. Decay and death or drastic change, the change understood in the word Revolution. Considered in this light the word loses its frightening connotation and assumes instead hope. THE ONLY REAL HOPE OPEN TO US AT THIS POINT IN HISTORY.

And still another Hate movement, writes:

> Once we have understood the necessity for revolution we can no longer sit around waiting for the time to be right. We must consciously and deliberately set about building the revolution. . . . Our race has never been in greater jeopardy than today. Neither Hun nor

Moor nor Mongol ever posed a more deadly threat to our racial existence than does the alien-controlled system. Revolutionary action is not parading . . . it is striking a blow at the System. It is sabotaging the means by which the System rules. It is killing the creatures who comprise the system. It is waging real warfare against the System using whatever means are most effective in ultimately destroying the System.

And a survey of the newspaper put out by this group reveals a regular feature called "Revolutionary Notes," where ways and means of making bombs and shooting guns are carefully detailed. When we consider that this is a group that speaks of the Jews who "are so zealously cramming their neo-liberal religion down the throats of our people, preaching to us a sermon of weakness and sickness, of degeneracy and decay, of national and racial death," we understand precisely what they have in mind for the Jew.

Indeed, the most striking thing about the Haters' propaganda is their deep, furious, and obsessive hatred for the Jew. It is a genuine hatred and, therefore, very dangerous; it is a hatred that never leaves them, that colors all their thinking on every conceivable issue, that gives them something for which to live and strive. It is a hatred that they transmit tirelessly and continuously to all who come in contact with them and their writings. It is a hatred they attempt to spread and of whose truth they try to convince all Americans. Above all, it is a hatred that cries out for a solution and, for expression, denying any conceivable coexistence, compromise, or solution other than that of the elimination of the Jew. It is a hatred that calls for violent destruction and war against the Jew. That hate and the violent solution of the Jewish problem is emphasized over and over again. Thus:

Jewish success is based on a vile system of 6,000 years of robbery, bribery, piracy, conspiracy, depradation, spoilation, distorting of all truth, plunder, fraud, blackmail, and the breaking of all laws, the smearing of others with the loot of their own crimes. . . .

The Jews are the greatest threat to the world! Every Jew should be investigated and then eliminated from society as soon as possible!

The brutal love of violence and violent love of brutality is summed up in a fascist poem (atrociously written, though that is not relevant to its fury and danger) by a young Hater, who, we are told, was once a member of the New Left. "Since joining us he has shaved, cut his hair to normal length, and placed his creative talents at our disposal . . . we might have another Horst Wessel on our hands." The poem:

The Aryan Stormtroopers

The trembling sheep all stare in wonder at the jack-booted march of Aryan thunder;
By the most heroic of men they are led under the banners in Black, White and Red.
Chests swell our gray shirts, lightening on armband; street battling saviours of the White mans' land.
Skin like leather, fists like a hammerhead, all enemies flee save the bleeding and dead.
We're not wage slaves of Banker and Jew, we reject the lying communists, too;
We know that one World can never be, only if we fight can our race breathe free.
So fight on, Stormtroops, down history's path; let all foes feel the Aryan wrath;
Hoist high the flag! March through the night into a new dawn of Aryan light.

And:

The first fact which strikes us in the face like a sledgehammer . . . is the overwhelming preponderance of Jews in the communication nerve centers. . . . No matter where we turn—newspapers, news magazines, news distribution, TV program production, broadcasting, textbook publication—we find an extraordinarily disproportionate Jewish influence. . . . We can also begin to perceive the motives behind the media's present course and we can see the goal toward which they are driving. . . . We know that they are forcing a great people to the wall, preparing them for the coming slaughter—as they have prepared so many other people before us. There is no greater power for good or for evil than this nation's mass media. That power is now in alien hands. It is therefore our foremost task, regardless of the difficulties involved, TO CUT OFF THOSE HANDS.

The spirit of Hitler is invoked over and over again, not only by the Nazi group which carries a different quotation from *Mein Kampf* in each of its newsletters nor by the birthday celebrations held for him, but by explicit praise and support for his teachings and actions. In commenting on the revival of naziism in North America and Australia, the Haters declare:

Yes, the aggressive power of National Socialism is once again with us. Adolph Hitler, the spiritual leader of all White Men has indeed, "risen from the grave" to take command of his movement. But this will be more than a "European" or "American" venture. . . . THIS TIME THE WORLD!

For the Jew, that kind of a thought invokes all the memories. The fact is that, after twenty-five years, a Hitlerian spirit has returned, for all the same reasons it rose in the first place, and aimed at the very same target with the very same solution.

The call for violence, destruction and death to the Jews is hardly thinly veiled: "Boating or should we do some killing? Should we cut off root and branch, the satanic Jews and their lackeys?" At other times, no attempt to hide the goal is made as at the rally in Washington, D.C. when the Nazis carried placards that read: "Gas the Jew Traitors," and "Death to Traitors."

What clearer and unequivocal statement of the intention of the Haters can be found than the following:

> We literary cynics have more than a touch of Wafton S.C. mentality: we know the right place for them is to swing from the end of a rope! We do not care whether they swing to the right or to the left as long as they swing by the neck.

The Nazis see themselves as the direct spiritual and ideological heirs of Hitler and his National Socialist movement. They commemorate the dead Nazis and thus identify themselves with all that they did:

> This month marked the 25th anniversary of the infamous ritual murder of 11 National Socialists at Nurenberg. In a special consecration ceremony the Commander gave a short address. Then, as the crucible was lit and the muted strains of "White Men at Arms" were played the Commander slowly read off the following names:
> "Hermann Göring, Joachim von Ribbentrop, Wilhelm Keitel, Alfred Rosenberg, Hans Franck, Julius Streicher, Alfred Artur von Seyss-Inquart. . . ."

Hatred of the Jew calls for his vilification and elimination:

> The combination of the vile Jewish mind and Satanic Jewish "religion" made the Jew a sadist by his very nature. He is not content unless he is inflicting misery, suffering and torment. The facts show that the most vicious atrocities against mankind have been committed by Jews. . . . The Jew has never

founded any civilization. It is foreigners who create and work for him; it is foreigners who shed their blood for him. . . .

The platform of one of the major Hate groups is explicit: "Our party stands for Jesus Christ . . . white supremacy . . . a free expulsion of all communists." Since all Jews are Communists in the eyes of these people, that is the best that Jews can expect. In the meantime the Haters declare:

> Ostracize all Jews, communists, negroes and negro-lovers. Have nothing to do with them. They are our enemies.

Or another, increasingly effective and gnawing Hate group:

> We must have an all-White America . . . an America in which our cultural, social, business and political life is free of alien, Jewish influence. . . .
> We must build a new society based on racial values rather than on monetary or materialistic values . . . (it) must not depend upon ability to adapt to an essentially Jewish system of values. . . .

The Jew can expect nothing but total elimination from society and violent extermination from Haters who print "Jew Surrender" passes for the eventual gas chamber and whose hatred for the Jew reaches the depths of paranoia:

> We'll let the people decide who is the idiot and who is the decent American . . . and that will be the end, Jew. For every individual who is proved in court to have been a traitor . . . it will mean the GAS and I don't mean the putride halitosis flavored vaporings of such as you, Jew.

(Letter from a leading Hater to Harry Golden)

There is a distinction between the evil, depraved and vicious MURDERS, such as the thrill-killings by teen-age gangsters in Central Park, and the righteous and necessary elimination from the earth of the human "disease germs" of the world: the rapists, kill-crazy criminals, TRAITORS and other anti-social vermin who badly NEED to be killed.

The key to the success of the Haters lies in the understanding by more and more of them that success will not come through genteel talk or methods. Only the open and direct appeal to the hate and violence that the Hater understands is what motivates the New Populism; why the kind of program that calls for the translating of that hate into action. The conservatives and fringe haters served their purpose in paving the way for a psychological change in the moods of Americans but the Haters know that success will come only to the group bold enough to expose hate and pledge violence to the "enemy."

This point was made more than a decade ago by a leading Hater to a "respectable" right-wing fringe group:

Your organization and methods can win the wealth, the intellectuals and the older people but it can never win the youth, the common working people [the masses] and the FIGHTERS who have been attracted and organized by us. These masses alone can give us the vote . . . these masses do not think and never have; they feel. They are won, as Franklin Roosevelt won them, by "emotional engineering."

The rich and powerful men with whom I have worked, have all failed to realize the deadly necessity of reaching the EMOTIONAL masses and have spent millions attempting to wake up the people with the "truth" alone. All of them constantly failed because what is needed to overturn the monstrous power of

the conspirators is an almost religious mass movement
WHICH IS THE ESSENCE OF COMMUNISM.

I know most of the conservative characters and
they dread being tossed into jails and insane asylums,
etc., like us. So they are "nice" and never mention
the arrogant, obnoxious, treasonable JEWS, who are
the source of most of our Communist Zionist, and
race mixing troubles.

And in speaking of right-wing General Edwin Walker:

If General Walker were not timid or "nice" about
his attack, nor too lady-like about the troops behind
him, he could mobilize the huge White Christian
majority of this perishing land . . . but I am not so
naive as to believe in any such improbable miracle. . . .

And that will leave us once more right where we
were before Walker; America's leaderless masses going
by default to the aggressive UN-nice Jews. . . .

Which in turn will put us one step closer to that
leadership and the power to hang and gas the swarm-
ing human rats. . . .

The Haters understand the new Populism and particularly the
emotions of most of the masses and of youth.

Most other right-wing gatherings look like convoca-
tions of the class of 1885. But hundreds of young
Americans come to us to FIGHT, for adventure! The
last thing we can expect is that masses of fighting
YOUNG men will be attracted by the stodgy "conservatism" and stories about taxes and economics.
They cannot resist the danger and challenge of the
party.

The public—the common ordinary Americans—the
truck drivers, carpenters, store clerks, etc., are sick to

DEATH of kikes, coons, communisms and queers and even sicker of 'nice' methods of dealing with them.

The point which we must make the patriots understand is that the only answer to the gutter demonstrations of these New York Jew agitators is to get down there in the gutter and run those rats right back into their holes.

Nothing will stop us from building steadily, man by man, until the great day when the right-wing too will have a mass action arm! And the first nasty little Yiddish Red who jumps up and opens his mouth . . . will find himself slammed back into his seat before he can take a breath.

To hell with conservatism! To hell with easy ways! To hell with talk, post office boxes and private meetings! The Jews and Reds and race mixers are on the march! They are out in the streets!

If the white race is to survive, the monster must not be talked about . . . it must be KILLED!

To kill it we must ATTACK! In the streets—in the Red meeting halls, everywhere the Jew-communist-Zionist-race-mixing machine sticks up its ugly Marxist face.

Smash it!

Crush it!

Kill it!

It cannot happen here? One prays to G-d it will not, for if it does these kind of people are totally capable of pushing history back thirty years.

CHAPTER 13:
UNLOOKED-FOR
HATERS

We have observed and analyzed the rise and growth of Haters whose existence occasions no surprise. They are the orthodox, the expected, Haters. They are the radical Right, Nazi and Fascist groups whose appeal is to the white, lower class and ethnic groups and majority fundamentalist and middle Americans. Hate groups of the Nazi radical Right have long been spotlighted by Jews and their defense organizations as enemies of the Jewish people.

But there is Jew-hatred today—and in alarming doses—from totally unexpected and unorthodox sections of the American public. The American Jew has always comforted himself by thinking of these sections as allies, friends, bulwarks against hate and people with whom and for whom he, himself, has done battle for civil liberties and equal rights. The fact that sections of these groups have either turned on the Jew or given passive acceptance to the attacks upon him proves yet again the hard truth that the Jew has no allies; that he cannot buy his peace and security by fighting for the peace and security of others; that equal rights may have relevance for others but not, necessarily, for the Jew.

Certainly, the ultimate danger of a holocaust or disaster for the Jew, comes from the Right, neo-Nazi camp drawing its strength from the white majority that controls the country. It is only that majority that has the capacity to rise up against the Jew in truly disastrous terms. But in no way should that allow us to close our eyes to localized Jew-hatred that, on a lower level, exists today in shocking terms and brings forth all the hate and violence against the Jew that could occur from others on a national level.

In no way should we refuse to see, and correctly assess, the very real local danger to Jews that comes—not from white, but from black Jew-hatred, that is of epidemic proportions. In no way should we ignore the Left acquiescence in Jew-hatred and participation in it. In no way should we underestimate the extent of liberal passivity and its latent acceptance of Jew-hatred.

In no way should we forget that upper-class and cultural and artistic non-Jews have joined the subtle battle to drive Jews out of desirable positions and positions of influence both out of feelings of guilt toward the minorities they—the non-Jews and their ancestors—exploited and also from envy and fear of Jewish talent and competition. All of these should be dealt with and understood.

For a long time, there was a blind, stupid, and dangerous unwillingness of Jews to recognize that Jew-hatred on the part of blacks existed and was growing; that it was a clear and present danger to many Jews in certain neighborhoods, professions, and schools. What would have brought forth massive and angry reaction from Jewish defense organizations had it been done by whites, was overlooked, explained away, and, indeed, condoned—simply because the haters in these cases were black.

Jews have suffered terribly because of this and it is important to understand just how dangerous this hatred is, and the role it has had and will have on the Jew who is its target, and on national feelings of Jew-hatred in the future.

For years it was the Jew who stood in the forefront of the struggle for civil and equal rights for the black. It was Jewish support for the largest and the greatest of the black groups, the National Association for the Advancement of Colored People (NAACP) that enabled that group to make the giant strides it did and to lay the indispensable foundation of progress upon which all recent progress for blacks has been built.

It was predominantly Jewish funds that supported the efforts of the Urban League, which, again, helped take the first painful and necessary steps in giving the black man his rightful share in American society.

It was the Rosenwald Foundation—established by Sears magnate Julius Rosenwald—that predominantly financed black colleges, literature, and science, at a time when whites made it all but impossible for blacks to receive a decent higher education. In its struggling years, before Congress agreed to help, Howard University survived only because of men like Rosenwald.

It was the "new" and more militant black groups, like CORE and SNCC, which received most of their funds and white support from Jews, and it was Jews who played a major white part in election campaigns and voter registration drives in the South, who went to jail and who died—let us not forget Schwerner and Goodman—for black rights.

Despite this—and as many astute observers might argue *because* of this—the Jew has become a target for black contempt and hate and has seen that hatred manifested in ways reminiscent of Streicher-type writings and physical pogroms.

Concerning Jewish support for the budding young black intellectuals, one of the tiny black intellectual magazines of our time, writes:

> Thus, we can see how the Jewish community used surplus capital to manipulate and control the fledgling Black intellectual community.

Or, concerning Rosenwald, the philanthropist:

> The Rosenwald Foundation, established by Julius Rosenwald, contributed in great measure to the dominance of Negro colleges and organizations by Zionists.

Jewish support for the NAACP, Urban League and other groups draws, not thanks but, the following:

> All of the so-called "civil rights" organizations are "influenced" in large measure as a direct result of being indebted to Jewish funding sources.

And then the gloves are taken off:

> Black people, living as colonialized subjects in America, have for years been ruthlessly exploited by the Jewish community. . . . The ingrained fear of being labeled an anti-Semite has prevented many a [sic] outspoken Black man from speaking up. The realization of the political, economic and social tyranny, induced by Zionist influence, has stilled the voices of many stout Black hearts . . . but never more. . . .
>
> The time for idle dialogue and non-functional intellectualism is over. The urgency of our struggle demands that we recall the words of a younger James Baldwin ". . . God gave Noah the rainbow sign, no more water, the fire next time."

And the fire came.

There is hardly a young black intellectual who is not prepared to fully agree with these sentiments. One cannot find a Black Power group on campus that is not as nationalist, extreme, and hating of Jews as the one who wrote those words. The days of NAACP and Urban League are over. The days of joint black and white efforts to create a better America and a more just and equitable society are at an end. Integration is out and sullen, hating, separatism is in. One may—and should—grieve for the death of the multiracial dream, but one dare not attempt to deny the existence of victory for black extremism among black youth and intellectuals. The Jew may grieve at the loss of a group he attempted to aid and which he believed would be the last to turn on him, but he would be worse than foolish to attempt to deny or to minimize black Jew-hatred. That hatred of Jews exists and is seen and heard in black writings, among black groups on campuses and in the physical attacks by blacks upon Jews and their property in the urban areas.

To begin with, a philosophical foundation for this Jew-hatred has been laid as a rationalization for attacks upon them. A whole series of charges and indictments have been leveled:

The Jew is plotting to keep the young black ignorant and politically docile. The Jew is an oppressor who enters black neighborhoods and robs him from Jewish-owned stores while exploiting him in Jewish-owned apartments. The Jew keeps him in slave wages while his wife, the black woman, serves as a maid for the Jewish wife. Conspiracy . . . conspiracy. All is a Jewish conspiracy and the Jew is the enemy.

And so we find Le Roi Jones, the black poet and hater, suddenly respected and wooed by supposedly responsible black and white leaders, the author of a poem that reads: "Destroy the Jews who stole from the Arabs/Destroy the Jews—/Put him in a box marked "dangerous germs."

And so we have the official Black Teachers group in New York City's public schools publishing an editorial that says:

> And the Jew, our great liberal friend of yesterday, whose cries of anguish still resound from the steppes of Russia to the tennis courts of Forest Hills, is now our exploiter! He keeps our women and men from becoming teachers and principals and our children ignorant.

And so, one of the officials of the group—at the time a teacher—reads a poem written by one of his students (one who obviously drinks from the Master's waters) over a radio station:

> Hey Jew boy, with that yarmulka on your head.
> You pale-faced Jew boy, I wish you were dead.
> I see you, Jew boy, now you can't hide.
> I got a scope on you, yeah Jew boy, you gonna die.

And a Black Militant, the host of the show, could only comment: "Beautiful." (And the white, Jewish-supported station never did apologize).

The catalogue of an exhibit of black photography, shown at the Metropolitan Museum of Art, claims that the Jew is the one who is keeping the black down. The WASP director denies that it is racist or bigoted.

Leaflets are placed in Jewish teachers' boxes that read:

> Get out, stay out, stay off, shut up. Get off our backs or your relatives in the Middle East will find themselves giving benefits to raise money to help you get out from under the terrible weight of an enraged black community.

And so "Jew pig" and "Jew stores" are common, and a speaker is invited by the Department of Afro-American Studies to Brooklyn College to blandly state that "it is the Jew in particular who has kept the black man in chains."

We find the Black Newspaper (subsidized by the school) at NYU, speaking of the Jews who "feed us alcoholic beverages, narcotics, pornography, and smut literature, making a mockery of the family as a necessary institution of life."

All these charges, all this black hate, exactly as evil and dangerous as the white kind and which, with bitter irony, is echoed by the late Nazi leader Rockwell who wrote:

> In every black ghetto in America the owners of the roach and rat-infested tenements who gyp the Negro

occupants are Jews! The ruthless dealers in vice, who sell the Negro liquor, dope, gambling equipment and other marks of Negro degradation are more JEWS! The owners of the grinding sweat shops which cruelly exploit Negro workers are still more JEWS!

Little wonder that a group calling itself the "Oppressed People's Theater" in the midst of a performance at New York's City College declared, "Hitler didn't burn enough Jews," and many in the audience applauded.

The results: a hatred that has spread throughout the black community and that sees large numbers of blacks with hostile feelings toward Jews with the vast majority of young ones and almost all of the intellectuals seething with hate.

In practical terms, this has meant burning and looting of Jewish stores that are in black areas. And let it be clear that these stores are are burned not only because they are white, they are specifically "Jew stores" and there is a special rage attached to the black anger here. It also means that Jewish teachers have become the target of open hatred and attacks and that they and Jewish supervisors are being forced out of the profession. It means that Jewish civil servants throughout the government are the target of blacks who claim that Jews have all the higher positions and who, therefore, demand quotas and preferential treatment. It means that poor Jews are the subjects of discrimination at the hands of anti-poverty officials, who are predominantly black, and the targets of physical attacks during voting for anti-poverty councils.

These specifically anti-Jewish attacks and the general anti-Jewish-tainted assaults on Jewish neighborhoods have resulted in Jewish stores that are looted and abandoned, Jewish property that drops to a fraction of its former value, Jewish jobs lost, Jewish neighborhoods abandoned, and Jewish poor left to fend for themselves. All this is not a nightmare of tomorrow. It is happening today.

And it will get worse as economic conditions worsen, and as the flight of whites will abandon the cities to black residents in bankruptcy and misery. Stores owned by Jews will be totally driven out, businesses destroyed and property seized. The establishment will say nothing.

What is the danger here? Certainly, the obvious one. That Jews are being oppressed in the America of our times by black-organized Jew-hatred and American establishment indifference and quiet support.

But more important is the fact that black hatred of Jews has ended the moratorium on anti-Semitism that existed since the end of World War II. The blacks had the "courage" to take matters into their own hands and to be open Jew-haters. They have made Jew-hatred respectable and fashionable again, and allowed non-Jewish whites, who have themselves always disliked Jews (but quietly), to once again say that, perhaps, they are right. The black hater of Jews allows the white gentile to openly hate Jews, to agree with the blacks that the Jew is indeed his main enemy, to impute to Jews all the real sins of the WASP and other gentiles, and to deflect black anger away from him to the eternal scapegoat—the Jew.

Finally, it allows the open and active rebirth of a white Jew-hatred. The moratorium is over, the embargo on hate is at an end. It is now fashionable to speak evil of dirty Jews again: the Auschwitz syndrome is buried. This is the inevitable result of allowing black Jew-hatred to escalate without a sound from the American establishment and with so little outrage from Jewish groups.

The role of the white Protestant establishment in this black hatred of Jews must never be forgotten. Nor the part played by so many liberals, fashionable radicals, intellectuals, and artists.

The refusal by the establishment to lash out at, and take a strong stand against, black hoodlumism and Jew-hatred may be understood as quiet but fervent relief that black anger is being aimed, not against its more logical target, the establishment that exploited and persecuted him from the days of slavery, but at the Jew. Far better for a Jewish store in the "ghetto" to burn or for a Jewish teacher to be displaced, than for Wall Street or the captains of industry and wealth to suffer. In a much more subtle way we see, from the white Protestant barons of

American, the czarist policy of deflecting muzhik anger away from themselves to the eternal scapegoat—the Jew. This is the reason for their silence as Jewish neighborhoods, stores and lives are made miserable and threatened. This is why they acquiesce and, indeed, enthusiastically join in the battle for preferential treatment and quotas which will leave them unharmed, but cripple the Jew. Let the Jew pay for the sins of the white Protestant and gentile establishment: there is no cheaper or older way to absolve oneself of one's sins. We can only expect things to get worse as the Jew is thrown to the dogs to assuage black anger and hunger. Black, Chicano and other minority-group power have grown so, thanks to liberal and Jewish efforts, that the politicians and barons fear them more than the Jew. The Jew is now expendable; he can be thrown to the alligators.

Non-Jewish liberals throughout the land join in the battle for all the underprivileged and deprived minorities since their own guilt feelings drive them to find some way to compensate for all the exploitation they and their fathers caused. How easy it is to soothe one's conscience by finding a scapegoat that is someone else. The white, non-Jewish liberal unloads all his guilt upon the Jew. How sweet and satisfying it is for him to hear that all the teachers, landlords, and storekeepers in the ghetto are Jewish. Suddenly, *he* is absolved of all sin. Suddenly it is not *he* who is at fault. The liberal leaps into the fray on behalf of the poor, deprived, and exploited blacks with gusto now that *he* will not be asked to pay. He sits quietly while black hatred of the Jew is poured forth. He watches silently while Jewish teachers, civil servants, and students are thrown out of the positions they deserve. He has little to say about Jewish stores and property that are burned and destroyed in the so-called ghettos. He is busy elsewhere as Jewish poor are denied the benefits that others receive. The liberal has not only become soft on Jew-hatred, he quietly supports it and encourages it.

The liberal is not immune to Jew-hatred. The liberal is not immune from hatred of any kind. For the most part his liberalism was born through his removal from the problems upon which he takes such dogmatic stands. He fights like a lion for people far removed from his own little world. His hypocrisy only emerges when the deprived for whom he loudly proclaims his fealty, encroach on his world and threaten his interests. The liberal is only liberal when it is inexpensive to be one. It has been both inexpensive and radically chic to be pro-Jewish. The years after Auschwitz made philosemitism an "in" thing. Today, it is not only no longer so, but it is to the interest of the non-Jewish liberal to side with others *against* Jewish interests. He is impelled by self-interest to throw the Jew to the wolves and, indeed, his own latent dislike and resentment of Jews is now given release.

How many non-Jewish liberals have long resented Jewish talent and competition! How many secretly smile to themselves as the arrogant and successful Jew now gets his comeuppance. How many are relieved to be both free of guilt and of competition as the Jew becomes the target of hate with their silent acquiescence.

It is important to note, especially, the sharp rise in Jew-hatred on the part of intellectual, literary, and cultured non-Jews in recent years. The supposed death of anti-Semitism and absence of prejudice was always indicated by the inflow and dominance of Jews in the fields of writing, theater, poetry, and the arts of all kinds. It was only natural, it was felt, that the non-Jews in these areas would feel no prejudice since they were educated, sensitive, literal, liberal, and radical. Prejudice and dislike for Jews, certainly violent hatred and jealousy, were the province of stupid masses and ignorant Fascist-types, and was certainly not to be found among the literary and artistic elite.

It is not true. The love affair of non-Jewish literary and art circles with the Jew was born in the same feeling of guilt they later acquired for blacks, Mexicans, Puerto Ricans, and Indians, in boredom and in a desire to "daringly" go against the prevalent stream of anti-Semitism, and by the temporary clinging to yet another fad that was temporarily chic and "in." Not only does such an attitude swiftly pass in the circles of the unstable types who inhabit that world, but the non-Jew suddenly saw that his relationship to his "adopted" Jew would not be the kind of comfortable, Kipling-colonialist-type of White Man's burden where he could condescendingly help the peasant rise a little higher, secure in the knowledge that he would never remotely rise to his own level.

The Jew, it was found to his horror, was clever and talented. Cleverer and more talented, in most cases, than he. He was a threat to his position, and it was no longer a fun game. Worse, the Jew was insufferably arrogant, loquacious, and sensitive and even more insecure than he. The Jewish intellectual was caught up in all sorts of guilt feelings even deeper and more twisted than the non-Jew. The non-Jewish intellectual and artist now became a victim of the same base and common drives as that of the masses he so loudly praises and quietly despises—jealousy, envy, hatred.

Suddenly, the love affair has cooled and changed into a secret and sullen resentment, jealousy, and envy. We see the tip of the iceberg; the rest is hidden just below the surface in hostility, resentment, and hate.

In discussing a speech by Norman Podhoretz, the Jewish editor of *Commentary* magazine (a publication of the American Jewish Committee), haters single out his comments citing, in the words of the haters, "the anger of Goy literary people over Jewish control of publishing media, cinema, and TV." This is their comment:

> It has been many years since the Jews worried about us Goy literary people. They simply blacklisted, mangled, bankrupted, and trampled upon us. We were regarded as people of no importance. Stupid and incompetent Jewish hacks reaped millions; we watched from the sidelines. Now suddenly Podhoretz is worried about us. Well he might be. There has been a sensational rise in the quality of anti-Semitic literature in the last few years. Our aim is simply to sink the dagger to the hilt in the corpse of the Jewish intellectual power system. . . .

> Podhoretz would do well to worry about dis-
> gruntled literary people. WE are the ones who will
> cook the goose of the Jewish ideologists. Our mission
> is entirely one of pure *destruction.*

Clearer and stronger language could hardly be found.
The non-Jews who have succeeded, do not give vent to this kind
of language since they are not desperate and are a great deal
more cautious than the hater who wrote the above words, a
disgruntled and frustrated failure with nothing to lose. But so
many of the successful ones *think* very much the same way and
are the repositories of latent and subtle jealousies, frustrations,
and envy of the Jew, who, through talent and creativity went to
the top and has taken the place of the non-Jew—*who wants it
back.*

I perceive a disturbing and dangerous possibility in the
coming years. In an era of Populist discontent, frustration, and
desperation, groups that are natural enemies and competitors
will temporarily join together against what they consider to be a
common enemy. "Outs" of all kinds will be prepared to join,
momentarily and bury their deep hatred and differences in
order to eliminate groups they consider to be the immediate
and more dangerous enemy. Particularly when that enemy
appears to be vulnerable and easy to destroy.

And so, one can see white ethnics, lower-class proletarians,
and the discontented joining for just a moment with blacks,
who are equally desperate and hating, in order to turn on the
Jew. For it is not the black man who is the primary target of
white hate as so many foolish Jews comfort themselves by
thinking. It is the Jew—affluent and successful, the target of
envy and resentment—who is the major target. And to destroy
him, the most illogical and unexpected of alliances will be
formed.

We have become conditioned to think of a white backlash in
terms of the poorer, lower-class blue-collar whites turning
against the blacks. What we did not contemplate is an alliance
of these lower classes, white, and black, turning against Jews.

The idea is hardly a fantastic one. White ethnics may fear the blacks and will, in the end, turn on them, but the possibility of their first joining together to attack the "haves" and particularly the Jews whom both resent, is a very real one. In a sense this is what the revolutionary Left is attempting to do when it seeks a lower-class alliance of all the poor. While the Left may not advocate specific attacks on Jews by this coalition, the result will be the same. On the other hand, the Fascist radical Right, despite its contempt and fear of blacks, has in the past already taken their side against Jews and would join with and promote a white-black alliance specifically aimed at the Jewish people.

In the words of Nazi Rockwell:

> And in the last two or three years, the Negroes are becoming anti-Semitic by the millions! Even more important, these Jew-wise Negroes are already at the bottom of the economic pile and have little or nothing to lose by fighting the Jews whom they finally begin to realize are exploiting and using them. The Negro anti-Jewish movement is a most deadly and immediate threat to the Jewish manipulators.

What Rockwell could see then, too many Jewish leaders do not yet see today. But the point to understand is the willingness of Rockwell, who looked upon blacks as "savages" and "apes" to sympathize with their plight so long as the target was the Jew. Both communism and fascism appeal, primarily, to the masses, to the little people, to the poor and disinherited. These people join them, not because of idealism, but because of self-interest. If that self interest means a temporary alliance of the bitterest of enemies against a common threat, they will join together to eliminate that threat and then turn on each other. This is what could very well happen in the case of frustrated and bitter black and white lower classes and the classical scapegoat, the Jew.

Of course in the end, the black man will fall at the hands of the white haters. Meanwhile, however, he serves a valuable function for them and all the guilt-ridden whites who are so overjoyed that he is blaming someone else. And the black hater, instinctively sensing that the Jew is the weakest link in the white chain, the one that few whites will grieve over very much, strikes at that link, at the white he can most easily defeat.

No, it is not the black man who is the main or first target of the haters but the Jew. And it is the Jew who is the main target of the black haters. For the American Jew, as for all his ancestors in other lands and times, there is no hope for allies or friendship when the die is cast.

A word for just a moment about the Left. One will not find the kind of open and explicit Jew-hatred in their literature that can be found among other haters. But they—with all the Jews that serve in their ranks—serve an invaluable function in the cause of Jew-hatred. The black haters, the revolutionaries who hate Jews, the nationalists who hate Jews, the Black Power groups who hate Jews, have no better allies and more vehement supporters than the radical Left. Never a word of criticism is heard from the whites and Jews in the Marxist-Leninist camp concerning the vicious Jew-hatred of black nationalist leaders. It is this lack of criticism and this unwillingness to speak out against black hatred that is the first step in its success. More, the Left does not stop with failure to criticize. It moves forward in active and enthusiastic support of the individuals and groups who—along with their black revolution—combine hatred of the Jew. It is the Left—with its Jews, for that is irrelevant to the Jewish apostate—that triumphantly supports the Panthers with their attacks on "Zionist pigs" and "kosher nationalism." It was the Left which fervently backed the black haters of Ocean Hill-Brownsville during the great school strike of 1968 with its obscene and open Jew-hatred. It is the Left which excuses and echoes the attacks on Jewish landlords, Jewish "gouging" merchants and Jewish oppressors. They give aid and comfort to the black haters, as well as moral, material, and physical support. It is unimportant that the Jews among them, will, in the end, go under too, and with even more contempt from the black haters for having aided them against their own people. The fact remains that before they go under, decent Jews will have suffered, thanks to them.

Finally, Left support for the Arab cause and fanatical attacks upon Israel are paying strong dividends for the cause of Jew-hatred in America. Only the naive and truly foolish will fail to recognize that, in the minds of the simple hating masses, there is no distinction between Jews and Zionist, and that Israel is the country of Jews. Only the willfully blind refuse to see that in the minds of the black haters the Arabs are "black" (and let us not waste time raising the issue of Arab slave traders and Arab genocide against blacks in the Sudan) and Jews are "white." Attacks upon the United Jewish Appeal and Israel Bonds invariably are linked to attacks upon Jews who work in black neighborhoods, "Oppress" blacks and then send "black" money to Israel. Attacks upon Israeli "genocide" and "oppression" of Arabs invariably lead to comparisons with Jews and blacks here. Israel is identified with Jews. The Left which, naively or not, persists in aiding the haters in attacks upon the Jewish state adds fuel to the fires of hate here.

Most important: in the months to come the issue of southeast Asia will slowly fade from the headlines and consciousness of the Left as the major issue upon which to build revolutionary hopes. In its place must be found another issue, another enemy, another target. It will be Israel.

The hatred and propaganda of hate that will be directed toward the Jewish state, in which Tel Aviv will replace Saigon as the major enemy of humanity and Dayan will take Thieu's place as the master criminal of humanity, will see such passionate attacks, demonstrations, and protests against Israel, that the Left will become the major sower of Jew-hatred. Its non-Jewish members, despite all their protestations, will exhibit more and more antipathy and hatred to Jews. The latent dislike of Jews that lies within the overwhelming majority of gentiles does not pass the radical left gentiles by. Marxists in Poland deceived no one as they expelled their "Zionists"—Jews who had been loyal Communists for forty years and more. Khruschev, the Marxist, was hardly immune to the disease of Jew-hatred when he told his Polish comrades: "You have too many Abramoviches in your leadership." The percentage of Milwaukee Socialists in the 1920s who were also supporters of the Populist Klan was more than a little disturbing.

There is more than a little dislike of Jews and the proportion of their leadership within the ranks of the Left. It is not only the fact that Marxists distrust intellectuals like the Jews, who are always questioning. The non-Jews in those ranks will be more than eager to believe their own propaganda and those of the militant blacks they support, when they speak of the sins of a Jew in the ghetto. The Left is destined to become more and more anti-Jewish, although cloaking it in terms of anti-Zionism. Their efforts among the poor workers of the ghetto and factories will do more practically to sow the seeds of Jew-hatred among the poor than the efforts of the radical Right despite the fact that, in the end, it will be the latter that will reap the fruits of most of their labors.

Hatred of the Jew. Silence in the face of that hatred. Indifference and apathy of the kind that decent and respectable Germans, Frenchmen, Italians, and Belgians displayed in the face of Nazi elimination of Jews. We can expect no more here. The Exile never changes and let us never forget that it is a condition of abnormalcy. Only home is normal for the Jewish people.

CHAPTER 14: THE REACTION

The most tragic and frustrating aspect of the impending disaster is the knowledge that Jewish leaders, along with millions of ordinary Jews, will scornfully and angrily dismiss the entire matter. Not content with heaping adjectives and labels—"paranoid," "absurd," "overreacting," "irresponsible," "dangerous"—scholarly efforts, based on "facts" and "history," will be made to disprove the danger to Jews in the United States.

The most universal and "triumphant" of these arguments will be the fact that Jew-hatred was virulent in the United States during the years of the Depression and that the Jew did not go under. Cited will be the massive numbers of Americans who were avid followers of Father Coughlin, who marched with the German-American Bund, who made the Yorkville section of Manhattan and many parts of Long Island and Brooklyn unsafe for Jews. They will cite an admittedly serious and critical wave of Jew-hatred and, victoriously, cry: "You see! Just as the American system overcame that crisis, so shall it, by its very nature of democratic guarantees, assure the Jewish future. This is not Germany; it will not happen here."

One would give a great deal to have these people proven right, but they are wrong. The very fact that such a virulent wave of Jew hatred arose in the thirties was, at the time, a terrible shock to the Jews of the United States. They did not believe that in the New World, a threat would even arise. At the time they were frightened and unsure as to what would happen. They saw a general drift to extremism, a gaining of votes by haters on Right and Left as people were driven by desperation and frustration. They saw a continuation of the trend that had frightened and shocked them a decade earlier as the Klan had risen to dangerous heights of popularity and gained genuine support. In a country that less than a decade earlier had gone to war with bright idealism and dedication on behalf of people threatened by tyrants, that for decades had been a beacon of light for the poor and oppressed peoples of Europe, that had gathered those people to its shores and allowed them to begin new lives, the Klan of the twenties and the Jew-hatred of the thirties was a shattering blow. Suddenly that which had not happened to the Jew in America when he was an insignificant and relatively unimportant and overlooked group, was happening. In its time it *did* give the Jew pause; it *did* shake him from the illusion that America was immune to the germ of Jew-hatred.

But more important we should ask ourselves the real reason why the Depression did not, in the end, result in a massive wave of persecution. This failure of Jew-hatred to continue, this dying away of the massive waves of hate that had been unleashed, had nothing to do with the ingrained constitutional guarantees of America or its traditions of democracy and freedom. In the face of personal crisis, anger, bitterness, frustration, and envy, all theoretical traditions of equality and freedom are swept away. The Constitution is a piece of paper at the mercy of the people's temper. What saved the democratic process and the Jew and what defeated the haters in the era of the Depression was not the "inevitable" triumph of American brotherhood and love, but the rise across the seas of German tyranny and hate.

Just as the hatred of the Klan floundered on the surge of good times in the twenties, so did the necessary conditions for continued flourishing and eventual victory of hate during the Depression, suddenly change—but not through any great success of the American economic system. And as conditions changed so did the hopes and chances of the haters. It was the sudden creation of new jobs by the approach of World War II and the immediate preparations for the war that saved the Jew. Ironically, it was that force that took the lives of six million *there* that may very well have helped spare five million *here*. It was the sudden creation of new jobs as the defense effort began here, and not constitutional guarantees, which was what took their most powerful weapon from the haters and from the American people their need to act out their latent hostility. It was the creation of new jobs by war in Europe and not the liberal efforts of the New Deal that finally broke unemployment and saved America from its steady drift to the haters.

It was the Japanese attack on Pearl Harbor and the declaration of war by the Nazis that suddenly turned Americans to the hatred of haters instead of their victims. Of course, the Bund would flunder as the Nazis it supported vowed they would kill American boys. Of course, the Fascists of America would lose support as the men they had been extolling began their efforts to kill Americans and to conquer the United States. In all this there is hardly great consolation and, surely, no proof that it cannot happen here. Indeed, the very arguments raised to disprove the threat to American Jews rather support and intensify the arguments that it can happen here—precisely because in our lifetime it *began* to happen here and was cut short by the ironic aid of a "providential" war.

More, a great and substantive change has taken place in America since that time. In the era of the Depression, America was just emerging from its simple and unique pioneering past. It was coming out of a relatively simple and unsophisticated era, free of all the wars and social passions that had wracked Europe and that had conditioned people to extremism and resolution. It was a simple America with much stronger traditions of discipline, virtue, acceptance of authority, of a work ethic, and of the individual's obligation to take his chances in the marketplace. He had been much more willing to accept his burden as his religion commanded him and as his social and economic ethics geared him to the belief that "making it or not" depended on his own efforts. He was a stronger person, more mature and better able to bear the burden of life. One does not become a revolutionary—even in ideology and thought—overnight. One does not revolutionize his own life in an instant. One does not simply discard the instincts, habits, and teachings of religion, and traditions of a lifetime in a moment of despair. The American of 1936 was not ready to wipe out the American traditional system, and the Jews around him. But, the American of 1972 is not the American of 1936.

The American today has come a long way in his thinking and his life-style in thirty years. The Great Depression shook him from many of his traditional concepts and his phlegmatic acceptance of hard times. The great economic boom that followed the hard times created a revolution in social and economic concepts. It created a more sophisticated, discontented, bored, dissatisfied, a more jaded, American; it was followed by great racial, social, and economic conflict, a different approach to work and to study. The American is weaker today than he was thirty years ago and hence less ready to accept difficulties. He is more defiant of authority and less willing to accept tradition based on experience—hence more willing to overthrow it. The Great Depression, the Second World War, the economic boom—all have combined to make a different American. That American is ready and able to challenge his problems, the American system that created it, and the democracy and freedom within it. He is much more apt to explode into violence and Jew-hatred in his discontent and frustration. The Great Depression shook the American tradition severely. The good times of post-World War II dangerously weakened the tough moral fiber. The American character has been sufficiently buffeted to make it vulnerable to things that were not possible before. Tradition has been fatally wounded. Revolution, violence, and fascism are ideas whose time has come.

"But how big are they? How many members can they boast?" Yet another of the arguments that will be brought to bear against those who fear the future for the American Jew. Those who play a political numbers game with us are capable of seeing life only in terms of tangible bodies, figures, statistics. In their total lack of understanding of the psychology of mass movements and extremism, they are programmed to think in terms of haters as being similar to members of a B'nai Brith or Knights of Pythias lodge.

As any simple student of history knows, numbers of members are hardly a real indication of the true influence and potential danger of an extremist ideological group. For evil to win out it is indeed true that only a relative handful of fanatic, committed individuals need sign party membership cards. The rest need only be passive voters or apathetic and indifferent opponents. In Maoist fashion, one need only work for a cadre of zealous proponents, ideologically to win over the hesitant supporters, and to neutralize the indifferent opponents. How many members did the Bolsheviks have when they seized power over the huge masses of Russia, and how many official Nazi party members were there among the millions who voted for Hitler in 1930, 1932, and 1933? One needs only support for an idea—not membership cards—to take power perfectly legally and democratically and this, indeed, is what Adolph Hitler did.

What is happening today is that a small, hard core of haters is planting seeds of hate in the minds of many millions of Americans whom conditions have made ripe for planting. They are winning minds and they will harvest the fruits of that labor in terms of real support at the proper moment of crisis. They are cleverer than those who deprecate the threat they pose. They are ploughing and sowing seeds, and only the ignorant city dwellers look at those fields that are incubating and see nothing.

The experienced know that beneath the empty spaces lie the quietly ripening, seeds beneath a proper diet of sun, water, and fertilizer. In time, they will suddenly burst forth into life just as the planter hoped they would from the time he began his laborious task.

So is it with the haters. They are concentrating today on winning minds. A huge number of hate books and publications are sold each year and they reach millions of people. Their titles are indicative of the poison they feed their readers: *Protocols of the Learned Elders of Zion, Jewish Ritual Murder, The International Jew; The Talmud Unmasked;* the *Myth of the Six Million; The Jew Comes to America; Iron Curtain Over America; Imperium, Judaism in Action.* There are literally hundreds of other such publications that reach millions of people each year. They are not insignificant; they dare not be ignored or underestimated.

Haters have begun to receive television and radio coverage in growing amounts. Groups have sprung up in cities where once it was thought to be out of the question. Nazis are active in Detroit, Cleveland, Connecticut, Philadelphia, Trenton, Washington, Los Angeles, Chicago, Seattle, San Diego, and northern California. Many of them boast bold storefronts with swastikas. A top hater has appeared at colleges and universities, been interviewed on radio and television and pockets of small Nazi groups have begun to spring up in high schools. A White Power telephone message has been established in different areas of the country enabling a caller to hear a hate message calculated to incite and to pander to his angry emotions. It reeks of Jew-hatred.

It is not without truth, what the head of one of the hate groups boasted to his members in a recent party bulletin:

> Right now the Party is stronger in every respect than it has ever been before. In the coming year, we must, as Adolph Hitler told us "adopt the highest embodiment of National Socialist thinking and

being." The possibilities are tremendous. . . . Everything is at stake. We have nothing to lose but the anti-White system and a heroic new order to gain.

A definite increase in the number and quality of the "storm-troopers" has taken place, with their uniformed shirts and helmets. The quality of the literature has improved and is now put out regularly. Obviously, there is money coming in from some source or sources. Although numbers are not the major criterion in judging whether haters are or are not a threat, the numbers *are* growing.

But America is a land of minorities and each will feel an interest in making sure that another minority is not persecuted.

How many times, in Europe and here, has such an illusion been pricked and shattered. Minorities in Poland joined with the majority in turning upon the Jews. Ukrainians, Poles, Hungarians, Rumanians, all the groups of Eastern Europe who happened to be minorities in different lands turned on the Jew in the hope that they would be spared. To the contrary, a land of minorities is a land that is not as secure and self-assured as a homogeneous country. It is wracked by majority fear of the minorities and by each minority's fear for itself. The Jew is the target of both majority and larger minorities; he is the scapegoat for them both.

America is no different. It is the melting pot that never melted; that is the fact of American life. The existence of many different nationalities, rather than aid in building tolerance of weaker minorities, invariably has the opposite effect—as witness that all the minorities never kept the blacks and Chicanos from persecution. A group that has once been persecuted does not learn tolerance and pity for others who are now in their former position. On the contrary, it usually takes its turn in the role of oppressor, having for so long been seeking that opportunity and hoping to deflect hatred away from itself. Men do not seek freedom and justice for themselves out of devotion to those ideals, but out of selfish desire to have them for themselves. Once obtained, they are not prepared to share them with others who are now below them. The difference between the haves and have-nots is not morality, but opportunity. Reverse their positions and a disgusting similarity results. The presence of cultural pluralism and many minorities has not the slightest relevance to the positive future of the Jew of America.

Sometimes the opponents of Return garb themselves in the garments of courage and heroism speaking of Jews who "no longer turn and run" and of themselves as being prepared to "man the ramparts." The outburst of sudden heroism and courage on the part of people whose timidity and unwillingness to stand up for rights of Jews is legendary, is remarkable. It is also hypocritical. It is also ludicrous.

Those who beat their Jewish breasts and suddenly don the mantle of the Macabbees after years of condemning those who did in fact, go into the streets for Jews, deceive no one. They bray loudly, not because they are ready to do battle, but because they either do not believe they will ever *have* to or because the thought of leaving the American fleshpots is so disturbing that they refuse to believe that it will happen.

In any case, I stand second to no Jew in my readiness to do battle for the Jew under conditions where success can logically be attained and, if there is no other choice, in desperation where one can at least salvage Jewish honor.

But there is a great difference between being brave and being a fool. Those who were so silent all these years in the face of Jewish problems out of fear of what non-Jews would say and making things worse for themselves strike ridiculous and foolish poses as they speak about losing an opportunity to leave the Exile in honor and with backs erect, and instead are prepared to gamble on winning a battle against overwhelming odds of people, arms, and government. It is one thing to fight a local neighborhood battle against hoodlums on behalf of Jewish rights and quite another to have to face an impossible array of national enemies. One is almost moved to admire the courage and bravery of the opponents of Return. I admit that I seek refuge in the cowardice of sanity.

There already exist large numbers of right-wing fringe groups that serve, and will continue to serve, as prime reservoirs for the haters from which to draw membership and support. Much of what the haters say is also said by large fringe and respectable conservative groups. Many Americans joined decent conservative and patriotic organizations in the hope that they would solve the problems that concern them. If these decent or fringe groups will be unable to do so, there will be a polarization and massive shift, out of desperation, to the haters. The latter already concentrate much of their fire on respectable and "do-nothing" conservative groups. Given more critical times these arguments will find their way into the hearts of many present-day conservatives and patriotic Americans whose anger and anguish will drive them into the arms of the haters. There is much truth to the Nazi assertion that, if the crisis is not too severe, the American people will not even follow a mildly rightist course, but if times are sufficiently bad they will flock to the most extreme of the haters.

> They are ludicrous figures and the arguments are so patently and obviously absurd, few people will believe them, let alone follow them.

Such an argument ignores the oft-proven fact that people are not students or adherents of logic. Given desperation they do not dissect arguments. They think with their hearts, not their heads, and they believe what they want to believe. Never laugh at the crudities or the absurdities; the people who are ripe for the haters are ready to believe the most incredible of them, because they *want* to believe, because they need to believe. Lies do not matter; indeed the bigger the lie the better, and this is one of the lessons the Nazis have learned from their Hitlerean mentor quite well. That which, to the Jew, is absurd on its face, is, to the Jew-hater, eminently true and logical because he has been saying it, himself, for such a long time—only quietly. When desperation and hate grow, reason flees and is replaced by wild mob willingness to find a scapegoat. Upon his head are put the most incredible and far-fetched sins. It does not matter what they may be, because he was invented for that purpose. Certainly, when a clever hater takes a large dose of reality—and the problems he raises are, indeed, real—and blends his arguments with a mixture of truths, half-truths and lies, the combination becomes a deceptive but effective one.

Earlier, I wrote of America, the violent. It is, sadly, true. The haters of our time sense that urge to violence and the readiness to explode what lies just beneath the surface of American frustration, boredom, restlessness, and rootlessness. Liberals, too often, dismiss the haters with contempt and deprecation. Again, their moral and spiritual sickness should not blind us to their danger or lead us to believe the comforting images that liberal, intellectual arrogance has created. The haters understand people, all too well. Their own base natures and sick souls empathize with the baseness and darkness that flit about all our souls.

The haters are not "little old ladies in tennis shoes." Many of them, and certainly those who are on the fringes, are younger, educated people. Most have long since evolved from purely religious fanatics to racial and political groups with hard-headed understanding of what people want, with a political program and methods to achieve those programs. They are a new breed. They are the new Nazis. They have patience and a fanatical faith that conditions are in their favor. They share with the Marxist-Leninist the same faith in the inevitability of their triumph, and they are prepared to put in long hours and years to achieve it. They have no private lives, and this secular-Jesuitism, this Nazi-Maoism, is a potent force that can overcome far greater numbers of opponents who are simply unwilling to sacrifice too much, who have no time to put into their fight to preserve democracy. A small group of dedicated, fanatical, haters can always overcome a great mass of apathetic selfish opponents.

The terrible sense of loss of purpose and aimlessness in life which has gripped whole sections of the country—particularly youth—gives haters a great market, *and they have something to sell. It may be horrible and nightmarish, but it is something which, for America, is new.* Along with the masses' demands for a better economic life, the haters have a terrible understanding of the weariness and disappointment of Americans with the general life of materialism as enunciated by both democrats and radicals, capitalists and socialists. They sense the hungering within youth and adults for a more spiritual, a more metaphysical ideology that will allow them to escape their boredom and the common drabness of their lives. They sense the search by people for romanticism, idealism, and an escape from rationalism and materialism. There is a deep envy of those who are capable of throwing off the ordinary, the expected, the accepted mores, the logical and sensible things of civilization. There is a desire to seize life, an emotional and primitive pagan desire to feel and sense and touch things—to bring excitement, pleasure, and change into the ordinary.

They understand that the death of authority, of the church and the family, has given man the right to be free—and the fear of that freedom. Man has cast off restraint and is terrified at his loss of moorings and direction. He has been cast out of the prison of authority and told: Go! But he does not know where to go and every place to which he turns is found to be hostile, dangerous, and spiritually unrewarding. And it is spirit that man needs—desperately. And if that spirit's thirst is no longer quenched by religion or church, he will seek some other drink. He cannot cope with the freedom of sterility and he runs to find himself a new master, who, while depriving him of his freedom, will restore to him some reason for being.

The young in particular are a tempting target for those who come with new wares. By the very nature of youth, and by the added uniqueness of the American impatience and inability to be permanently satisfied, the American youth is a victim of quick change, easy, emotional love and easy, emotional rejection. Fad has been elevated in the United States to a fine art and movements, fashions, and trends come swiftly and disappear just as rapidly with little warning and with little remembrance. Like a group of mindless cattle, herds of Americans are maneuvered. They pound the ground with their running hooves as they stampede in the direction of yet another mindless and meaningless fad.

Today they are liberal; tomorrow radical; the next day, completely capable of hate. Of all the lost and wandering souls of our generation it is the young, who have no remembrance of an authority of church, family, or government, who are the most lost and bewildered, the most desperate and searching and, consequently, the most easily led into every new fad and trend. The products of an era of permissiveness; the belief that life is a thing to be savored and its purpose to enjoy oneself; that life owes man happiness and contentment—they are total slaves to their passions and desires, terribly incapable of the discipline and self-restraint that allow the individual to control his direction and decide his own fate. Indeed, violence, sadism, and brutality are the ultimate fads for discontented, frustrated, and bored people. Youth that has tasted all can easily be drawn to the ultimate in excitement and thrills—murder of the Jew.

Brooding, unhappy, permanently dissatisfied, so many youths march for causes, not so much because they are idealists, but because war threatens them or their pursuit of life, out of sheer boredom and an opportunity to lash out and destroy. This irrational lashing out and desire for violence is not a small thing in the United States. Millions of Americans are afflicted with a terrible spiritual boredom and dissatisfaction with a life that sees them, in their own eyes, under the thumb and guidance of someone else.

The adult of a generation before who secretly seethes against a life that saw parent, teacher, employer, and spouse set boundaries about his freedom and limit the things he would have liked to do, longs, so often, for the opportunity to be savagely, primitively and violently *free*. His child is even more disturbed.

And so the hater understands full well the nature of the

human beast—better than his liberal counterparts who are so remote and alienated from the realities of man. The intellectual may build and study his society in a classroom. The hater lives with it in the streets, the factory, the bars and the church. He sees and understands the elements that comprise the society of the American lower class and lower middle class. He knows the ingredients well: violence, boredom, frustration, rootlessness, purposelessness, fear, anger, irrationality, violence. He knows that the American is a frightened man—fearful of all the dangers and crises that surround and plague him. He knows that he is deeply disturbed and terrified by the racial, political, social, economic, and psychological crises that grip the nation and that threaten him and his family. He knows that frightened people become desperate people and desperate people will do desperate things—things they would not do in times of normalcy and peace of mind.

He knows that such a man wants and *needs* an enemy—a tangible one that he can blame, cast his sins and anger upon, strike at and destroy. The hater is prepared to give him that enemy. He is prepared to give him an outlet for his anger, hate and frustration.

That enemy, the major, implacable, unceasing enemy is not the Communist; he is not the Negro; he is not the liberal. He is all of them rolled into one—the Jew.

He knew that people forget quickly—so terribly quickly— and that they can forget the most obscene and vicious of crimes. The searing memory of the Holocaust fades into semi-consciousness and then near-oblivion, given the balm of time and the press of personal crisis. The most terrible things—the Holocaust of thirty years ago and its descent into Hell—are easily forgotten. And, because they are forgotten, the propensity to repeat them is strengthened and the psychological bar is lowered until it disappears from view and memory. All this the hater knows and understands.

He understands, too, that the emotions and values of yesterday are not necessarily those of today, while those of today can easily be changed tomorrow. There are no sacred cows that cannot be slaughtered and no values that cannot be changed by an earnest, determined, fanatical, single-minded group. The fact that Jew-hatred may be anathema today can be changed by diligent work and pervasive crisis. There is something shameful about being anti-Jewish and people are afraid to proclaim their feelings of hostilities to Jews. But that, the hater knows, is only a psychological barrier. It can be knocked down, and he works unceasingly toward that end. He knows that when the day comes when it will no longer be unfashionable or impolite to speak openly of dislike of Jews, the battle will be on its way to being won.

So he paints a world that is sublimely simple and clear, totally black and white, with clearly demarcated good and evil. On the one hand there is the Aryan and on the other, the Jew. On the one hand there is Christ and on the other the Anti-Christ, the Jew. One one side there is the Christian patriot who loves America and on the other the Jew who is disloyal and a Communist. On one hand there is the simple, hardworking, laborer, farmer, housewife, and on the other is the international Wall Street capitalist and exploiter, the Jew. On the one hand there is the virtuous Christian American and, on the other hand, the pornographic, lascivious Jew. All that is good and virtuous is presented by the hater in terms of the greater and wondrous white, Anglo-Saxon Aryan racial genius, while all that is dark, polluted and evil is represented by the satanic, hook-nosed, racial Jew.

The entire system of today is Jewish planned, Jewish operated and Jewish dominated. That system, with its futile democracy that leads only to chaos and anarcy, must be overthrown, that system that panders only to weakness and that rewards the unfit and racially impure must be destroyed. In its place the haters offer the weary, weak, angry and frightened American a Faustian dream. "Give up your soul that you call freedom and democracy and we will give you a new world of racial purity, power, order, and security for you and those you love."

Is it so inconceivable that such a message will bear fruit in the days of crisis that lie ahead of us?

In a world of materialism and technological loss of identity, daily repetition of boredom and unsatisfying fads, monotonous rationalism and complex problems, the haters offer a grandiose and visionary world of race, strength, discipline, goals, simplicity, and power. Is this not appealing to a hopelessly confused citizen with nowhere to go and no future beyond his job and home—which leave him empty?

The haters know their people when they write: "We are the new BARBARIANS of our times. They are degenerate and effete; we are vigorous and masculine. They are passive and cringing; we are dynamic and aggressive, the way nature intends all living creatures to be. They moan for 'security' and 'peace.' We eagerly seek out combat and danger as the natural means of testing and improving us.

"And there is the key to our coming victory over those dark mutineers!"

Who is prepared to argue that the following words by the Nazis are not immensely effective?

> America has a bad case of "Jew-itis." We're supposed to have a majority democracy here where the majority rules. Yet somehow we get things the great Aryan majority just doesn't want. We've got anti-gun laws, legalized pornography, Communist hell-raising in the streets, integration laws and now this last straw [busing]. They want to offer our kids on the altar of this obscene nigger worship that nobody really wants!
>
> It's the weirdest thing in the world. The liberal bureaucrats don't believe in it. The Jewish judges don't believe in it. You don't catch any of them living near the niggers. Why do we have these things? What's at the bottom of it? One thing. One dirty four-letter word: Jews!

In places like Detroit, Waukegan, Middletown, Ohio, Wilmington, St. Petersburg, and Jacksonville, Seattle and all the hundreds of other localities where schools have been closed down and remain hotbeds of racial tension because of fights between blacks and whites, much words are applauded, quietly. And with ever increasing frequency—loudly.

It is fallacious to believe that Jew-killers are only a godless, pervert, lunatic fringe. Goebbel's diaries are replete with "may G-d give us success" entries, and as Heinz Hohne wrote, the concentration-camp system and the rhythm of mass extermination were not dictated by sadists, but by "worthy family men brought up in the belief that anti-semitism was a form of pest control." The potential Jew-killers exist in America among the men who pump gas, who drive trucks, who erect buildings and among corporate managers and our intelligentsia.

The Talmud tells us that, with the destruction of the Temple, prophecy was given over to the young and the fools. Even if this were not so, it would be presumptuous and dangerous for a man to prophesy with certainty what is to come. No man can do that and no man can say with sureness that what occurred thirty years ago must undoubtedly happen again, this time in America.

But surely one is entitled and, indeed, obligated to point out the overwhelming probability of its happening and the fact that it has already *begun* to happen. Surely one can point to all the signs that are so obvious and clear to the honest eye and ear and ask whether one has the right to keep silent. Surely one has the right to ask, in view of everything we see, whether we dare gamble, in the face of the historical presumption that it does happen under such conditions as those that exist now in America.

It is important for us to ignore the fury of the opponents of the call to go home. Those who oppose this call have had their counterparts in every generation of Jewish suffering, including the German, where "it could not happen."

People who say unpopular things must be prepared to earn the opposition of frightened, little, people. Those who say unpopular things, *that people really know to be true,* are sure to draw down upon their heads all the anger and hate that can be mustered

It does not matter. A generation ago those who warned of a holocaust were sneered at and persecuted. Innocent Jews paid the price of their refusal to listen. It dare not happen again. Over and over our voices must be raised in the cry that it is time to go home. That across the sea lies a land, the land of the Jewish people. Eretz Yisroel, the land of Israel. For two millenia we waited for it. Now it waits for us.

PART IV
TIME TO
GO HOME

CHAPTER 15: ERETZ YISROEL

The people of Israel and the land of Israel stand in unique unity. One cannot be separated from the other. For the Christian, there is no one single land that lies at the center of his aspirations and imposes a religious obligation to dwell there. For the Muslim or Buddist or Hindu there is no one particular country that is set aside—not only as a sacred place for a pilgrimage, but also as a mandatory place in which to live. The Jew, as in so many other things, is different.

Despite attempts by those who have reformed Judaism in so many other ways, to mutilate, bury, and ignore it, the fact remains that for the Jewish people and the Jewish faith, from its very beginnings, Eretz Yisroel—the Land of Israel—has remained central to Judaism as a place where a Jew was *commanded* to live, and a home to which he looked with agonized longing during centuries and ages of pain and persecution.

The shouts of outrage from assimilated Jewish leaders do not matter. No one can deny that the All Mighty told Abraham: "And I shall give thee and thy seed after thee all the land of Canaan for an everlasting heritage." The anger of those who speak of America as being "different" and not really *galut* (exile), but *tifutzot* (diaspora) pales into irrelevance before the fact that there is a clear Biblical injunction, "And thou shalt settle in it [the land] ," a thing that causes the Rabbis to declare that settling in Israel is "equal to all the commandments of the Torah." (*Sifre Re'eh*, 60). All the denials and self-assurances will not wipe away the fact that the Torah could think of no greater punishment than exile from his land. The Bible is filled with innumerable admonitions that violation of the Torah commandments would bring exile from the land of Israel. "And the Lord shall scatter you among the peoples and you shall be left few in number among the nations whither the Lord shall lead you away." And twice in the Five Books of Moses does the Jew read, yearly, in hushed tones and swiftly (lest the pain overwhelm him) the *Tochacha* or criticism, which warns of that most dreaded of all curses—exile from the Jewish land. "And the Lord shall scatter thee among all peoples from one end of the earth even into the other end of the earth. . . ."

Exile—even to the most temporarily beautiful of all lands—has always been a curse for the Jew. It remains so.

It is only the land of Israel that is held up to us as the blessing on our heads. "It is better to lodge in the deserts of Israel than in the palaces of other countries," state the Rabbis. "A man should forever live in the Land of Israel, even in a city that has a majority of gentiles, rather than live outside the Land even in a city with a majority of Jews, for he who lives in the Land of Israel is considered as having a G-d, while outside the Land he is considered as not having a G-d." For those who go to the Land of Israel, the Rabbis permit leniency in certain Sabbath prohibitions and give a wife grounds for divorce from a husband reluctant to go there to live with her. The religious obligation of a Jew to go live in the Land of Israel is clear and unchallangeable despite the denials and anger.

But it is more than merely a religious obligation for the Jew. The reality of the impossibility of permanent immunity from gentile hostility; the reality of pogroms, Crusades, Inquisitions, humiliations, discrimination, tension, and gas chambers, all led to a deep yearning and an instinctive understanding of the uniqueness of the Land as the sole solution to the Jewish agony and a deep Jewish yearning for it that became a passion. I can think of nothing more to add to this magnificent obsession of the Jew for his home than what I once wrote:

And the Jew scattered to the far corners of the earth, and the winds that blew in every nook took him with them. And wherever he went, he looked back—to home.

The Byzantines oppressed him, and he grew more stubborn and prayed each morning, "And may our eyes behold your return to Zion in mercy. . . ." The Church scorned and cursed him, and he grew tougher, praying each afternoon, "Sound the great horn for our Freedom. . . ." The Crusaders burned him alive and the feudal Christians refused to allow him to own land or join guilds, and he prayed each evening, "And unto Jerusalem, Your City, return in mercy. . . ."

The Arabs drove him out of Granada and stole his children in Yemen, and he broke a glass at his wedding . . . not to forget the destruction of Jerusalem. He was exiled from Spain and from France and from England and Portugal, and Cossacks delighted in pogroms in Russia, and he proclaimed each Passover: "Next year in Jerusalem. . . . Now we are slaves—next year free men; now we are here—next year in the Land of Israel."

And the more they burned your grandfather, the more stubborn he became, and the more they beat him, the tougher was his defiance. The more they strove to drive him from this world, the more he determined to live; the more his G-d tried to make him lose faith in Him, the more defiant your obnoxiously obstinate zeyde became.

He was obsessed with one thing. Return to Israel. He was driven by it; he was a man possessed. And so, when he prayed, it was always facing home. How curious it is. Arabs, you see, also face one way— Mecca, land of slavery, city of Saudi Arabia. But Jews face home. Sephardic Jews in Baghdad pray to the west, Polish Jews in Warsaw to the east, the Jewish four corners of the earth turning to face a common dream—Israel.

And when he died—still in exile—the Jew was buried in a simple white pine box (this is the real and traditional "Jewish way of death") and with one other thing—a tiny sack filled with soil from Eretz Yisroel—the Land of Israel. If his eye could not see it in life, this stubborn old Jew was determined to clutch it in death.

Listen, young Jew: This is how the world determined that he should die and this is how—in his gentle, humble way—he told them, NO!

Because he knew that there was no place in this alien world where he could ever find . . . peace and security, he knew that he must return home. Because he knew—so much better than we—that all the utopias and all the ideologies and all the Marxism-Leninisms and Trotskyisms and Maoisms hold no place for the Jew; because he knew that the Trotskys and Zinovievs and Kamenevs and Radeks who worshipped so eagerly at strange altars would be devoured by their false gods; because he foresaw the Soviet version of Babi Yar and the Polish Gomulka expulsion of loyal communists, because of their "Zhid" origins; because he was so much more perceptive and wiser than his grandchildren he was never tempted by the siren call of exile. He chose to return home.

Listen, young descendent of a stubborn zeyde. Listen and try to understand the tenacity of the Jews who sat in countless synagogues on the night of Tisha B'Av with flickering candles and tear-stained Book of Lamentations, with stockinged feet and bearded face as befits the mourner for Zion and who mournfully remembered the anniversary of the destruction and sadly intoned the words: "How doth she sit solitary; the city that was filled with people hath become a widow."

Listen to all this and ask yourself the question: Was it truly United States oil that created Israel? Was it truly the military-industrial complex that gave birth to a Jewish State? Was it the United Nations that brought us home? Was it British imperialism that created this dream?

There was no Esso when Jews were driven from the land in which they had lived for centuries and to which they vowed to return. There were no Arabs when Bar Kochba went down to defeat, and Jews were already turning to Zion three times a day. There was no Pentagon when Yehuda Helevi, the greatest of medieval Jewish poets wrote: "My heart is in the East and I am at the end of the West."

Israel came into being because it never came out of being. Israel came back to life because it never died. It was the Jewish State in the days of Joshua: it was the Jewish State when there were Pharaohs; it was the Jewish State when Assyrians and Moabites and Edomites and Philistines and Babylonians and Persians and Hellenes and Romans drifted through history and passed out of it again. It remained Jewish because Jews never left it and there was never a time when Jewish communities did not remain in Zion.

Do you think Theodor Herzl created Zionism? Not so! Zionism came into being the day the Jews went into exile and was nurtured by every religious law and custom. Every Jew who practiced his faith and every Jew who observed his tradition was a Zionist. Herzl was merely a man whose time had come, and Jews simply put into practice the goal and dream and aspirations of two millenia. Had there been no Balfour Declaration—there would still have arisen the State of Israel. Had there been no United Nations—there would still have come into being a Jewish State. The stubbornness of Jewish zeydes can be denied for only so long.

For two thousand years the Jew bombarded his G-d with pleas, entreaties, tears, promises, repentance, threats, recriminations, and yet more tears. Home, was his persistent and nagging plea to his Maker. When shall we be allowed to go home?

Even the All Mighty can endure just so much. The unceasing persistence of a Jew can even wear down Omnipotence, and at last He consented. In a drama unrivaled in the history of man, a people that had begun its long journey into exile twenty centuries earlier, returned. The maddening patience was blessed, the unshakable memory of the hills of Judea was rewarded by return to their barren and rocky slopes. The mind boggles! Can one really grasp the magnificence and impossibility of it all? Can one appreciate our fortune in having been, for some inexplicable reason, chosen as the generation to behold that which all the prophets of old never saw? The return of a scattered, weak, government-less, and defenseless people to a land it had left at a time when most modern-day peoples were attaining the cultural level of swineherd in dark and dank backwardness. The rebirth of a language that moved from the petrified atmosphere of library and study hall into the streets, laboratories, and jet fighter planes of today. The clear and unmistakable fulfillment of prophecy; the miraculous realization of vision. For thus did the Jewish seers and visionaries of old speak as the Divine hand touched them:

Thus says the Lord: A voice is heard in Ramah, lamentation and bitter weeping; it is Rachel weeping for her children; she refuses to be comforted, for they are away. Thus says the Lord: Restrain your voice from weeping and your eyes from tears; for your work shall have its reward, says the Lord; they shall return from the land of the enemy. And there is hope in your future, says the Lord, that your children shall return to their own land (Jeremiah 31).

And He said unto me: Son of man, can these bones live? And I answered: O Lord G-d, Thou knowest. . . .

Then He said unto me, Son of man, these bones are the whole House of Israel: behold, they say: Our bones are dried up, and our hope is lost. . . . Therefore prophesy and say unto them, Thus saith the Lord G-d: Behold, I will open your graves, and cause you to come out of your grave, O my people; and . . . I will bring you into the land of Israel (Ezekiel 37:3, 11).

Words spoken millenia ago; visions dreamed and dreams envisioned. And today they have come true. Indeed, there can no longer exist atheists among us—only men who are blind.

When the first foolish intellectuals and students arrived from Russia to a Holy Land that was filled less with the Presence than with deserts, swamps, malaria, and poverty, it seemed impossible for the land to come back to life at all—how much more so at the hands of the amateurish Jews who could never become tillers of the soil. Tailors, yes: toilers, never. When a Viennese journalist erupted one day from assimilation to Jewishness and began to rave about a Jewish State, he was properly condemned as a madman by all the proper people. But Herzl was to succeed and, when he rose in 1897 to declare that "surely in fifty years we will see a Jewish State," he was to be proven right. When Arab armies rushed to wipe out the outnumbered and out-gunned Jews of the newborn Jewish State the Jews, weak and cowardly, suddenly emerged as victors, and a state, larger than the absurdity offered by the United Nations, came into being. Miracles no longer happen. . . .

And in 1967—as the primitive Jewish enemies whose cruel and barbaric makeup had been translated in 1920 and '29 and '36-39 into mutilations, torture, rape, and murder—poised for a Middle Eastern version of the "Final Solution" the fire of G-d through the courtesy of the Defense Forces of Israel exploded into the most awesome military victory of modern times.

> And five of you shall choose a hundred and a hundred of you shall choose ten thousand; and your enemies shall fall before you by the sword.

All that was dreamed has come true—in our times. "Blessed art thou O Lord our G-d . . . who has enabled us to live, and sustained us and allowed us to reach this time." Are we not truly blessed and is our lot not beautiful?

After two millenia of a drama of suffering and endurance that shames the most imaginative of fiction by its poignancy, horror, and unbroken continuity, the Jew, again, has a home. It stands today, a beautiful state and a large one. Indeed, after 1967, it is no longer the tiny and precarious thing of Lake Success. It is a large state and a beautiful state and it is all Jewish.

It is a state where our children and theirs can grow tall and proud and free and Jewish. It is a state where the abnormality, insecurity, and gnawing reminder of minority status does not exist; where the problems of majority culture are reflected, not in Jewish children's exposure to Christmas patterns in public schools, but in the children of the foreign embassies coming home to *their* parents and wondering why *they*, too, cannot light Hanukkah candles as all the other children do. . . .

It is a state where "kike" and "zhid" and "hep" and "death to the Jew" are not heard and where the Saturday Sabbath is the one observed, where *Jewish* holidays are the days off, where the language of the prophets is the language of daily life, where longshoremen curse in Hebrew and policemen give traffic summonses in the holy tongue.

It is a state where Jewish rabbis and schools keep the spirit alive while Jewish generals and frogmen keep its body safe. It is a state where one cannot walk in the present without colliding with the past, where one daily trods upon the footsteps of his ancestors. Here is the Wall which is never left unattended, and is a symbol of its children's devotion. Here are the children looking at the remnant of glory past and of future promise. It is a beautiful state and a large state and it is all Jewish.

And if so, why do we sit here? If so, why will next Yom Kippur find our synagogues filled with Jews who watch the clock ticking away the final minutes of the solemn holiday and as the service draws to its conclusion and we turn to the last page and the last line in the prayer book, a million voices throughout the great land will shout forth:

"Next Year in Jerusalem!"

And next year we shall still be here in exile. . . .

What is wrong with us? Do we not understand what is happening and will yet happen to us in exile?

Do we not realize that remaining in the Diaspora is equivalent to making a decision to assimilate, either for ourselves or for our children, and do we not know that if we do not return to the Jewish homeland our children's Jewish identity may be swallowed up in the self-delusion of alien philosophies?

Do we not see the assimilation, the intermarriage, the alienation of our young? Do we not see the murder of their souls and their identity, tragedy of their wanderings in a culture that is not theirs and in a world in which they are strangers, rootless and a minority? It is unnatural to be a minority. It is abnormal. One cannot grow up normal and healthy when one is a stranger and different. And we *are* strangers in this land and we *are* different. Do we not realize what is happening to us and do we not behold the spiritual and cultural genocide into which we are walking? Are our children and our children's children that unimportant to us that we ply them with material gifts and let them die of spiritual starvation?

Are the fleshpots and the good life more important than the preservation of our children as Jews and the guarantee that they will marry Jews, have Jewish children of their own and live in a

Jewish atmosphere that breeds confidence, normalcy and mental, spiritual, and physical strength!

And after the Holocaust of our own times do we not yet realize that remaining in exile is to see the endless repetition of tragedy, of hatred of the Jew, physical persecution, pogrom and Holocaust? What is there in us that allows us to sit with neo-Nazis and Panthers and an angry, restless, envious and hating majority whose idea of Jew-hatred merely awaits a time to come?

The fires of thirty years ago have barely been extinguished, the smell of the gas still pervades the nostrils of millions and the graves of six million, who never imagined it could happen, are still fresh. And, already, we forget; we already attempt to put it from our minds. But we know. Deep in our hearts we know and all the brave platitudes and speeches fade away into the insignificance and mirages they are when a George Wallace is shot and a million Jews falter for a moment and fearfully ask: "Was it a Jew who shot him?"

We have a land, at last, and—in mad flight from logic and sanity—we prefer to sit here with our own Nazis and haters.

It is time to go home; it is time to return. Out there is a land that awaits its children. Only there can one be a complete and a completely normal Jew. And in the face of all these things that we *know* to be true we continue to sit here. In the face of all the terrible specters of assimilation on the one hand, and physical annihilation on the other, we remain in exile—a self-imposed exile. In the end, the Jew remains a victim of his refusal to see that which he does not wish to see. In a frenzy of fear that he will be convinced he conjures up all the arguments:

"But if we leave America who will support Israel through political pressure and influence?"

Let us not delude ourselves and let us not create for ourselves a political ego that will contribute to that delusion. In the end it is not American Jewish political pressure that will create a favorable or unfavorable American foreign policy climate toward Israel. American Jewish political power is at its lowest ebb in decades and, with the growth of ethnic identity on the part of groups far larger than the Jew, it will become less significant yet. In addition to all this, is the fact that Jews, in a lemming-like refusal to make Jewish self-interest their yardstick and measuring rod, have let the major parties know that there is almost nothing that any political leader can do that will not see the great majority of Jews vote liberal Democrat and oppose conservative Republicanism. The great majority of Jewish eggs are in one basket; and why should the owner of that basket be worried about losing eggs that are guaranteed to him? And why should his competitor ever dream of acquiring them when there is apparently nothing he can do that will ever tempt them his way?

The myth of Jewish political power was severely damaged when, in an election year, President Dwight Eisenhower criticized Israel for its Sinai campaign and publically pressured it to withdraw. The impossibility of getting Jews to vote for their own interests and thus give themselves political leverage is revealed by a Jewish insistence on voting for a New York City mayor who has eroded Jewish power and interests to an incredible degree; by a persistent Jewish support for a presidential candidate who preaches isolationism for abroad and woos groups and circles that are diametrically opposed to Jewish interest at home; by a regular and unshakable knee-jerk kind of politically blind voting pattern that finds Jewish votes taken for granted by those who have always had them and despaired of by those who are convinced they can never acquire them.

Any support for Israel on the part of the United States will come, not through American Jewish political pressure or appeals for support of the "democracy of the Middle East," but through that most open and honest of all reasons—American self-interest.

In recent times American military, political, and economic support of the Jewish State came about because Israel was able to convince America that it was to the *American* interest to stop the Soviet Union in the Middle East. As long as arguments along the lines of the community of American and Israeli interests are considered logical and convincing by Washington,

Israel will get its support. When the arguments begin to sound weak or when other interests begin to take precedence, American support will end and there will be little that the small and divided American Jewish community will be able to do.

Far more tangible and far more effective support for the existence of Israel will come—not from some overblown vision of American Jewish political lobbying strength, but—through the millions of soldiers, investors and citizens that American Jewry can pour into the Jewish State.

"But who will give Israel the financial support it needs if all American Jews leave?"

Have no fear; unfortunately they are not all leaving. Not all, and not half. But if all American Jews *did* leave for Israel and if they did take with them their wealth, property, and capital, who would ever again need a United Jewish Appeal and what an economically healthy state it would be! All that capital could not be matched by another 100 years of UJA fundraising. . . .

"But Israel cannot hold all the American Jews should they decide to come there."

I have already spoken of Israel the beautiful—and Israel the large. In 1947 the Jewish authorities, spokesmen for the proposed new Jewish state, agreed to partition Eretz Yisroel, the Land of Israel. Eretz Yisroel, the ancient home of the Jewish people consisted of far more than the absurdity contemplated by the United Nations. Jews had reigned with sovereignty not only over the land that was now called Tel Aviv and the citrus groves of the coastal plain. They had ruled over the lands of Judea and Samaria and Jerusalem and Golan and what was now called Transjordan. The latter had been ripped away by British fist in the early '20s while the rest was sadly waived in the hope that Jewish reasonableness and compromise would bring the peace Jews so desired and at least a tiny beginning of the redemption. As usual Jews were saved from their own foolishness by the hatred and stupidity of their enemies.

And so, today, Jews have returned—*not to captured territories but to liberated ones.* If Hebron, resting place of the patriarchs is not Jewish, then nothing is. If Bethlehem, city of

Ruth and David, is not Jewish, then nothing is. If Shechem, where Jacob wandered and the first Jewish king, Elimelech, was crowned, is not Jewish, nothing is. If Judea and Samaria, where the Bible came to life and where one cannot take four steps without colliding with the Jewish past, are not Jewish, nothing is. If the land where the patriarchs lived, the Judges fought liberation battles for their people, the prophets dreamed their vision of exile and return, and the kings ruled in splendor, is not Jewish—nothing is.

But the land *is* Jewish and it will *remain* Jewish and it will be able to hold, not hundreds of thousands, but many millions—all the millions of Jews who can return from America and the Soviet Union and all the lands of their dispersion. "The Land of the Deer" is what the rabbis called Eretz Yisroel and they explained that just as deerskin stretches so does the Jewish land expand to take in its children—all its children. How true and how correct. It is only for Jewish hands that the land has given forth its fruit and the desert bloomed. It is only with Jews that so many people live today in an area that critics warned could not hold more than a few hundred thousand and that, tomorrow, can hold as many as will desire to come.

"But if America turns upon the Jews and withdraws its support, then, surely, Israel is no longer safe, and it too, will go under."

There remain with us—as always—men of little faith and little vision who cannot grasp the fact that the Jewish people have been chosen by their Creator for a greatness from which they cannot escape and for a permanence that no one—neither they themselves nor their enemies—can destroy. The suffering of the Jewish people is undeniable, but so is their indestructibility. History is not a mere game of chance. It is a planned and ordained series of events with purpose and reason to it and the Jewish people, their lot, their past, and future are all part of the Divine scheme.

And that plan speaks of an end to the long night of exile and a return home. Are there people so obtuse that they really believe that the return, after two millenia, was not a miracle that partakes of the most permanent of meanings? Are they so lacking in understanding that they think that such an event came about only to collapse after thirty or fifty years? Men of little vision, little faith, and little intelligence!

To be sure, there is no promise and there is no guarantee for the exile except that of suffering, persecution and terror.

> And the Lord shall scatter thee among all the nations. . . . And among these nations shalt thou have no repose and there shall be no rest for the sole of thy foot but the Lord shall give thee there a trembling heart, failing of eyes and languishing of soul. And thy life shall hang in doubt before thee and thou shalt fear night and day and shalt have no assurance of thy life.

Yes, this is the reality of the Exile.

But the Land of Israel and the people who will return there are assured a pledge of continuity and permanence, rebirth and rebuilding. When the late Chief Rabbi of Israel, the saintly and scholarly Rabbi Yitzhak Isaac Halevi Herzog, of blessed memory, heard of Jewish fears of Nazi extermination of the Jewish community of Eretz Yisroel in the dark days of the Afrika Corps' approach to the gates of the Holy Land, he reacted angrily and with sublime confidence:

"It is impossible. The Prophets speak only of two destructions and not a third one."

And the faith and confidence of the Chief Rabbi was echoed by a simple, pious Jerusalem Jew, who on the day in 1967 that Jordanian Hussein signed his military agreement with Egypt's Nasser and the Jewish world was plunged into deep gloom and foreboding, smiled and said:

"You'll see, by Shavuot—Pentecost—we will be praying at the Wall again." It is through the mad confidence of such foolish dreamers and impractical visionaries that Jewish life continues.

Disaster for American Jewry? The destruction of the Jewish community in the new world exile? All possible. But the Land of Israel cannot be destroyed again and stands as a fortress of safety for Jews, beckoning them home. Its guarantees are not from France, that turns upon it, or America that can do the same tomorrow. "O Lord, my strength and my stronghold and my refuge in the day of affliction"—this is the weapon of Israel, this is the Guarantor of the survival of the Jewish state.

> Behold, I will bring them from the north country, and gather them from the uttermost parts of the earth, and with them the blind and the lame, the woman with child and her that travaileth with child together; a great company shall they return hither. They shall come with weeping, and with supplications will I lead them: I will cause them to walk by rivers of waters, in a straight way wherein they shall not stumble: For I am a father to Israel, and Ephraim is my firstborn.
>
> Hear the word of the Lord, O ye nations, and declare it in the isles afar off, and say, He that scattered Israel will gather him, and keep him, as a shepherd doth his flock. For the Lord hath redeemed Jacob and ransomed him from the hand that is stronger than he. Therefore they shall come and sing in the height of Zion . . . (Jeremiah 31: 8-12).

The Land calls us and we stand in the midst of the burning and trembling exile. It is time to go home.

CHAPTER 16: TIME TO GO HOME

If there is any certainty left in this world it is that events have a depressing tendency to repeat themselves. The controversy that has already arisen over my calls to American Jews to escape another possible disaster, the calls which will undoubtedly rise to a crescendo with the publication of this book, are merely echoes of events in the not-so-distant past.

The cast of characters was the same; only the people playing the parts bore different names. Zev Jabotinsky, the giant of our era, strode, raced, tore through Eastern and Central Europe of the 1930s calling upon Jews to evacuate the "zone of Jewish distress." It was the zone that he saw, all too clearly, was becoming untenable for the Jew and which was destined to explode in a fury and anger that would consume them. The Jewish leadership of the time opposed him with a vehemence that might well have been better reserved for the Jew-haters who would soon be upon them. Jabotinsky in their eyes was an "alarmist." He was "unrealistic." He "exaggerated" and "dramatized" too much. He suffered from "paranoia." More, he was "irresponsible" and, himself, would cause the very anti-Semitism of which he warned. They were furious that he would allow the Jew-hater to win his battle to drive out the Jew. They boasted that they only wished that Poland had, not three and a half, but seven million Jews. That would make it safer for them.

And even those who understood, lacked that sense of urgency, that sense that of time rapidly running out. They could not see what he saw. They looked at the same events, read the same newspapers, heard the same voices but only *he* rose in fear. They saw nothing, no need for alarm. No one really believed it possible. No one really thought that the terrible things of which Jabotinsky spoke could come about in the twentieth century. But he did. He looked ahead and saw it in all its madness.

It was the time of growing Polish, Hungarian, Lithuanian, Slovak economic misery and nationalism. Jews were battling for scarce positions with traditional Jew-haters. It was the time of the rise to power of Adolph Hitler. It was a time when there was still time, but precious little of it. It was a time when a bold evacuation would have saved untold numbers of Jews, but when people lacked the courage and the daring to do what they instinctively knew was correct. "I am sure that elemental floods will soon break out all over East European Jewry," Jabotinsky declared.

He was right, but no one listened. They came by the thousands to hear him speak. They glowed at his words, they tingled to his concepts. They roared, they cheered, they applauded, they adored him. But they did not do what he pleaded with them to do. They came, they heard—and went home. They stayed in the home that he warned would be their graves. He was correct, and only too late was he vindicated.

The drama that unfolded in the '30s was only a newer version of yet an earlier one. The name of the hero in 1920 was Max Nordau, the grand old man who had served as the right hand of political Zionism's founder, Theodor Herzl; the emancipated Jew who had become a renowned psychiatrist, literary writer, and critic; the man whom Herzl's family, deeply disturbed over his mad obsession with a mad Jewish State, had persuaded him to see; the man who told Herzl after sitting with him for three days: "You may be mad, but if you are, I am too. . . ." Now, in 1920, at the age of 72, he remained as vigorous and as impatient as always. He, too, was a man who understood Time. He knew that there are moments when time seems to stand still for an instant and one has an opportunity to make history move in one of two directions—to greatness or to abysmal failure. It was 1920, and the bloom of the Balfour Declaration which promised support for a Jewish homeland was still on the Zionist rose. Nordau had no patience for the timid, for those who cautioned against moving too quickly, for those who insisted on being "practical." He had no patience with practical people when time was of the essence and when Jewish destiny was in the balance. He only knew that we needed the land of Israel:

> We need it for the people that we may establish there, those millions of our brethren who are being threatened with massacre or rapine in the Ukraine, whom Poland is trying to strangle slowly but inexorably by means of economic boycott and whom Austria, Hungary and Germany want to push back into the ignominy of the ghetto.

He called for an audacious resettlement, immediately, and without delay, of 600,000 Jews from Poland, the Ukraine and Rumania. People thought that he had gone mad.

"It is not possible, there are no houses to live in," they cried.

"They will live in tents to begin with," he replied. "Rather that than to have one's throat cut in pogroms."

"They will have nothing to eat," cried the critics. "We will feed them until the first crop," he answered.

"It will cost billions!" was the horrified protest.

277

"No," he retorted, "but many millions, and they must be found . . . quickly, to save Jews from assassins and make them a valiant, vigorous Jewish nation rejuvenated, planting their roots deep into the nourishing holy soil.

"There are not several, not two, there is only *one* single method of overcoming this difficulty; we must by all means and with the utmost speed see to it that our numbers are equal to the Arabs of Palestine and that we outnumber them as far as possible, however large the difference may be at first."

It was too much, it was too daring for the little men who could not see, see through the walls of tomorrow. They rejected the plan. The 600,000 never came. They and ten times that number perished, the victims of Hitler and timid practicality.

But Jabotinsky's was the first presentation of the drama. That took place earlier still, when a totally improbable Viennese journalist, assimilated, lost from his people, was suddenly struck by a terrible nightmare of Jew-hatred and an equally marvelous prophecy—a Jewish State.

The Jews must get out of Europe where there was no home for them. Emancipation was a delusion, and anti-Semitism the reality. Jews, there is only one solution—a Jewish State; Jews it is time to go home. In the face of howls of protest from the happy and emancipated Jews of Europe, from those who were beginning to feel free and equal and rich, Herzl wrote:

> Is it not true that, in countries where we live in perceptible numbers, the position of Jewish lawyers, doctors, technicians, teachers, and employees of all descriptions becomes daily more intolerable? Is it not true that the Jewish middle classes are seriously threatened? Is it not true that the passions of the mob are incited against our wealthy people?

No. Not 1972, but 1896. Yes, as true today as it was then. "I shall now put the question in the briefest possible form," wrote Herzl. "Are we to get out now and where to? Or may we remain? And how long?"

"Let us first settle the point of staying where we are. Can we hope for better days until the princes and peoples are more mercifully disposed to us? I say that we cannot hope for a change in the current of feeling. And why not? Even if we were as near to the hearts of princes as are their other subjects they could not protect us. They would only feed popular hatred by showing us too much favor. By 'too much' I really mean less than is claimed as the right by every ordinary citizen. The nations in whose midst the Jews live are either covertly or openly anti-Semitic."

Emigration. Evacuation. Exodus. Leaving the exile. That was Herzl's answer. It was shocking to all the Jews of Europe who maintained the friction that they were, indeed, "home" and that emancipation had brought them equality, love, and respect. Herzl was condemned and denounced. He did not retreat:

> Again people will say that I am furnishing the anti-Semites with weapons. Why so? Because I admit the truth. . . ?

And again, today. Here are some of the voices of recognized Jewish *and Zionist* leaders in response to the warnings of potential disaster and holocaust for Jews in the United States: "We disagree utterly with the hysterical opinion that Jews in the United States face a new holocaust . . . and therefore must emigrate en masse to Israel if they are to survive." "America 1972 is not Germany 1932 and any attempt to equate the two constitutes recklessness and irresponsibility." ". . . irresponsible merchants of doom. . . ." "Defeatism that is harmful in the long run to Israel as well as to American Jewry. . . . We do not need, nor desire, the scare tactics and sensational claims of the Aliyah propaganda of the JDL." It is quite true. America 1972 is not Germany 1932 and no such contention was ever made. But it is most certainly Germany 1925 and 1926 and 1928 and 1929. It most certainly is a country with startling and unnerving similarities to the Weimar of those years, both in respect to society and its conditions as a whole, as well as in respect to the Jewish relationship to that society.

Nor does one know for whom the sleek and healthy Jewish leader who intoned that "we" do not need such Aliyah propaganda, speaks. She may, indeed, not need it since she has no intention of going to Israel aside from state visits and vacations. But she surely cannot speak for the "we" who suffer at the hands of inner-city Jew-hatred—white and black; who feel the sting of quotas and criminal violence; who are, perhaps, better judges of reality than those who allowed all the crises of today to fall upon Jews without seeing them coming and without stopping them when they were upon us.

In general, American Jewry suffers from a massive lack of greatness, from a deplorable and tragic absence of talented leaders. Never in Jewish history has so large a community suffered from such an awesome mediocrity of leadership. It must pay for that.

American Jews will survive if they learn to perceive and expose that mediocrity. If they will understand the dwarflike nature and the timidity and shortsightedness of those they have crowned their leaders, there is yet hope for them. But if they continue to follow the men and groups who led them into disastrous assimilation, into the destruction of Jewish neighborhoods; into the desert of quotas, preferential treatment, affirmative action, numerus clausus, into the ability to overlook Jewish poor and needy, and into a world where Jewish interests were made secondary to non-Jewish ones—then we can be assured of the most awesome disaster ever to befall any Jewish community in history.

For these people and organizations—and they are the very same who led us so blindly and negligently into our crises over the past years—are utterly incapable of the breadth of vision needed to save us today. They are victims of their own smallness and their contracted vision. They do not wish to see and so cannot see. The task of saying things that are so awful terrifies them and they shrink from the absoluteness of the chosenness, the inwardness and the isolation of the true Jew.

We cannot depend upon them and we dare not listen to them. Now is a time for greatness and we must achieve that.

We must immediately move to bring into being a national organization whose purpose will be to create the machinery for the mass return of American Jews to the Land of Israel. It must create within the American Jew that sense of urgency that is so lacking today and that, consequently, fails to inspire him with a sense of danger and the need to make his move. We must create a great national Jewish debate so that the issue will be removed from our fears and openly discussed.

Never in the history of the Jewish people has there ever been a successful or major Aliyah of significant proportions from lands of apparent wealth and freedom based on positive motives. From the days of the first Return, that of the Jews of Babylonia, in which barely a little more than 40,000 made their way back, until our days when the Herzlian call was met with such extremes of apathy by western Jews, it has only been the negative fear of Jew-hatred that has brought any remotely significant Aliya from lands where oppression of Jews was not in force, at the moment.

The contention of opponents of "scare tactics" that Aliyah should be promoted on positive grounds, those which emphasize the *positive* reasons to go to Israel, are models of fraud and hypocrisy. They know full well that such efforts have been made for decades by many organizations and that they, quite naturally, have been dismal failures in terms of the insignificant numbers of Jews that have been moved by the arguments to return. Their sole interest in demanding that the "negative" arguments about Jew-hatred cease, is due to their fears that this will create personal problems for them from gentiles, in the Exile they have little intention of leaving.

No amount of gentile persuasion and positive thinking will create a mass Aliya from the United States. The incentive of living among Jews in a Jewish cultural environment on the ancient Jewish soil is simply not powerful enough to pull the American Jew in any large numbers from the land of his birth, from his deep roots, from familiar surroundings, and economic advantage to a land that—however he may love it—is strange, economically disadvantaged, and poses a challenge that the average man is simply not courageous enough to accept.

I am afraid that it is only fear that will provide the incentive for most people to make such a truly radical move as leaving the land of their birth and culture and uprooting their lives. In the words of our rabbis, the positive words of forty-eight prophets and seven prophetesses failed, but the seal of Haman that decreed death to the Jews was successful.

Certainly, if there were no real grounds for fear of Jew-hatred, raising the issue merely to expedite Aliyah would be fraudulent and reprehensible. But the fear is, indeed, a real one and the dangers we warn of, exist. *Not* to speak and *not* to warn is what would be truly reprehensible.

No, it is clear that practical efforts to create the machinery for mass American Jewish Aliyah is immediately necessary. The formation of a national organization for that purpose is essential. I suggest that the name of the organization be Habayta—Homeward or Return—and that it be nonpolitical and non-aligned with grassroot links in every city, town, and hamlet synagogue and institution where Jews may be found. For its program I suggest the following:

RETURN (HABAYTA)

1. To begin an immediate, urgent drive in every Jewish community to convince Jews of the gravity and reality of the situation and to persuade them to take immediate, urgent steps to return to Israel
2. Toward this end, speakers to be trained and sent all over the country into every local Jewish community
3. Literature to be printed which will emphasize this theme and include facts and arguments concerning the deepening American crises, the dangerous effects they will have on the Jew, the manifestations

of those dangers in the form of existing anti-Jewish groups and the cancer of assimilation

4. To educate, also, toward the *POSITIVE* reasons for Jews living in Israel, i.e. the normalcy of a Jewish people in a Jewish State with a Jewish culture

5. To register individuals, families, and whole institutions to RETURN. This registration will include complete information on background, profession or occupation, skills, family, and income in order to help these people obtain employment and inexpensive housing in appropriate areas

6. It will concentrate particularly on mass door-to-door campaigns in urban areas where social and economic conditions have worsened to a point where Jews are seriously willing to consider RETURN

7. It will place specific emphasis on the religious obligation of observant Jews to RETURN, and to propagandize in religious institutions and neighborhoods

8. It will create local branches of RETURN in every Jewish community. These branches will lead the educational drive in the communities as well as serve as the national movement's vehicle to register those who wish to RETURN

9. It will inform itself fully of the social and economic problems involved in mass Aliyah, particularly in the field of housing, employment, and education so as to act as the agent for individual American Jews seeking RETURN

10. It will gather long lists of names and present them to the appropriate Aliyah agencies and departments for the purpose of working with them to create viable cities, villages, and settlements for returnees with inexpensive housing accommodations, planned facilities and jobs; 15-20 percent of the population in those areas will be Israeli

11. It will go over the professions, occupations, and skills of each individual with Aliyah authorities so as to ascertain who can be placed and which individuals need to be found jobs

12. It will induce private investors to create employment for the returnees by investing in industries, factories, etc., which will create jobs for them. Chairmen of local branches will seek out local investors

13. It will work with the Israeli government and private investors to ascertain exactly what kind of industries and factories are needed and to guarantee a fair profit, sufficient to induce private capital to invest

14. It will establish regular local meetings of Jews wishing to return, at which time discussions of Israel, Aliya, and Jewish identity will be held

15. The cities, villages and settlements will be aimed as far as possible to Aliyah in the liberated areas

16. It will urge the setting up of stronger defense groups to protect Jews as conditions become worse, to win time for the Jews to understand the need to leave.

IMMEDIATE STEPS

1. The election of a provisional Board of Directors which will oversee the operations of RETURN (habayta) and which will have the authority to make all necessary decisions

2. The choosing of local chairmen for RETURN, one chairman for each synagogue or local Jewish community organization. These people will immediately publicize the creation of RETURN to the community and press, their own appointments as local chairmen, the first meeting of interested

people in the community, and immediate registration of first members

3. The setting of a quota of at least ten registered families from each delegate to be sent into the national office within six weeks

4. The immediate opening of a national office with Executive Director and Secretary

5. The placing of national ads announcing the formation of RETURN as well as ads and interviews in all local Jewish publications

6. The announcement of a national WEEK OF RETURN during which the mass registration of Jews will take place

7. The interest of at least one local investor in every community to invest in an industry

The above is only a brief outline of the Movement of Return that must be created immediately. Yesterday was the proper time for the beginning of such a movement. Today is very late. Tomorrow may be too late.

The key word here is "urgency." We must instill that feeling of urgency within the American Jew. He must be made to understand the danger and the awful possibilities. He must be made to realize that we have not the luxury of time to wait. Our world is very different today from what it was only a few years ago. Time moves much more swiftly, events catch up to us and inundate us with unexpected and awesome speed. We no longer have the time to anticipate and to plan that we once did; we no longer have the time to carefully plan our answers and escape from danger.

There may be those who do not reject our contention out of hand but who feel that there is yet time. They may agree that a permanent future for Jews in America is out of the question but that disaster will not occur so soon. They may, therefore, plan on keeping a careful eye on events over the next few years and, meanwhile, accumulate more money. They are foolish people, living in a world of illusions.

First, let it be clear that people who plan on waiting until the last moment are people who overstay that moment. One can never gauge with a jeweler's measure the exact moment of danger or even come close to it. But more important, is a most practical danger.

We blithely assume that the fiscal policy of the United States, which has been to allow dollars to leave the country in unlimited supply and with no restrictions, will never be changed when in reality such a policy can—in all sanity and logic—no longer be continued without at least some modifications. The huge dollar gap that grows worse, buffeting the credibility of the American dollar, must somehow be narrowed. No economy, not even the American one can continue to survive as its dollars leave in such staggering numbers. There is no question that the government will take measures to limit the outflow.

It is difficult to gauge exactly what those fiscal steps might be. Presumably they will be such things as limiting the dollars that tourists may take out of the country or the investments of American corporations overseas. But, surely, the possibility arises of a general limitation of the withdrawal of dollars over and above a certain minimum figure. Nothing is more calculated to discourage Aliyah if the individual knows that he will be forced to leave behind a significant amount of property. Indeed, to wait the number of years that too many people calculate as "safe" may be to see their assets frozen and to shut the doors of their own minds to emigration.

The time, therefore, is not tomorrow—even a clever tomorrow—but today. The memory of Six Million who did not believe it could happen and whose leaders assured them that it would not happen must spur us on to the difficult decision.

Six million. Yet again. But this time unlike their predecessors who had no precedent for a holocaust; who had the right of logic and history on their side when they said it could not happen; who had the right to question the sanity of men who warned of such barbarism in the twentieth century; who had the privilege of not being able to conceive of a cultured, social democracy as Weimar descending into the depths of the inferno

—we have no such excuses and no such logic and no such right.

We have seen what happened in our own times. We watched while naive Paradise was lost and Hell broke loose with all its unspeakable terror and madness. We KNOW. Deep in our hearts WE KNOW that it could happen again.

And we know, too, that there is an answer. We know that there is a place to which we can return. Shall we have the courage to fear or shall we fear to have courage?

Home. It calls us. Let us Return.